PEACEBUILDING AND RECONCILIATION

Peacebuilding and Reconciliation

Contemporary Themes and Challenges

Edited by Marwan Darweish
and Carol Rank

Assistant editor: Sarah Giles

PlutoPress
www.plutobooks.com

First published 2012 by Pluto Press
345 Archway Road, London N6 5AA

www.plutobooks.com

Distributed in the United States of America exclusively by
Palgrave Macmillan, a division of St. Martin's Press LLC,
175 Fifth Avenue, New York, NY 10010

British Library Cataloguing in Publication Data
A catalogue record for this book is available from the British Library

ISBN 978 0 7453 3288 8 Hardback
ISBN 978 0 7453 3287 1 Paperback
ISBN 978 1 8496 4758 8 PDF eBook
ISBN 978 1 8496 4760 1 Kindle eBook
ISBN 978 1 8496 4759 5 EPUB eBook

Library of Congress Cataloging in Publication Data applied for

This book is printed on paper suitable for recycling and made from fully managed and
sustained forest sources. Logging, pulping and manufacturing processes are expected to
conform to the environmental standards of the country of origin.

10 9 8 7 6 5 4 3 2 1

Designed and produced for Pluto Press by Curran Publishing Services, Norwich, UK.
Simultaneously printed digitally by CPI Antony Rowe, Chippenham, UK and
Edwards Bros in the United States of America

CONTENTS

ACKNOWLEDGEMENTS

We would like to thank our contributors whose perspectives and experiences comprise this book, and our assistant editor, Sarah Giles whose tenacity and attention to detail made this book possible. We would also like to thank the Vice Chancellor of Coventry University, Professor Madeleine Atkins, for her encouragement with the book, and our colleagues at the Centre for Peace and Reconciliation Studies for their support.

Marwan Darweish
and Carol Rank

INTRODUCTION

Marwan Darweish and Carol Rank

Processes of peacebuilding are complex and interconnected. The chapters in this book highlight particular facets central to peacebuilding and reconciliation in societies experiencing or emerging out of violent conflict. Some of the themes and challenges presented are:

- 'top down' versus 'bottom up' approaches and the need for local ownership of peacebuilding processes
- attempts at building national unity through truth and reconciliation commissions
- promoting reconciliation through grassroots traditional processes
- the challenges of dealing with secessionist movements and terrorist groups
- the issue of refugees' right of return and reintegration
- the reintegration of former combatants, particularly child soldiers
- the role of interreligious dialogue and public health systems in building stable, peaceful societies.

Case studies in this book are drawn from Afghanistan, Canada, Democratic Republic of Congo (DRC), Ethiopia, Kosovo, Sierra Leone, Nepal, Lebanon, Palestine and Sierra Leone.

All of the contributors to this book are scholar-practitioners, many from the global south, who have been working in conflict areas. They bring fresh perspectives and insights to peace, justice and reconciliation, gained from their experiences of living and working in the conflict situations they describe and analyse. The articles presented here thus represent a bridge between theory and practice, drawing on both academic research and observation in particular conflict settings, and exploring how to meet the challenges involved in peacebuilding and reconciliation.

WHAT IS PEACEBUILDING?

Three major schools of thought have contributed to the evolution of the peacebuilding field:

- the United Nations
- peace research
- sustainable development theory (Bercovitch and Jackson, 2009: 169–71).

The origins of the peacebuilding concept go back to the contribution of former United Nations (UN) Secretary-General Boutros-Ghali's *Agenda for Peace* (1992) which presented a new development that went beyond the scope of conflict management, settlement and prevention. The book gave a broad definition of peacebuilding as 'action to identify and support structures which tend to strengthen and solidify peace to avoid a relapse to conflict' (1992: 11).

The emerging normative consensus of the late 1980s and the beginning of the 1990s on sustainable development, human rights, gender, the human security agenda and the realization of the centrality of the UN role, along with the end of a number of long and complex violent conflicts, raised the demand for coordinated efforts to move toward reconstruction and peacebuilding. Both developments accelerated the evolution of the concept of post-settlement peacebuilding and reconstruction, and became central to UN operations.

The peacebuilding concept was expanded by the Brahimi report (United Nations 2000), which recommended the adoption of clear strategies and specific peacebuilding tools and the establishment of a UN peacebuilding unit. Former UN Secretary-General Kofi Annan's contribution systematized and synchronized peacebuilding activities, and during this period the terms 'conflict prevention' and 'peacebuilding' were used interchangeably. Broadly, peacebuilding was seen as any activity that contributed to peace and to the formation of structures that can contribute to peace.

In summary, since 1992 the United Nations has moved from a simplistic linear understanding of the transition from violence to peace to a more integrated, comprehensive understanding. Peacebuilding requires a range of military, security, political, humanitarian, social and economic capabilities and skills, and has been described as a holistic approach to transform the political, social and economic structures and conditions within society that give rise to the violence. Peacebuilding utilizes a range of options for interventions in order to achieve a lasting peace. These interventions are multi-level, long term and comprehensive.

Other contributions to the development of our understanding of peacebuilding come from peace research, such as Galtung (1975) and Ramsbotham, Woodhouse and Miall (2011). Galtung introduced the concept of structural violence, which referred to the systems, structures, laws, regulations and policies that cause exploitation, discrimination and social injustice. Hence, peacebuilding requires dealing with the root and structural causes of violence. Galtung (1971) also noted the various forms of cultural violence based on sets of values and beliefs that reinforce and legitimize direct and structural violence.

Other peace research scholars such as Lederach argued for a focus on relationship building between conflicting parties as a way to transform conflict. Lederach (1997) described peacebuilding as all the efforts employed to transform the underlying structural, cultural and relational roots of violent conflict. Therefore, peacebuilding is a comprehensive, continuing process that is bottom up but also addresses society at all levels, from the grassroots to middle-level actors and at the national and international levels. The actors at the national and international top levels are involved in negotiation and peacemaking, while the grassroots, bottom-up level are aiming to promote peace and reconciliation at local and community level, acknowledging the local context and culture. The middle-level process, focusing on political and social community leaders, aims to facilitate linkage between the top and grassroot levels to sustain peace and reconciliation. (Lederach, 1997).

Another important contribution to the evolution of the peace-building field came from sustainable development theory. This was because development, reconstruction and relief were seen as critical in war-torn societies – societies emerging from violent conflict need to meet immediate humanitarian needs. It was also recognized that long-term sustainable development is critical, and can only be implemented when there is a cessation of violence and a movement towards peace. Consequently, many development agencies established peacebuilding units and became more aware of the link between development and conflict, and the need for conflict sensitivity when agencies operate in conflict zones.

As Ramsbotham and colleagues (2011: 236–7) point out, there is now another shift going on towards a 'transformative cosmopolitan model' of peacebuilding. The 'liberal peace' model of peacebuilding in post-conflict societies has been critiqued as being a paternalistic 'one size fits all' approach that aimed at stability through the imposition of Western-style democracy and a liberal market economy. Such a peace can be more in the interest of the rich and powerful of the West, than in the interests of local people. A more emancipatory, civil society-led approach was proposed as an alternative, with a focus on local capacity building and what Lederach called 'indigenous empowerment'. However, equally there were pitfalls in that approach, because although it was important to promote local 'ownership' of peacebuilding, such processes could also be subject to power asymmetries, patriarchy and other elements that it would not be desirable to help maintain and reinforce (Ramsbotham et al., 2011: 235).

Addressing this problem, Oliver Richmond (2008: 163) proposed a middle way to bring together both the 'top down' and 'bottom up' approaches; local capacity building linked to international and global systems. As described by Liden (2009: 616), this new model is cosmopolitan and transformative in that it 'exemplifies a model of global governance where a cosmopolitan human rights agenda is consistent with the communitarian defence of political autonomy and cultural diversity'.

This new shift toward a more inclusive and integrative approach seems very positive. As Ramsbotham and colleagues (2011: 238–40) point out, at the heart of this approach is a commitment to nonviolence, and peace education – education that is liberating and which promotes mutual understanding, peace and tolerance.

RECONCILIATION OR COEXISTENCE?

While there has been a critique of the 'liberal peace' model which includes promoting democratic systems in societies emerging from violent conflict, democracy does in fact provide an effective means of dealing with conflict. As Bloomfield (2003: 10–11) notes, democratic systems based on principles of equality, representation and participation in government provide ways of handling internal conflicts, civil war, ethnic rivalry and the oppression of minorities. Bloomfield goes on to say that democratic compromise produces solutions to the issues of conflict, and that reconciliation addresses the relationships of those who will implement the solutions.

In other words, for peacebuilding to occur, people must trust both the system and each other. Rigby (2011: 243–4) distinguishes between 'vertical trust' – between citizens and their institutions – and 'horizontal trust' – between people in their everyday lives. Reconciliation is about relationships between individuals, groups and communities as well as their relationship with the state. But what does reconciliation really mean, and should we even use that word? As Chayes and Minow (2003) point out, reconciliation may remain an elusive or even insulting notion to people still reeling from the murder of their loved ones or their own torture or rape. Rigby prefers to use the term 'coexistence' rather than reconciliation, as people can live parallel lives or even live side by side without having reconciled with each other.

Likewise Crocker (2002: 509–49) criticized Desmond Tutu's call for forgiveness in the context of the South African Truth and Reconciliation Commission, and said that his notion of *ubuntu* or social harmony was unrealistic. Rather than reconciliation, Crocker uses the term 'non-lethal coexistence' because it demands less of people and does not require forgiveness, yet it provides for 'democratic reciprocity' – people respecting each other as citizens. Kreisberg (2001: 48) also provides a more narrow definition of reconciliation as 'processes by which parties that have experienced an oppressive relationship or a destructive conflict with each other move to attain or to restore a relationship that they believe will be minimally acceptable'.

Reconciliation is a long-term process, and as conflict and enmity can be inherited from one generation to the next, it may take generations to deconstruct enemy images and build trust. Reconciliation is not a linear process; there can be progress made but there might also be relapses, particularly if violence re-emerges. There are a number of factors that can help people deal with the past and envision a shared future with a former enemy. These include:

- security (an end to violence and an assurance that it will not recommence)
- truth (acknowledgement of the wrongs of the past)
- justice ('making things right' through punishment or reparations) (Rigby, 2011: 237).

Another important element of reconciliation is healing – at the individual, community and societal levels.

One way to promote reconciliation is through a 'truth and reconciliation commission', the most well known of which was that for South Africa. Such commissions are far from a panacea; these top-down approaches to building national unity and promoting reconciliation have been criticized as not really reaching people at the grassroots and in some cases failing entirely, as in the Democratic Republic of the Congo (DRC). Local-level reconciliation efforts by civil society groups using traditional practices and rituals, can be more effective as well as culturally appropriate and less expensive. However, it is also possible that national initiatives can create the 'cultural space' for local initiatives and that top-down and bottom-up approaches can work together and reinforce each other.

While reconciliation involves building trust and overcoming psychological hurdles in coming to terms with past wrongs, and being willing to live beside if not with the former enemy, it also requires structural changes to foster the kind of 'vertical coexistence' and trust in institutions described previously. Politics and reconciliation are intertwined; economic justice and political power sharing are the basis for reconciliation (Bloomfield, 2003: 11), and reconciliation enables former enemies to work together toward a just and equitable form of government. Thus reconciliation – or at least 'non-lethal coexistence' – is essential for peacebuilding

STRUCTURE AND CONTENT OF THE BOOK

The chapters in this book address many of the issues raised above in the discussion on peacebuilding and reconciliation. We have divided the book into the following sections:

1 Peace: but what kind of peace?
2 Reconciliation and dealing with the past
3 Cultural processes and initiatives
4 Challenges to peacebuilding and reconciliation.

Peace: but what kind of peace?

A starting point for discussion on peacebuilding is to define what kind of 'peace' is being built or imposed. One challenge is the tension between internal and external influences and the requirement for local ownership of peacebuilding processes, as evidenced in Afghanistan and Kosovo. The need to acknowledge indigenous culture and tradition to deal with peacebuilding initiatives is examined by Chrissie Hirst in 'How has the liberal peace served Afghanistan?' Hirst critiques the UN 'standard operating procedure' and the imposition of a peacebuilding 'formula' of liberal democracy and a market-driven economy. According to Hirst, the attempt by the United States to install a stable and cooperative regime in

Afghanistan in the 'war on terror' has resulted in 'armed humani-tarianism' – a convergence of state building and development with the security agenda, rather than a focus on human security. In 'The obstacles to sustainable peace and democracy in post-independence Kosovo', Gëzim Visoka notes that likewise in Kosovo, the presence of the United Nations and other international agencies continues to block local control and delay the full democratization of an inde-pendent state. As in Afghanistan, internal conflict continues, in this case between the Albanian and Serbian Kosovars, which both justifies the continued international involvement whilst also hindering the sovereignty of Kosovo.

Moving to an African context, in 'Ethnicity, ethnic conflicts and secessionism in Ethiopian politics' Bezawit Beyene analyses the diffi-culties involved in creating a stable peace in Ethiopia. She notes that although Ethiopia did not experience the kinds of ethnic divisions that were created or exacerbated by a colonial history, nevertheless the country is a tenuous union of competing ethnic groups, with threats to the state by secessionists. Beyene explores the debate over unification versus subjugation, and concludes that there needs to be more government-level recognition of the kinds of unjust and unequal relationships between ethnic groups that were promulgated in the past, along with processes to build trust and cooperation between rival groups in order move beyond federalism to a form of power sharing by regions, and greater decentralization.

Reconciliation and dealing with the past

A key aspect of building peace is how to face and deal with the past after violent conflict in order to promote peaceful coexistence and ideally, reconciliation. The template of the South African Truth and Reconciliation Commission has been reproduced elsewhere, including in the Democratic Republic of Congo, where as noted earlier, it failed. In 'State failure and civil society potential: reconcili-ation in the Democratic Republic of Congo', Verity Mould explores why the Truth and Reconciliation Commission failed in that country to the extent that it was dubbed a 'truth omission'. She notes how in the first year of the TRC the decision was taken not to investi-gate human rights abuses but to offer amnesty to rebel groups in order to secure their participation in a power-sharing government; in other words, to protect a fragile peace rather than to secure justice. Mould notes in contrast the potential for civil society organizations to promote reconciliation, including through the use of traditional mechanisms and rituals. In order to do this, civil society needs sufficient human and financial resources to fulfil its potential in this role.

In contrast to state-sponsored processes that promote reconciliation, Steve Kaindeneh in 'Remembering the past and reconciling for the future: the role of indigenous commemorative practices in Sierra Leone' explores the importance of traditional mechanisms and rituals in helping to heal the emotional damage of the civil war in Sierra Leone (1991–2002). He describes the remembrance practices of his own ethnic group, the Mendi of southern and eastern Sierra Leone, which include confession, symbolic cleansing and rituals in sacred spaces. He argues that while former fighters were given amnesty, such purification rituals helped to reintegrate these former fighters back into their communities and to 'cool the hearts' of the people.

In a very different context, Patricia Elgersma in 'Decolonization and reconciliation: the colonial dilemma of Canada's residential school apology and restitution' critiques the dominant attitude in Canada that its treatment of indigenous peoples, while once brutal, is now safely in the past and that only certain former practices require apologies. She examines the history of the government-led policy (1874–1996) of removing indigenous children from their homes and placing them in boarding schools where they were taught English and Christian doctrine, expunging their traditional culture and language. She concludes that there needs to be a 'decolonization' of the Canadian 'settler' mindset and a more robust acknowledgement of the wrongs of the past, along with greater attempts to promote social and economic justice in the present day.

Cultural processes and initiatives

Peacebuilding in its broadest sense encompasses social, political, economic and cultural processes. Two important areas to consider in working to move from cultures of violence to cultures of peace are religion and public health. Sarah Bernstein, in 'Is "interreligious" synonymous with "interfaith"? the roles of dialogue in peacebuilding' notes the dual capacity of religion to foment conflict and violence or conversely to be a force for peace. She makes a distinction between interfaith and interreligious dialogue, and highlights the strengths and weaknesses of both. She defines interfaith dialogue as focusing on theology (the faith), seeking doctrinal change from exclusivist to inclusivist views, whereas interreligious dialogue aims to bring individuals from different religious communities together, to have a dialogue which enables them to 're-humanize the other', to correct misperceptions and to work together for peace, justice and social change.

In 'The role of health in building peace: the case of Afghanistan', Wossenyelesh Kifle, highlighting Afghanistan as a case study, provides a compelling analysis of the health problems caused by war from direct killing, food shortage and disease, but also emphasizes the potential for health service organizations to be involved in peace-building, from grassroots activities to involvement in international diplomacy and negotiation. She notes that health care is concerned with people's day-to-day survival and is a universal concern and right. Health is thus inextricably linked to peace, human security and development.

Challenges to peacebuilding and reconciliation

A formidable challenge to peacebuilding is the threat of terrorism, and it is essential to examine the rhetoric surrounding the debate on the 'war on terror.' In 'The new economy of terror: motivations and driving forces behind contemporary Islamist insurgencies', Peter Keay critiques the traditional view that Islamic extremism is fuelled primarily by religious motivation. While he acknowledges that religion is more than just a recruiting tool, he puts forward the view that a primary driver behind terrorist groups is financial: terrorist groups, however decentralized, are funded through an international, illegal economy. Terrorism is financed through the smuggling of arms, drugs and narcotics, partnership with crime, and money laundering. To fight terrorism the financial structures that maintain it must also therefore be targeted.

In the intractable Israel–Palestine conflict, the challenges are so great that the word 'peacebuilding' cannot yet realistically be used to describe the political situation in the area. One challenge is the continued exile of the Palestinian people and their right, as refugees, to return to their homeland. Abigail Bainbridge in 'The question of home: refugees and peace in the Israel–Palestine conflict' notes that while the right of return for Palestinian refugees has been expressed in international law and a UN resolution, many see the issue as 'more symbolic than real'. Bainbridge asserts, however, that the right to return is very real to Palestinians living in refugee camps, who continue to live in unjust, impoverished conditions, and that even improving living conditions in their exile in Lebanon, Jordan and Syria is not a sustainable solution unless refugees become integral and essential players in any future peace process. The question of the status of Palestinian refugees and internally displaced people remains a major obstacle to the Israel–Palestine peace process.

Not only are the Palestinian people in conflict with Israel, they are also dealing with severe internal conflict which has prevented the emergence of a unified government able to encompass both the Islamist Hamas and secular Fatah political parties. In 'Hamas: between militarism and governance', Ibrahim Natil charts the birth and rise of Hamas as a resistance movement and its latter transition to a governing body, exploring how and why the shift from militarism to governance occurred. This chapter highlights the challenges at national and international level that Hamas faced in order to make this transition. Recently, the Arab Spring in Egypt and Tunisia has impacted on the relationship between Hamas and Fatah, and with mediation from Cairo, reconciliation has now been initiated between the two parties with an agreement to form a national unity government and hold new elections in a year's time.

Another challenge to peacebuilding in post-conflict societies is the reintegration of child soldiers. In 'Returning home towards a new future: Nepal's reintegration programme for former child soldiers', Dilli Binadi discusses how children were used in the Maoist insurgency in Nepal from 1996–2006, exploring the factors that motivated them to join the Maoists, and examining what is now being done to help these former child soldiers reintegrate into society. Unlike child soldiers in other parts of the world, such as some African countries, the majority of Nepalese child soldiers joined voluntarily as an attractive alternative to their oppressive reality. Binadi demonstrates that the root cause of their involvement in the military stemmed in part from their need to earn money; furthermore many joined because of peer pressure, for the cultural programmes offered by the Maoists, and for the empowerment offered by enlistment. He concludes that the reintegration of former child soldiers requires psychosocial care, educational support and vocational training for income generation.

PEACEBUILDING AND RECONCILIATION: THEORY INTO PRACTICE

The chapters in this book represent grounded scholarship that seeks to find solutions to the problems of violence, war and injustice through addressing the personal, relational, cultural and structural aspects of building peace in societies experiencing or emerging from violent conflict. The authors effectively manage to reflect on their own knowledge and experience of the difficult environments they describe, because they have direct experience from their personal and working lives of the conflicts and peace processes they are examining. The contributors seek to put their theoretical understanding into practice to promote sustainable peace in their countries and in the world.

PART I

PEACE: BUT WHAT KIND OF PEACE?

1

HOW HAS THE LIBERAL PEACE SERVED AFGHANISTAN?

Chrissie Hirst

LIBERAL PEACE: DEFINING THE MODEL

The end of the Cold War brought crucial changes to the global context of conflicts in the developing world. With the lens of superpower rivalry removed, the role of international organizations to intervene was strengthened, in particular the role of the United Nations (UN). The 1992 UN Secretary-General's *An Agenda for Peace*, and the 1995 *Supplement to An Agenda for Peace* (Boutros-Ghali, 1992 and 1995) outlined an array of steps or measures (for example, disarmament, demobilization, security sector reform, election monitoring and regulatory reform) which have become standardized elements of post-conflict peacebuilding intervention, also described as 'state building' or 'nation building'.

The 1990s saw the consolidation of this 'standard peacebuilding formula', involving post-conflict elections and market-oriented reforms, often followed shortly after by a declaration of peacebuilding 'success' (Paris, 2006: 175). Some analysts have termed the United Nations' post-settlement peacebuilding package as 'standard operating procedure' (SOP), closely linked to the pursuit of the goals of 'liberal internationalism', understood as the pairing of liberal parliamentary democracy and liberal market capitalism. The term 'liberal peace' or 'liberal peacebuilding' came to be used to describe the intended process and outcome of applying this SOP.

While the liberal peace SOP has gained ground over the last decade, some writers have highlighted its fragile foundation – the

15

SOP is based on the assumption that 'liberalization' is the optimal recipe for lasting peace in post-conflict countries. As the number of SOP interventions undertaken increased, in some cases it appeared that interventions had been counterproductive, and by the end of the decade the 'liberal peacebuilding' model was increasingly called into question.

Afghanistan, alongside Bosnia, Kosovo and East Timor, is an example of a country where the liberal peacebuilding model has been applied, and where the results are unclear at best. Written in May 2010, as elections in Afghanistan were rescheduled because of the insecurity, and revisited in February 2012 alongside discussion of deadlines for international withdrawal, this chapter reviews the record in Afghanistan, and assesses the validity of different critical perspectives on 'liberal peace'.

CRITICAL PERSPECTIVES

In the last decade, criticism of liberal peacebuilding has grown. Hoffman groups critics into two main camps (2009: 10). The first are those who argue that while the premise itself is not unsound, the implementation of the model has been overly top-down, formulaic or pushed ahead too quickly with structural reform and electoral processes (for example Paris, Sisk, Rotberg). Hoffman's second camp includes those who see the problem in the liberal peace model itself, perceiving it as merely 'a cover for the political and economic interests of the West' (for example Chomsky and Ignatieff).

A number of critics have focused on the conceptual framework for liberal peace, highlighting problems with specific yet fundamental aspects of the model, forming what can be considered a third camp. Duffield positions the emergence of liberal peace in the context of the conceptual convergence of development and security in the 1990s: the 'new security framework', where a wave of 'new wars', inter-national crime and terrorism arise from underdevelopment, now seen as dangerous. He argues the liberal peace model is 'a political project in its own right', and reflects a radical and specific political, developmental and security agenda 'to transform the dysfunctional and war-affected societies that it encounters on its borders into cooperative, representative and, especially, stable entities' (2001: 11).

Mac Ginty describes the 'near hegemony' of the 'liberal demo-cratic peace model' applied to post-conflict states, arguing that the dominance of this model has had 'a profound impact on the manage-ment of contemporary violent ethnonational conflict in standardising the core elements of peace initiatives and accords and reducing the space available for alternative (non-Western) approaches to peace-making' (2006: 33). In his review of the United Nations as one of the key institutions of liberal peace, Chesterman makes further references to colonialism, describing UN transitional administrations as 'benevolent autocracy' and post-conflict transformation projects as 'modern colonial enterprise'. He argues that greater honesty about the motivation behind the international community's state-building projects would be beneficial for all parties (2004: 47, 127).

THE LIBERAL PEACE AND AFGHANISTAN

Given increasing sensitivity to overly bureaucratic and top-down, outside-in interventions by the international community, at first glance the model applied in Afghanistan appears to break with previous interventions of the 1990s. In many ways this is true, with the approach defined as the 'light footprint', reflecting the greatly reduced UN mission role and size, and the commitment to bolstering Afghan capacity – a move away from earlier more colonial and prescriptive interventions such as Kosovo.[1]

How has this new, much-heralded 'light footprint' version of liberal peace served Afghanistan? Mac Ginty identifies three characteristic liberal peace pitfalls that have the capacity to seriously jeopardize the quality of peace achieved:

- a lack of local ownership
- a reflection of external rather than internal concerns
- a premature withdrawal of external support (2006: 162).

The record of international intervention so far in Afghanistan is reviewed below in relation to the first two pitfalls – it remains too early to judge the third, although the announced 2014 deadline for international military withdrawal certainly appears ambitious. This section also considers aid distribution more broadly, with reflections focusing on key elements of liberal peacebuilding, primarily elections and 'democratization', and additionally human rights, rule of law, disarmament processes, development assistance and market reform.

Lack of local ownership, lack of a genuine peace process

Despite the 'light footprint' approach, it is clear that the process of state building in Afghanistan has been almost entirely controlled by external parties, primarily the United States, working alongside international institutions such as the United Nations and the World Bank. Mac Ginty's first pitfall was apparent from the early days of the intervention – a lack of local ownership: a lack of full involvement of Afghan stakeholders in shaping, and thereby valuing and committing to, the peace process.

From the outset of the post-2001 liberal peacebuilding project in Afghanistan, the international actors leading the process and convening the Bonn conference determined which constituencies would have 'local ownership'. This local ownership has been incomplete, selective and based on groups acceptable to Western powers. Although the Bonn Agreement was broadly presented and accepted as a 'peace deal', analysts observe that the UN-sponsored talks reflected the distribution of power that resulted from the US strategy, and was more an agreement among those on the winning side than a settlement based on negotiations among conflicting parties. Johnson and Leslie argue that:

> The problem started with the Bonn agreement itself ... [and] took place in the shadow of a massive military campaign in retaliation for the events of 11 September 2001. Although the agreement that emerged is often referred to as a 'peace agreement', the circumstances that gave rise to it were not those from which peace agreements are usually forged .... The major party to the conflict, the Taliban, was not even at the table. Rather, the Bonn agreement was a victor's sharing of the spoils of war in the wake of the forcible removal from power of the Taliban.
>
> (Johnson and Leslie, 2004: 157)

In discussing peacebuilding success factors and key roles for outsiders, Liklider highlights 'inclusiveness', the need to involve all major parties, noting that 'It is tempting to negotiate with the moderates and try to leave the extremists out .... But this is often a mistake' (2001: 701). Many writers emphasize the importance of including all stakeholders in peace processes: excluded parties are far more likely to continue with violence and reject a settlement that has been imposed by others. Bonn excluded various key groups within Afghan society, but the exclusion of the Taliban as a major party in the conflict has been particularly criticized. Commentators argue that the Taliban represent deep-rooted values and interests in Afghan society that must be included in any peace process for it to succeed, regardless of how acceptable such values and interests might be to Western actors (Johnson and Leslie 2004: 209; Sisk 2008: 206).

While some analysts feel the Bonn Agreement reflected the best chance available for a peace deal, in the period following the settlement there was widespread recognition that Bonn was not a comprehensive peace agreement. Others describe it as a mechanism for distributing power and profit among the victors, and a senior UN leader has referred to the Agreement as the 'original sin' (Bennett et al., 2003: 15). Sadly, little has changed in the years since Bonn. Wijeyaratne completes her review of the prospects for peace in Afghanistan under the subtitle 'The missing peace process', with the observation that although limited efforts are continuing, they are fractured and ultimately 'There is no clear peace process bringing together all sides of the conflict' (2008: 5). She emphasizes that Afghanistan is not in a post-conflict situation, the Bonn Agreement and Afghanistan Compact 'are insufficient as they do not provide a roadmap to peace', and she sees Bonn as a key factor in the post-2002 conflict (2008: 31).

Where previously any moves to reach out to the Taliban were strongly censured by the international community, the last year has seen a major shift in approach. A decade after their exclusion from the first meeting, the December 2011 'Bonn II' international conference included open discussion on political engagement with the Taliban. As plans for Gulf-sponsored talks to include Taliban and Afghan leaders take shape in early 2012 (amidst some level of regional political controversy), a new, more inclusive phase of peace negotiations may now be approaching.

External rather than internal concerns – prioritization and legitimization

With the basis of the liberal peace state-building exercise undermined from the outset through a failure to establish local ownership at Bonn, the process continued much as it had started, faltering into Mac Ginty's second pitfall as external concerns took priority over internal concerns in many vital areas.

Beyond the exclusion of the Taliban from Bonn, a crucial point here is the inclusion of leaders who had supported the West and who were important to continuing US efforts to eliminate Al Qaeda. The inclusion in the Bonn talks of the Northern Alliance and other groups responsible for atrocities and abuse during the war sent a strong message: these warlords were legitimized as national leaders, rewarded with support from the international community. As Johnson and Leslie observed, 'The US decision to engage certain factions to pursue its ground war not only returned to power the very people who had been responsible for Afghanistan's plunder, but also ensured that they obtained significant supplies of new arms and useful quantities of hard currency' (2004: 157–8).

The subsequent steps in the process of transition and legitimization of interim institutions have included the holding of two *loya jirga* meetings and four rounds of elections. Implementation practice has reflected the lack of adherence to liberal peace principles: internal concerns for the need for representative and fair processes were subordinated to external security concerns.

As a key element of liberal peace, elections are valued for the inherently peaceful checks and balances they place on elected leaders, and within the liberal peacebuilding framework for their power to legitimate. Election of post-war leaders is also in many cases legitimization of the peace process in question, and is therefore seen as having enormous potential for strengthening a peace process. In Afghanistan's case, the use of the traditional *loya jirga* decision-making mechanisms (a large meeting of community or tribal representatives from across the country) was arguably an appropriate cultural adaptation of the liberal peace SOP and avoided the risks of an early election. While the first 'emergency' *loya jirga* was widely criticized, the second, 'constitutional' *loya jirga* went better than many had dared hope as the United Nations took a stronger role and managed to reduce manipulation. Given the many ethnic and political divisions in Afghan society, commentators saw the second *loya jirga* debates and the first presidential elections in 2004 as significant successes, in many ways high points for electoral democracy in the country.

However, as both critics and proponents of the role of democratization in peacebuilding warn, elections may also bring negative consequences. In the sensitive post-conflict contexts of inter-group division, elections incur 'validation risks', as in the case of Bosnia, where extremist parties emerged from wartime factions. Post-war elections risk reinforcing conflict dynamics and playing a negative legitimizing role:

the Liberian outcome is similar to Afghanistan's, following elections there in 2005: the inclusion through the legislative arena of a number of factions involved in the war who have either emerged as 'warlord' figures or whose hands are not clean in terms of the widespread atrocities that occurred.

(Sisk, 2008: 199)

The damage done by the first *loya jirga* in 2002 and the 2005 elections in Afghanistan is widely discussed. Several analysts observe the manipulations and abuse apparent at the first *loya jirga*, essentially the first step towards forming a government. Death threats were made against some speakers by warlords and commanders, and a secret ballot was lacking for many positions – the violation of *jirga* principles by the US intervention to ensure Hamid Karzai's position is another key criticism. Rubin also outlines the high levels of abusive and threatening behaviour evident at the 2002 *loya jirga*, linking this problem to the US-led coalition's policy of supporting commanders and warlords, and noting that the same factors 'bedevilled the constitutional process which followed' (2004: 9). A policy of accommodation with warlords is identified as a key factor in international and Afghan government policy; lacking international or US support for confrontation, Karzai is seen as having no choice but to allow many commanders to register for the 2005 elections, despite a procedural ban on candidates who had links to illegally armed groups.

Only a year after the 70 per cent turnout of 2004, disappointment and disenfranchisement resulted in only 49 per cent of the electorate voting in 2005, with even lower rates of 33 per cent in the urban, middle-class stronghold of Kabul district, which was expected to provide the core constituency of the new democracy (Suhrke, 2007a: 8). Local human rights monitoring reports indicated that over 80 per cent of the winning candidates in the provinces and 60 per cent in Kabul maintained ties to armed groups, with possibly as many as half the seats in the lower house of parliament going to former *mujahideen* or warlords; additionally, a significant amount of fraud was experienced, with 680 polling stations quarantined, although the international monitoring team ruled the integrity of the elections was not affected (Sedra and Middlebrook, 2005: 2).

The 2009 presidential elections without doubt further damaged voters' remaining trust in the electoral system. Widespread fraud in the first round saw almost a quarter of the votes cast for President Karzai (1.3 million) ruled as invalid, and a second round did little to counter perceptions of elaborate international manipulation. In an increasingly negative and accusatory environment, the parliamentary elections scheduled for the following May were postponed because of a lack of international funding. Held in September 2010, these parliamentary elections were perhaps the worst exercise of this kind so far: rather than demonstrating the consolidation of democratic processes in the country, they resulted in public protest and serious political instability for over eight months. Despite certification of the results by the Independent Electoral Commission (IEC), President Karzai ordered the establishment of a special court to review the results: the court disqualified 62 out of 249 parliamentary seats, although negotiation led to the final result of only nine members of parliament being removed (HRW, 2012).

Criticism has been harsh, and primarily directed against the international community, focusing on the 'check-list' attitude to the election component of the SOP (ICG, 2009).

> The recent fraudulent elections in Afghanistan cost over $250 million, and added to growing dissatisfaction among the Afghan people. This money was spent on staging an elaborate political exercise – an exercise aimed at demonstrating that the 'West' had brought democracy to Afghanistan. The exercise failed.
>
> (Adlparvar, 2009)

Certainly in terms of Afghan popular opinion this appears to be the case, with field surveys reflecting deep cynicism. Lough's research found that public scepticism has increased since 2009; elections are associated with violence, and 'are widely viewed as fraud-tainted, lacking in procedural transparency and controlled by powerful national leaders or foreign actors' (2011: 12,13). This echoes Coburn's earlier research on public opinion: 'While opinions were mixed on the role of figures like Karzai and Abdullah, and institutions such as the IEC, there was almost uniform condemnation of the role of the international community' (2009: 5).

Arguably a key factor has been the multiple roles of the international community. An underlying tension of the liberal peacebuilding approach is that while the United Nations in general has civilian responsibilities, it tends not to have control over the military command beyond the limits of traditional peacekeeping roles. Chesterman argues this can lead to conflicts of interest between the two 'arms' of the intervention, as in the case of Bosnia, or Afghanistan, where UN political objectives and the objectives of the liberal peace were subordinated and military priorities ranked well above political goals (2004: 253).

Peace and prosperity in Afghanistan, for example, was less important to the United States than ensuring that the territory was not used as a haven for terrorists; this military agenda at times ran against the broader aims of peacebuilding (Chesterman, 2004: 191–2).

The outgoing head of the United Nations in Afghanistan,

Kai Eide, offers an inside perspective – in a new account of the process he expresses his regrets and frustrations in relation to the overbearing role of the United States and the prioritization of military over political objectives (Eide, 2012). Suhrke also notes the incompatibility of policy objectives, in particular the tension between political reforms and security issues, and related decision-making over the inclusion of warlord figures in the democratic process:

> the principal reason for the US-led intervention in Afghanistan was not to promote political democracy, but to eliminate suspected terrorists and install a stable and cooperative regime in 'the war on terror'. The requirements of this strategic imperative did not always coincide with the promotion of democracy. US empowerment of local warlords who assisted American forces in the fight against the Taliban and Al Qaida is an oft-cited example.
>
> (Suhrke, 2007a: 1)

As the single most important foreign actor, the United States exerted strong influence over the UN 'civilian arm' of the intervention, even in classic political areas such as democratization and human rights – core elements of liberal peacebuilding. The continuing power of the warlords, and more specifically the 'warlord strategy' of the United States, has been identified as the primary problem for human rights, peace and stability in the country: there has been substantial criticism of the shallow commitments of the United States to democratic and human rights principles. Analytical reports from early on in the Afghanistan mission point to the United Nations' reluctance to take up its full responsibilities and unique mandate to investigate human rights abuses, especially those committed by key figures within the new government who had supported the US-led war effort. It seems that rule of law was not a priority, and these policies and prioritization demonstrated to local communities that warlords' positions would not be challenged by international actors.

> These [warlord] actors were lionized after Bonn, made into heroes .... Nothing was done to punish them for past atrocities or for crimes being committed now. Fighting the Taliban has led to turning a blind eye to other actors, and as a result, criminalized behavior has become legitimized and entrenched.
>
> (Wijeyaratne, 2008: 9–10)

The support given to warlords by international actors was a

significant factor in creating a culture of impunity and the accept-ance of double standards. At a level of principle as well as in practice this deprioritization of human rights by the international community and United Nations critically undermined liberal peacebuilding. By 2008, the United Nations' own experts found that national insti-tutions capable of systematically defending human rights had not been created and that impunity was entrenched and widespread. The 'Wikileaks war logs' released in 2010 revealed previously unreported and large numbers of civilian casualties, including cases where human rights were clearly subordinate to military goals (*Guardian*, 2010b). The Wikileaks material also served to highlight that the continued presence of foreign troops is itself a factor perpetuating instability in Afghanistan.[2] In early 2012, Human Rights Watch raised various concerns in relation to Afghanistan: continued increases in civilian casualties, continued torture and abuse of detainees, and widespread violations of women's rights, observing that 'For many interna-tional actors, particularly the United States, a desire to bow out of what increasingly appears to be an unwinnable war has entirely overshadowed concerns about human rights' (HRW, 2012).

In other key priority areas for the liberal peace, the warlord strategy has also trumped policy in practice. The vital disarma-ment component of the intervention, run by the UN Development Programme (UNDP) through the Disbandment of Illegal Armed Groups programme, struggled in an ambiguous environment of uncertain political support. Undermined by official support for local militias and warlords, UNDP's programme has been described as 'hobbled from the start by lack of will in Kabul, particularly within the Ministry of Interior, whose staff has militia ties' (ICG, 2007: 13). Security sector reform was equally affected by a lack of political will to address the problems surrounding the Ministry of the Interior.[3]

Jointly implemented by UNDP, the Afghan government and the International Security Assistance Force (ISAF), the 2010 Afghanistan Peace and Re-integration Programme sought a fresh start, and to combine demobilization with political peace efforts, underpinned by an international military push to force insurgents to the table. As Lamey and Winterbotham observe, 'It should not come as a surprise that a peace process implemented alongside an international military surge has not proved effective' (2011: 17). The creation and arming by different actors of informal security forces such as the Afghanistan National Auxiliary Police, Afghan Local Police, and more nebulous 'community defence volunteers' at various points in different regions, patchily applied in order to combat insurgent activity, has also proved extremely damaging to the consolidation of governmental structures and rule of law. The results of these competing security and peacebuilding objectives have been inconsistently applied policies, increased inter-ethnic and regional tension, and in several regions the reported rearming of communities anticipating more violence (Saltmarshe and Medhi, 2011: 4).

DISTRIBUTION AND DEPENDENCY

The distribution of development aid is another vital component of the liberal peace model, and in Afghanistan another example of where external concerns, including military priorities, have taken precedence over longer-term development goals with dangerous consequences. Significant disparities exist in the geographical distribution of aid, often because aid is being used to achieve military or political objectives – rewarding allegiance or complementing the 'hearts and minds' campaigning of international troops in the area.[4] With insecure or strategic areas awarded far higher amounts of aid, these disparities have resulted in increased inter-ethnic tension, resentment and negative incentives for peaceful approaches. The establishment of military teams tasked with humanitarian or development activities and funding of 'quick impact projects' in key military areas compounds the problem.[5] Aid distribution according to security priorities has actively undermined progress towards achieving security, with communities outside the conflict areas seeing armed violence rewarded with resources.

While international development assistance has had a positive impact on many aspects of the Afghan economy, the methods of its distribution have undoubtedly fed corruption, and arguably facilitated 'the emergence of warlord politics' (Mac Ginty and Williams, 2009: 171). A brief review of funding only serves to underline the fact that military objectives are prioritized. By 2008, the United States alone was spending nearly US$100 million per day on its military activities in Afghanistan, whereas the average volume of all international donor assistance to the country between 2001 and 2008 was only US$7 million per day: 'reconstruction assistance is a fraction of military spending' (Waldman, 2008: 1). The 2009 figures are telling: government revenue, US$1.3 billion; aid, US$6.1 billion; foreign military operations, US$63.1 billion (Poole, 2011: 1).

A final component of the liberal peace tool kit, the reforms required to create a market economy, have made significant progress from the SOP perspective but the results overall are mixed. Privatization has proceeded, reforms have liberalized investments, foreign exchange and trade, and by 2007 the gross national product and per capita income had doubled. However, debilitating poverty continues and substantial economic challenges persist; 2011 also saw the near-collapse of the national bank.

Extreme dependence on international assistance has been identified as a key problem for economic recovery, also undermining stability and democratic accountability as the Afghan government reports to foreign donors. In general, the lack of perspective in the provision of funding to the fledgling Afghan government was damaging; with an operating budget that by 2005 was based almost entirely (over 90 per cent) on international aid rather than domestic revenue, credibility and democratic accountability were inevitably undermined. This percentage and level of dependency has not changed. Although macro indicators and GDP levels have improved, late 2011 saw many expressing serious concerns over the country's economic survival, with warnings of threats to stability and post-2014 recession as international forces withdraw coming from key institutions such as the World Bank (Rubin, 2011; World Bank, 2011).

> The main argument regarding democratic development is that accountability follows the direction of resource flows. With the national budget mostly financed by foreign governments and institutions, the Afghan government's main responsibility in accounting for the use of these funds is towards the donors, rather than its own people.
>
> (Suhrke, 2006: 4–6)

Additionally, liberalization is seen to have fed political manipulation of the market and corruption. Johnson and Leslie note the lack of regulatory frameworks and argue that 'current policies of market liberalisation run counter to the needs of state building on many levels' (2004: 212). Discussions at the US Institute of Peace recently highlighted the inequalities created by the market system itself, identifying corruption, alongside security, as the two biggest challenges to Afghanistan's economy. There is also evidence of criticism of the market economy model from within Afghanistan, with claims that an open market has 'deteriorated the economic conditions in Afghanistan and increased the poverty rate in the country' (Khelwatgar, 2008; Thabat, 2006). Current analysis argues that a focus on national indicators disguises the ground-level situation, and that poverty reduction has lost ground to economic growth: 'Rural communities across large parts of Afghanistan are getting poorer ... livelihoods of many people ... are even less secure now than they were ten years ago' (Kantor and Pain, 2011: 7). Although important progress has been made recently on curbing the drugs trade, statistically one of Afghanistan's leading economic activities continues to be the illegal cultivation and trade of opium, closely linked to insecurity and the culture of impunity. Here again, military objectives have overridden state- and peacebuilding needs to bring criminal activity under control.[6]

While the debate may continue over whether market liberalization has brought overall benefit to Afghanistan, and indeed whether SOP economic liberalization programmes are advisable per se, there can be no doubt that the continuing insecurity is a critical obstacle to economic growth.[7]

THE LIBERAL PEACE ASSESSED: FLAWED OR HIJACKED?

Over a decade since the intervention in Afghanistan began, progress towards the liberal peace goals of stable, functioning democratic and market economy systems is most uncertain. In 2009, a context of rapidly deteriorating security and spreading insurgency led the United States and other close allies to increase military commitments. By early 2012, discussion now focuses on military withdrawal and accompanying reductions in development aid and activity. Where does this leave the liberal peace?

Hoffman's first camp of critics have some evidence for their purist argument that the failure is because the liberal peace model was never implemented correctly. The adaptation of the classic electoral recipe for Afghanistan appeared to bring some positive results initially, and the 'light footprint' emphasis on Afghan leadership may also have been a very positive alternative to heavy Kosovo-style UN institutions. However, with instability preventing effective implementation, this camp can claim that it is impossible to judge the success of the model, as it was never given a real chance in the highly insecure context. As Rotberg for example contends, the special circumstances of Afghanistan and Iraq mean they cannot be used as examples of failure, and the liberal peace paradigm still holds despite the new states' inability to achieve security (2006: 28). Yet the model was followed, and the intervention initiated and implemented despite high levels of insecurity from the start.

The case of Afghanistan also offers much fuel for the critics of Hoffman's second camp, those who see liberal peacebuilding as a cover for Western ambition, particularly given the clear priority accorded to the overt US military agenda above liberal peace objectives. However, the argument that the entire state-building project in Afghanistan is merely a 'tool of the West' is too simplistic an analysis. The adaptation of the UN SOP to the 'light footprint', as well as the efforts and programmes of many donors, international agencies and NGOs, are important indications of commitments to support peace and development in Afghanistan independently of the US-led coalition security agenda (the strong debate around civil–military relations and roles serves to reinforce this point).

In conclusion therefore, the arguments of the third camp of conceptual critics provide the most useful lens to view the liberal peace intervention in Afghanistan. Key points raised by writers such as Chesterman, Duffield and Mac Ginty – the colonial subtext for state-building projects and the proposition that the liberal peace agenda represents a convergence of development and security – are supported in a number of ways by the record in Afghanistan.

Following Duffield's earlier critique of the radical social trans-formation programme inherent in liberal peace, Mac Ginty and Williams' recent work discusses the 'armed humanitarian':

> A new phenomenon has emerged, that of the 'armed humani-tarian', who is seen by some hostile locals as delivering not only aid but also a message of alien 'democracy' and western mores. For a conservative Afghan elder, bringing education to the women of his area, as UNICEF has done for example, is not a 'neutral' act; it is one that threatens his legitimacy as a lawmaker, and the very culture of his society.
>
> (Mac Ginty and Williams, 2009: c167–8)

Suhrke also highlights the dangers in the application of overtly Western models in Afghanistan: 'the standard programme for post-conflict reconstruction entailed as its outer limits a declaratory strategy of radical social change', and represented an inherently conflictual and comprehensive 'reconstruction-cum-modernisation project' (2007b: 1293,1299). The growth of the insurgency, inter-ethnic divisions and resentment of international actors are therefore logical outcomes of the 'social engineering' pursued. At another level, the creation of such extreme dependency on international aid has also proven fatal for genuine local ownership and sustainable state building, resulting in a rentier state, dysfunctionally over-reliant on the support of external actors.

Chesterman observes that 'the recognition and accommodation of interests on the part of local and international actors continue to be central to the project of transformation, which justifies this modern colonial enterprise in post-conflict territories' (2004: 47). The domestic interests of donors and aid have long been discussed and articulated, and past support for liberal peace interventions has hardly been perceived as altruistic. This notwithstanding, the necessary recognition of international actors' interests must also have limits for the liberal peace model to survive. Some external interests are simply too divergent and contradictory to be accommodated within the liberal peace model, however flawed the model may be.

CONCLUSION

The premise that liberal peacebuilding in Afghanistan would also bring security for the West was false; the theoretical convergence of development and security was not functionally possible given the specific and unsatisfied military objectives of the United States. The long-term process of state building cannot be used as an instrument to deal with international terrorism: 'Waging war while trying to build peace was fundamentally contradictory' (Suhrke, 2006: 3). Tortuous discussions and numerous policy rethinks and efforts to create an 'integrated approach' or a 'comprehensive approach' combining military and development action in the 2007 and 2008 period reflect an international intervention that was in conflict with itself.

In conclusion, liberal peace has served Afghanistan poorly: the conceptual criticisms of the third camp are borne out on the ground. While effort was made to adapt the SOP to the Afghan context, social conflict and disenfranchisement have resulted. Crucially, the subordination of peacebuilding and development objectives to US security objectives resulted in increased instability, and the insurgency, or more accurately the civil war, continues. Given that the agenda and prioritization of military goals was clear before the intervention began, the fundamental failing of the liberal peace model in Afghanistan is arguably its *accommodation* of contradictory external interests, and the willingness of leading liberal peace protagonists, primarily the United Nations, to provide for a 'liberal peace' framework to house these interests. It remains to be seen whether the model will survive this legacy of accommodation, and further critical review of the liberal peacebuilding SOP may be one positive outcome of the Afghanistan intervention.

NOTES

1   Chesterman comments on the inherent contradictions in the UN approach to Afghanistan:

> the 'light footprint' approach. Such a departure from the expansive mandates in Kosovo and East Timor substantially reduced the formal political functions of the UN Assistance Mission in Afghanistan (UNAMA) ... [and] represented a philosophical challenge to the increasing aggregation of sovereign powers exercised in UN peace operations since the mid 1990s... As [a] senior UN official put it, 'we are protecting a peace process from the hubris of the international liberal agenda as promoted by donors'. Such an agenda might include setting policy (on, for example, human rights, democracy, gender, the rule of law) in accordance with donor requirements and time-lines rather than on the basis of what was locally feasible.
> (Chesterman, 2004: 89–90)

2   'The intensification of the international military presence from 2006 onwards, meant to contain the insurgency, has had the opposite effect, with greater numbers of troops eventually presiding over an acceleration of the insurgency's expansion' (Giustozzi and Ibrahimi, 2012: 2).

3   Experts also concluded that reform efforts were seriously undermined by the conflicting expectations of the police force to be created, and the 'need to reconcile the "German vision" of the police as a civilian law and order force, and the "US vision" of the police as a security force with a major counter-insurgency role' (Wilder, 2007: x).

4   Advocacy reports on aid effectiveness highlight the disparities:

> A number of major donors direct a disproportionate share of their funds to the southern provinces where the insurgency is strongest; if it were a state, Helmand alone would be the world's fifth largest recipient of funds from USAID. These disparities are also reflected in the pattern of combined government and donor spending: for 2007–2008 the most insecure provinces of Nimroz, Helmand, Zabul, Kandahar and Uruzgan have been allocated more than $200 per person, whereas many other provinces are to receive less than half this amount, and some, such as Sari Pul or Pakhar, are allocated less than one third ... the resentment which these significant disparities has generated ... the perverse incentive created for secure areas, which perceive the insecurity attracts aid, this approach is dangerously short-sighted and has contributed to the problems of insecurity.
> (Waldman, 2008: 2–3)

5   A controversial approach pioneered in Iraq and Afghanistan, the

creation of military 'provincial reconstruction teams' (PRTs) represent a mixing of security and development activities as military teams, sometimes including civilian advisors. They undertake humanitarian or development activities with the objective of gaining support and demonstrating an 'instant peace dividend' (often through 'quick impact projects') to the communities in the target area for the military units concerned. The PRT concept has been greatly criticized for contributing to the dangerous blurring of lines between civilian and military actors, and reducing safety for development workers and humanitarian space – as well as for providing poor-quality development programming (BAAG/ENNA, 2008). Subsequent assessments of development progress also point to the PRT model as problematic, noting the 'fundamental tension' in military-delivered development assistance (Saltmarshe and Medhi, 2011: 4).

6   Suhrke's observations are shared by a number of analysts and commentators: 'Taking on the top players in the opium economy might jeopardize the fragile state structures and shatter political alliances that were useful in US-led counter-insurgency operations. The prospect effectively blocked efforts to attack the problem at its core' (2007b: 1302).

7   Recent discussions within the United Nations highlight growing calls to adapt the 'SOP' approach of market liberalisation for developing countries currently implemented by international financial institutions – this approach is increasingly being called into question, particularly in the context of the global economic crisis (UNCTAD, 2010).

2

THE OBSTACLES TO SUSTAINABLE PEACE AND DEMOCRACY IN POST-INDEPENDENCE KOSOVO

Gëzim Visoka

INTRODUCTION

Even after ten years of international administration and four years since its declaration of independence from Serbia, Kosovo continues to face ethnic and socio-economic problems, as well as fundamental challenges to its governance and sovereignty that have the potential to undermine the progress achieved and threaten Kosovo's stability. Kosovo already illustrates some of the signs of a weak state: it does not exercise sovereign control over its northern territory; it has a weak economy and high unemployment. There are high levels of corruption and institutional weaknesses in the justice and law sectors, and Kosovo is making only slow progress towards international recognition and participation.

Between 1999 and 2008, the United Nations Mission in Kosovo (UNMIK) aimed to establish a 'liberal peace' through establishing democratic institutions and a market-oriented economy. However, the imposition of such an agenda for 'democratization' has arguably left a weak democracy, fragile peace and fragmented sovereignty in Kosovo.

The purpose of this chapter is to examine how the building of a sustainable peace, the establishment of a democratic polity and the consolidation of sovereignty is frustrated and constrained in Kosovo. The chapter highlights the fundamental factors that fragment Kosovo's sovereignty both domestically and internationally, and delay socio-economic development within the country. It will argue that this fragmentation is affected both by the existence of parallel Serb institutions in the north of Kosovo, and by the presence of international bodies and agencies with overlapping and divided agendas. Meanwhile, the potential for social emancipation in the country is obstructed by weak domestic governance, ethnic power sharing and social injustice.

KOSOVO: FROM UNMIK TO AHTISAARI AND BEYOND

In 1999, following the intensification of the conflict between the Serbian regime and Kosovo Albanians, and NATO's intervention, the United Nations was tasked to govern Kosovo through an Interim Administration Mission (UNMIK), as outlined in UN Security Council (UNSC) Resolution 1244. The Resolution specified neither the scope of UNMIK's authority – whether it would exercise sole authority or share power with local institutions – nor the structure the mission would have (Zaum, 2007: 132).

However, UNMIK later decided to transfer its competencies gradually to the Provisional Institutions of Self-Government (PISG), pending the determination of Kosovo's future status. A broad and temporary power-sharing mechanism was established within central and local government to reserve seats and secure space for ethnic minority participation in politics, which was rationalized as a way to facilitate the reintegration of communities and ethnic reconciliation.

However, from 1999–2003, UNMIK delayed transferring power to local institutions, and did little to promote local ownership of reconstruction processes. This was partly because of Kosovo's unresolved political status and the fear that transferring power to Kosovo's local institutions would be viewed by Kosovo-Serbs as a threat. In an attempt to balance these fears, the UN Special Representative of the Secretary-General to Kosovo, Michael Steiner, outlined benchmarks in April 2002 that had to be achieved before Kosovo's political status could be discussed (UNSC, 2002: 3). By 2004, however, events on the ground, including the March riots, put the discussions of Kosovo's status firmly on the agenda.

Two years and two rounds of UN-led negotiations between Serb authorities and Kosovo representatives failed to achieve a consensual solution. Given the deadlock, a group of mainly Western countries saw no alternative but to support UN Special Envoy Ahtisaari's recommendation to grant independence to Kosovo, 'supervised initially by the international community' and to implement his

Comprehensive Status Settlement (CSS) (UN Secretary-General, 2007: 3). As the Ahtisaari Proposal did not receive sufficient support within the UN Security Council because of the expected veto by Russia and China, the United States together with a group of the European Union member states facilitated a unilateral declaration of independence (Bolton and Visoka, 2010).

Accordingly, on 17 February 2008 Kosovan political representatives declared Kosovo 'an independent and sovereign state' (Kosovo Assembly, 2008). The Declaration of Independence was framed 'in full accordance' with the Ahtisaari Proposal and expressed a commitment to cooperate with the international community to ensure the 'future peace, prosperity and stability' of Kosovo (Kosovo Assembly, 2008). Despite its contested status, Kosovo so far has been recognized by 86 out of 193 UN Member States.

The Ahtisaari Proposal envisages a new format for the international presence, tasked to supervise the status settlement and gradually to pass full governance power to local authorities. However, the international presence in post-independence Kosovo does not operate as defined in the Ahtisaari Proposal. Because of a lack of consensus within their respective organizations, UNMIK, the Organization for Security and Cooperation in Europe (OSCE) and the European Union Rule of Law Mission in Kosovo (EULEX) remain neutral with regard to Kosovo's status. However, although they remain formally status-neutral under the framework of UN Security Council Resolution 1244, the three organizations each take a distinct approach in how they cooperate with their Kosovo counterparts, and in their recognition of the sovereignty of Kosovo.

The International Civilian Office (ICO) is the only status-supportive international body. The ICO is mandated to strengthen Kosovo's domestic sovereignty by supporting decentralization and the protection of minorities, and by improving governance and abolishing Serbian parallel structures – in theory at least – to minimize Serbian interference in Kosovo's domestic affairs. However, it is expected that its mandate will not be renewed after 2012 owing to a lack of funding.

Although EULEX operates under UN Security Council Resolution 1244, its mission aims to strengthen the sector of law and justice by advising, mentoring and monitoring the work of courts, police and customs, which function as institutions of independent Kosovo (European Commission, 2008). Notwithstanding its commitment to status-neutrality, the UN presence in Kosovo undertakes three main functions: monitoring and reporting, facilitating dialogue between Prishtina and Belgrade on issues of practical concern, and facilitating, where necessary and possible, Kosovo's engagement in international agreements (UN Secretary-General, 2008: 5). UNMIK still holds some administrative functions in northern Kosovo, where its key partners are Serb institutions within key public sectors. The OSCE continues to support local governance and communities in Kosovo, but operates under a status-neutral framework. OSCE activities are now reconfigured to focus on early warning and proactive monitoring of local institutions and community rights.

During the two phases of international administration (before and after Kosovo's independence), the international community, together with local actors, failed to lay the seeds of a stable peace in Kosovo. While the international community was interested in maintaining a fragile peace and stability, Kosovar authorities demanded independence and state-building at any price, and this dual agenda allowed Belgrade to exploit this situation in order to promote its own national interests in the bargaining process in Kosovo.

The consequences of Kosovo's independence not being universally accepted and a lack of clarity regarding the goals and mandate of the international actors, combined with insufficient coordination of their roles and responsibilities, challenge newly-independent Kosovo in three ways. First, this enables the 'parallel' Serb institutions to influence and interfere in northern Kosovo, through tolerating the former's illegal activities and restricting the capacity of Kosovar authorities to extend their administrative and political involvement to the north. This creates divided loyalties among the population in the north, and undermines Kosovo's territorial integrity and domestic sovereignty. These parallel structures are tolerated because of the high antagonism between the ethnic communities living in northern Kosovo, but also because of the broader issue of Serbia and its international supporters. Second, a divided international response to crucial post-status peacebuilding and state-building cannot effectively pressure Kosovo's institutions to implement vital reforms in the justice and governance sectors. Third, as a consequence of the previous situation, the international presence tolerates corruption and political unaccountability amongst local politicians in exchange for ensuring stability.

Finally, the ambiguity over Kosovo's status limits its sovereignty externally. The overlapping agendas of the international presence and its internal division exacerbate the situation, further discouraging international recognition of Kosovo and preventing it from participating in international organizations. The international presence therefore contributes both to Kosovo's domestic failure to establish the rule of law and good governance, and to delay in consolidating Kosovo's sovereignty internationally.

SERB PARALLEL STRUCTURES

Following the war in 1999, Serbs in Kosovo established parallel structures within the sectors of security, education, health and public services, which were supported by and relied heavily on the Belgrade authorities. Created initially to boycott the UN administration of Kosovo, their main function became to resist UN-created, Albanian-led, self-governing local institutions. Belgrade uses these structures to influence local Serbs, to manipulate and destabilize processes in Kosovo, and to retain bargaining incentives for Serbia's own interests. This creates a volatile environment; the mayor of Mitrovica Municipality (South), Avni Kastrati, described northern Kosovo as a place where the lack of rule of law and the activities of parallel structures and criminal groups result in frequent violent incidents; bombings, attacks against non-Serb citizens and even murder (*Gazeta Express*, 2010).

As a predominantly Serb area, northern Kosovo is therefore under the de facto control of these Serb parallel structures, which substantially limits the capacity of Kosovar institutions to extend their authority in this part of the country. These structures also constitute a significant obstacle to the representation and participation of Serbs in Kosovar institutions; they constrain the functioning of these institutions within Serb-populated areas and therefore threaten the overall territorial integrity and internal security of Kosovo. In some respects the Serb parallel structures in Kosovo have the attributes of 'states within states'; micro-entities that can emerge from a secession, protracted civil war or state collapse, which perform revenue collection and extraction, public and service-oriented activities, and challenge the legitimacy and authority of the central government (Kingston and Spears, 2004: 3–7).

Indeed, the problem of northern Kosovo is the main source of potential destabilization in Kosovo. Although any intervention by Kosovar authorities would trigger a violent reaction, the international presence could play a fundamental role in restoring law and order. Since the Kosovo government cannot access northern Kosovo, the presence of status-neutral institutions such as UNMIK, the OSCE and EULEX is expected to help bridge this gap. However, these institutions are producing mixed results, largely because of their constrained mandates.

Following Serb anti-independence riots in 2008, district and municipal courts in North Mitrovica ceased to operate and UNMIK failed to restore them. EULEX attempted to reinstate the courts, installing Serb, Albanian and international judges, but the initiative stalled following objections raised by the Kosovo government concerning the nomination of Serb judges from Belgrade (Koha Ditore, 2010a).

Equally, EULEX has not yet established a functioning customs regime in northern Kosovo. During the 2008 anti-independence riots, Serbs destroyed the two border crossings in northern Kosovo (Gates 1 and 31), creating a vacuum that facilitates the smuggling of people and untaxed goods between Serbia and Kosovo. Currently, these border points are managed by EULEX officials who merely record the entry and exit of goods; they do not however collect revenues, as they have not yet established where to send the revenues. The profits arising from this unresolved customs regime generally provide income for the Serb parallel structures and often line the pockets of criminal gangs (Medija Centar, 2010). Indeed, EU and UN officials concur that other criminal activities, notably drug trafficking, are exacerbated in the area and pose a significant regional problem (Crisis Group, 2010: 19).

In January 2010, the Kosovar government, in consultation with the ICO, produced a common 'Strategy for northern Kosovo', which aims to strengthen the rule of law, address governance issues in the three northern municipalities, implement decentralization to create a North Mitrovica municipality and improve the social and economic situation. Despite its comprehensive approach, the strategy received limited support from UNMIK, EULEX and the OSCE. The main obstacles were strong objections from the Belgrade authorities and those running the Serb parallel structures; they interpreted the strategy as a dangerous provocation and called on UNMIK and EULEX to remain status-neutral and to condemn the strategy (UN Secretary-General, 2010: 4).

Responding to the inaction of the international community, the Kosovo government attempted to regain control over the two northern border points by dispatching special police forces on 25 July 2011. However, this 'unilateral' action triggered a negative reaction from EU member states and the United Nations, as well as triggering furious resistance from the local Serb population. Their resistance resulted in the burning of a border checkpoint, the killing of a Kosovo-Albanian policeman and the establishment of barricades all over northern Kosovo by the local population (Balkan

Insight, 2011). Although the checkpoints were gradually regained by NATO peacekeepers, the situation remains fragile and freedom of movement constrained. Following these events, the international community, Kosovo and Serbia have finally taken the question of northern Kosovo seriously. It is expected that during 2012 an internationally mediated political process will determine the future of this region, which is likely to receive a light autonomous status, backed by a special international presence and substantial developmental assistance from the European Union (Crisis Group, 2012). Such an agreement will ultimately legitimize local parallel structures and eventually provide amnesty for their criminal and informal activities over the last twelve years.

THE STATE OF GOVERNANCE IN KOSOVO

For fragile states and countries in democratic transitions and in post-conflict situations, prioritizing good governance is seen as a key requirement in order to address high levels of corruption and unaccountable practices, unequal distribution of resources, and social division (Smith, 2007: 6). However, Kosovo's potential to enable socio-economic development and a functioning democracy is restricted by poor governance, contested ethnic power-sharing arrangements, and social injustice.

Freedom House, an international non-governmental organization, and others acknowledge that prior to 2010, national democratic governance in Kosovo was stable, and that election processes were free and fair. However, the national elections held in November 2010 were viewed locally as undemocratic and to some extent manipulated, because political parties in several municipalities misused votes, manipulating the election results in favour of the incumbent Prime Minister Hashim Thaci (Koha Ditore, 2010b). Despite the positive assessment of international observers, local pressure by political parties and social movements resulted in the recount of 40 per cent of ballots and repeat elections, in three contested regions. Over 1,300 cases of vote manipulation and irregularity were initiated for prosecution in Kosovo. This certainly poses questions about democratic practices, the legacy of international investment in democratization, and the legitimacy of the next government in Kosovo.

The 2011 Freedom House Report acknowledged an improvement in ensuring the smooth functioning of local authorities, as well as the completion of the legislative process for decentralisation (Freedom House, 2011). The report acknowledged that civil society groups do monitor corruption, compliance with human rights statutes and the implementation of fair laws, but warned that the financial sustainability of Kosovo NGOs is weakened (Freedom House, 2011: 287).

> The judiciary is one of the weakest sectors in Kosovo's rule of law. The 2010 Freedom House report blamed this situation on the 'legacy of the previous nine years' as Kosovo's body of applicable laws remains a series of divided areas between UNMIK regulations, laws adopted by the Assembly of Kosovo in accordance with the new Constitution, certain former Yugoslav laws, and the laws of Serbia through Belgrade's parallel Kosovo structures in Kosovo Serb areas, especially in northern Kosovo.
>
> (Freedom House, 2010: 276)

Indeed, the 2011 EU *Progress Report* reasserted that the justice system remains weak, inefficient and vulnerable to political interference, and that Kosovo's judiciary is still in need of reform (European Union, 2011).

Problems with inefficient governance, high levels of corruption, election irregularities and the failure to establish the rule of law has impacted negatively on civic trust in institutions, on participation by citizens at the local level, and on civic activism. In the 2000 elections (the first post-war elections) nearly 80 per cent of Kosovo citizens turned out to vote, but by 2007, turnout had dropped to 40 per cent. Civic satisfaction with Kosovo's main institutions shows a similar decrease. In 2003, the Kosovo government and assembly enjoyed over 70 per cent of citizens' support, this dropped in 2006 and 2009 to approximately 40 per cent. Similarly, while UNMIK enjoyed 40 per cent satisfaction in 2003, this was at a mere 15 per cent by 2009 (UNDP, 2010). Consequently, events on the ground show that social dissatisfaction as a result of fragile governance is constantly being articulated through protests and social unrest.

ETHNIC POWER-SHARING IN KOSOVO

As part of the overall democratization process, the international community in general has favoured ethnic power-sharing, autonomy and self-governance as a strategy to encourage the integration of all ethnic groups and to avoid partition. As a result of power-sharing deals, a quota system of representation in the central decision-making bodies is reserved for minority ethnic groups (Roeder and Rothchild, 2005: 31). This strategy includes the decentralization of power (that is, the transfer of authority and responsibility for public functions) to intermediate and local governments. This strategy aims to accommodate ethnic interests more effectively by bringing institutions of local government closer to the people.

One argument though, is that power-sharing arrangements empower ethnic elites, which risks escalating the conflict and delaying the prospects for a self-sustaining peace (Roeder and Rothchild, 2005). Ethnic power-sharing can further limit democracy by discouraging political competition, restricting the electorate's choices and by disabling public accountability. Ethnic elites can harm the peace agreement through abuse of power and by exploiting the government resources under their management, by increasing governmental inefficiency through higher administrative costs and the duplication of decision-making agencies, and finally by complicating political and social change through governmental rigidity (Roeder and Rothchild, 2005: 36–41).

Ahtisaari's proposal emphasized the importance of addressing the needs and concerns of Kosovar-Serbs through extensive government decentralization. Decentralized regions, where the Serb community constitute a majority, enjoy extensive financial autonomy; they can accept transparent funding from Serbia and can participate in inter-municipal partnerships and cross-border cooperation with Serbian institutions (UN Secretary-General, 2007). After 2008, most international and local politicians acknowledged that decentralization and the creation of new Serb majority municipalities was essential for sustaining and stabilizing the Serb community in the new state and for overcoming the unsettled political and administrative situation in northern Kosovo (KIPRED, 2009: 3). Despite this, the decentralization process is progressing very slowly, mainly because of Serbia's objection to Kosovo's independence and objection to the modes of municipal power-sharing.

The loudest voice against decentralisation in Kosovo is from Levizja Vetëvendosje (Movement for Self-Determination). According to Vetëvendosje:

Through decentralization, Serbia is intending to expand and define the borders of enclaves, create continuous territory through enclaves with the planned return of Serbs by the government of Serbia, take the high peaks of hills and mountains with indisputable strategic and military importance, and legitimize its parallel structures in Kosovo.

(Vetëvendosje, 2006: 13)

Even though there is evidence that the Serbian population wants to participate in and support decentralization, the strong presence and influence of Belgrade through its satellite network of local leaders does not appear to allow this (ECMI, 2009). This clearly shows how powerless the Serbian population has become, mainly as a result of their dependency on self-appointed leadership and the external influence of Belgrade. This self-imposed exclusion by local leaders – not the Serb population in general – has the immediate effect of 'discouraging the Serb community from participating in and shaping the structures of the Kosovar state, creating a real risk for margin-alisation and long-term division, even if the parallel structures cease to exist' (ECMI, 2009). Although these obstacles continue, in the last two years ethnic relations have settled in almost all the new and mixed municipal units, which provide optimism for the prospect of peaceful co-existence among communities in Kosovo in the near future.

SOCIAL INJUSTICE IN KOSOVO

As part of the post-conflict reconstruction of Kosovo, the interna-tional community has installed the framework for a market-oriented economy. Although this economic system has shown modest progress and macroeconomic stability, Kosovo's economy is highly dependent on financial and technical assistance from the interna-tional community and the Kosovar diaspora. Nearly one-third of Kosovo's economy comprises remittances from the diaspora, donor-financed activities and foreign aid. As poverty is high, a large number of people, particularly unemployed and vulnerable groups, receive social protection in the form of social assistance, or pensions and special schemes for war invalids (World Bank, 2007: 28).

Nonetheless, despite the low-income inequality gap, remittances from the diaspora, and social assistance, Kosovo's citizens remain the poorest in Europe with an average per capita annual income of US$2,500 (World Bank, 2007). High unemployment (over 45 per cent) is the main concern for Kosovar society; it encourages migration and promotes an informal economy and the black market, but also creates the conditions for social unrest, and is a trigger for wider destabilization.

One of the attributes of liberal peacebuilding is establishing market-oriented economies, which in many post-conflict cases has resulted in social exclusion and threatening of peace. The situation in Kosovo shows a low investment in the welfare and security of individuals

(Beha and Visoka, 2010). Although the international community has been largely focused on the issue of inter-ethnic violence, the Internal Security Sector Review found that 'for the people of Kosovo high unemployment, a lack of economic development and widespread poverty have created an atmosphere of insecurity' (UNDP, 2006: xiii). The same report goes further to argue that 'economic instability has exacerbated problems such as ethnic violence, corruption, increased crime rates and contributed to a growth in mistrust of Kosovo's key institutions of government, both international and indigenous' (UNDP, 2006: xiii). The EU 2011 *Progress Report for Kosovo* points out that 'the weak rule of law, corruption, high level of informal activities, and ad hoc policies have increased economic uncertainty and deep structural problems continued to hamper the economy' (European Commission, 2011: 30). Hence it is suggested that the process of economic reform should prioritize welfare and empowerment of the most marginalized; international actors should support and provide guidance, but leave local actors and communities to take the lead in the development of a market-orientated economy (Richmond, 2010: 33).

CONJECTURES FOR KOSOVO'S FUTURE

Today, peace in Kosovo is stable but not sustainable. The path to sustainable peace is obstructed by fragile governance, fragmented ethnic power sharing and social injustice, as well as by the overlapping and contested international presences that allow the functioning of Serb parallel structures and hold the situation of northern Kosovo in limbo. These obstacles are the key factors that will shape the future of Kosovo.

There are two separate developments that will influence the next stage of Kosovan politics. The first is related to the continuing EU-mediated dialogue between Kosovo and Serbia, where the fate of northern Kosovo and the normalization of political relations between the two countries are determinants of stability in Kosovo and beyond. The dialogue so far has produced a number of technical solutions to integrated border management, mutual recognition of university diplomas, exchange of civil registers and overcoming the obstacles set by Serbia on Kosovo's regional cooperation. The fate of Serbia's EU integration dynamic is linked to concessions with Kosovo. Equally, the survival of the incumbent government in Kosovo depends on external support. In this regard, the most sensitive issue remains the political status of northern Kosovo. The parties are gradually heading towards a solution that will provide the region with light autonomy and self-governing authorities beyond those envisaged in the Ahtisaari Proposal, as well as legitimizing and recognizing the existing parallel structure in northern Kosovo. However, such a solution is likely to trigger violent reaction from radical opposition in Serbia and Kosovo, eventual changes in the government, and stagnation of the process.

Second, the transformation of Vetëvendosje from a social movement into a political party and its participation in the November 2010 national elections in Kosovo, signified the emergence of a new populist political agenda in Kosovo. Vetëvendosje's political agenda, which is gaining extensive popularity, seeks on the one hand to encourage active citizenship, a welfare state and economic development in the area of production and employment, and on the other hand seeks to end international governance and supervision in Kosovo, and in doing so to establish a new partnership between locals and internationals that facilitates and supports the socio-economic development of Kosovo (Visoka, 2011).

However, a critical issue here concerns the emerging ethnic politics that risk further segregation between the Albanian majority and the Serb minority (and other minorities), which could effectively delay ethnic reconciliation and social cohesion in Kosovo. This ethnic-based confrontation could be transferred to the institutions, where Vetëvendosje is constantly increasing its influence both within Kosovo's parliament, and outside, through protests and exclusionary practices that promote nationalist ideology and implicitly deny ethnic difference and pluralism in society. Although such practices are part of political change, they should not endanger the multi-ethnic character of the state and constitutional order in Kosovo.

Arguably, to avoid any potential destabilisation in Kosovo, certain changes are necessary, including the creation of a functioning, democratic state with coherent, legal, and representative political structures, a sustainable peace between Kosovar-Serbs and Kosovar-Albanians, and mutual recognition and cooperation between the Republic of Kosovo and the Republic of Serbia that would finally open the way for common integration within Euro-Atlantic structures, as a guarantee for long-term stability in the entire region.

3

ETHNICITY, ETHNIC CONFLICTS AND SECESSIONISM IN ETHIOPIAN POLITICS

Bezawit Beyene

THEORETICAL OVERVIEW

Ethnicity is one aspect of identity around which people organize themselves; it is often the core element by which people mobilize and seek political power. Harff and Gurr define ethnic groups as 'psychological communities' whose members share a persisting sense of common interest and identity based on some combination of shared historical experience and valued cultural traits; beliefs, language, ways of life, or a common homeland (2004: 3). Moreover, 'ethnicity is not a thing or a collective asset of a particular group; it is a social relation in which social actors perceive themselves and are perceived by others as being culturally distinct collectivities' (Malešsevic', 2004: 4).

Ethnic groups and their characteristics are viewed in a number of different ways. For some scholars, ethnic groups have a certain characteristic unique to the group that is consistent and inherent, whereas for others, elements of the group character are mutable, and marked only when viewed in relation to other groups. It is important to understand, however, that these characteristics are not always consistent and that changes are almost inevitable. Solidarity within the group is often strong, which creates the potential for the group to mobilize members around their shared ethnicity in order to protect common interests or needs.

Human needs theory explains the causes of identity (ethnic) group mobilization and conflict as the consequence of a failure to fulfil human developmental needs. John Burton and Edward Azar argued that 'protracted social conflicts' are caused when people are not able to acquire the means to meet their basic needs. Basic needs, as explained by Azar, include 'security, recognition and acceptance, fair access to political institutions and economic participation', in general referred to as developmental needs (1990: 7–10).

Azar argues that individuals predominantly attempt to meet these developmental needs through the formation of identity groups, and that the rise of politically active identity groups stems from two sources. The first of these sources is the colonial legacy, from the period when various European powers used the 'divide and rule' system, privileging certain groups over others. The second source is an historical pattern of rivalry and contest among communal actors. In this case, the capacity to fulfil human needs presupposes the ability to access political and economic power, which is thwarted if power is dominated by a single group or by a combination of groups that tends to discriminate against others. The inability to share power and ensure equitable distribution is influenced by the acceptance or rejection of group identity (Azar, 1990: 7–10). In most instances dominant groups try to assimilate other groups by coercive means (Burton, 1990: 37).

When ethnicity is not managed through peace-oriented and democratic policies, it inherently involves and perpetuates conflict; notwithstanding that ethnicity is also a major cornerstone of social organization. Ethnic politicization and conflict occur for various reasons, the major ones being economic, political and cultural inequalities.

Harff and Gurr describe ethno-nationalist groups as 'relatively large and regionally concentrated ethnic groups that lie within the boundaries of one state or of several adjacent states; their modern political movements are directed towards achieving greater autonomy or independent statehood' (2004: 23). Secession 'is the formal withdrawal from membership of a polity by section. It is the attempt by an ethnic or regional group(s) to withdraw its region from the control of the state of which it is part' (Baker, 1998: 6). Most African countries in the post-independence era are facing rebellious tendencies from secessionist groups which in one way or another consider themselves different, marginalized from the existing system of governance and culturally discriminated against. Political secession is pursued either by groups who have no hope of achieving their political and economic interests (their developmental needs) within the existing state system, or by those who believe their national identity is totally distinct and would be better expressed through the existence of a separate state.

ETHNIC POLITICS AND SECESSIONIST MOVEMENTS IN ETHIOPIA

Historical background

The political history of Ethiopia is permeated with ethnic rivalry and conflict. Since the early dynasties, the rulers were descended only from certain ethnic groups, reinforcing the belief that they were the people chosen by God to lead the country. The Amhara dynasties in particular traced their origin from the Old Testament, claiming that the first king who founded the dynasty in the first century AD was Menelik I, the son of King Solomon of Israel and Queen of Sheba of Axum (Axum was the first dynastic state from which the later Abyssinian dynasties had their origin). This line of ancestry, sustained until 1974, received strong support from the Orthodox Christian Church, and the history of the Axumite and Amhara dynasties was glorified and used to give legitimacy to the ruling power.

Throughout the *Zemene Mesafinet* (Era of Princes) from 1769 to 1855, competition and conflict between the central power or emperor and the regional lords or princes was prevalent (Aalen, 2002: 2–3). Since this period, when control over central power was pursued by lords, sultans and chiefs organized along ethnic lines from different regions, Ethiopia has exhibited precisely such a pattern of rivalry and contest amongst key actors and, as Azar noted, this is one of the reasons for the emergence of ethnic-based political groups (1990: 7).

The process of consolidating central power in Ethiopia was started by Emperor Tewdros II in 1855. His actions included reducing the power of regional lords and establishing a 'national army'. Emperor Yohannes (1872–89), who succeeded Emperor Tewdros II, tried to continue the centralization, but using different techniques. His approach could be described as 'controlled regionalism', but it failed to achieve its objective (Zewde, 1991: 44). It was during the reign of Emperor Menelik II (1889–1913) that Ethiopia assumed its current territorial boundaries.

Emperor Menelik II pursued an expansionist policy and launched several military campaigns, subjugating and annexing the various ethnic groups and communities that occupied the southern and western parts of the country. Following this expansionist political movement, ethnic entities like the Oromo, the Wolaita, the Sidama, the Gurage and the Kafa came under the rule of the central ruling power. However, the expansionism of Menelik II was subject to different theories and interpretations; some groups argue that the process was one of unification, while others consider it internal colonization (Aalen, 2002: 3). For example, the internal colonization argument was widely used by ethno-national groups such as the Oromo Liberation Front (OLF) and Ogaden National Liberation Front (ONLF). The subjective nature of these arguments, or 'rewriting' of history, is an inherent challenge, allowing nationalist groups to select the interpretations that facilitate political mobilization and domination by one or more groups.

The proponents of the internal colonization argument cite evidence that the system applied by the expansionists was exploitative, allocating a different status to individuals based on their ethnic background. Central government representatives (Amhara) were dispatched throughout the country, and were referred to as *neftegna*, literally meaning 'bearers of guns', by the groups under their control (Tronvoll, 2000: 12). Since the 1890s, the Abyssinian forces arrived with the intention of incorporating new areas by enforcing taxation and the Abyssinian system of governance. In some areas such as Welaita and Kefa, they faced resistance and used violent measures to subjugate the people. They used cultural stereotypes, which regarded people in specific areas as 'backward' and 'pagan', in order to find justification for this domination.

The proponents of the unification theory, however, view the process as 'primarily an outcome of internal power struggles between Menelik and competing forces' (Aalen, 2002: 3). They consider Ethiopia a truly 'multi-ethnic national society' which emerged from centuries of interaction and acculturation between ethnic groups (ICG, 2009: 2). Other perspectives on Ethiopian history recognise the injustices and the domination of one group over others at various times, but view expansionism as a natural process of state formation.

Emperor Haile Selassie (1930–74) continued consolidating central power and nation building, which was strengthened by the introduction of a constitution. However, continued inequalities and injustice led to various peasant rebellions and the emergence of ethnically based liberation movements in such areas as Eritrea, Tigray, Oromiya, Sidama and Ogaden (Alem, 2004: 100).

From 1855 to 1974, successive imperial rulers from Emperor Tewdros to Emperor Haile Selassie attempted to end ethnic political rivalries and to consolidate the rival constituencies under a central power dominated by the Amhara or Tigre ethnic groups. They aimed for the 'cultural homogenization' of the country, which was achieved through the centralization of state power and a one-language policy (Alem, 2004: 99). Rulers attempted to assimilate other ethnic groups into the Amhara culture while simultaneously rejecting the culture and identity of those groups.

The Derg, a Marxist military regime led by Mengestu Hailemaryam, took power in 1974, by overthrowing the imperial rule, which had been feudal and characterized by economic and political inequalities and exploitation that favoured the dominant ethnic group and local lords. However, from taking power in 1974 until its overthrow in 1991, the Derg too continued to promote a centralized unitary state. The new regime maintained the one-language (Amharic) policy and changed little of the feudal nature of the previous regime (Firebrace, 1983: 17).

However, the imposition of the Amharic language could not be tolerated by other ethnic constituencies; language was believed to be a key factor of identity and valued as an essential means of cultural preservation and political participation. The Marxist rule of the Derg used more coercive policies which led to the emergence and growth of different ethnically based political groups (Tronvoll, 2000: 14).

Prior to the military regime, successive rulers had been deaf to the demands of different ethnicities. Most rulers pursued a united Ethiopia slogan without recognizing the rights and cultures of different ethnic groups, a policy which led to the growth of ethnic-based political groups. Progressive demands by these groups were made in response to coercive treatment by central government, and some began their struggle during Emperor Haile Selassie's rule.

The Eritrean liberation movement for independence from Ethiopia (1961–91) was distinct from that of other ethnic groups in Ethiopia, because of Eritrea's earlier experience of 'occupation' by Italy. The inability of successive Ethiopian governments to recognize the unique identity and needs of the Eritreans contributed to their decision to secure their identity through the establishment of a separate state. Factors such as ethnic dominance by central government, inability to exercise political power, and cultural and economic underdevelopment were significant in the struggle against successive Ethiopian governments.

The Tigrean People's Liberation Front (TPLF), which has been in power since 1991, ruling under the umbrella of the Ethiopian government (Ethiopian Peoples' Revolutionary Democratic Front, PRDF), was itself the product of ethnic grievance against Amhara dominion. The Tigrean people expressed their discontent with the governing system as well as with the unfair taxation by the emperor and their own 'feudal lords' in the Wayyane rebellion of 1943 (Firebrace, 1983: 17). The TPLF began armed struggle in 1975, with the objective of 'self-determination' by Tigreans. A major factor in the emergence of the TPLF movement was their exclusion from power; therefore, having experienced political alienation, the TPLF later recognized the concerns of other ethno-national groups and proposed the establishment of a federal system that would address these problems within Ethiopia.

The Oromo Liberation Front (OLF)

The OLF began its quest for self-rule during the military regime and still seeks independence for the Oromo people. The Oromo people form one of the largest ethnic groups in Ethiopia, with a population of around 17 million across approximately 600,000 square kilometres. The Oromo liberation movement grew out of the Mecha-Tulema Self-Help Association in 1973, which developed a political awareness of the unequal relationship between the Oromo people and the Abyssinian people in terms of economic, political and cultural rights. This grievance became the motivation for the Oromo to organize themselves politically.

The OLF had been fighting central ruling governments since the Derg, and since the 1980s in alliance with the TPLF. This alliance enabled the OLF to consider an alternative option to that of separation from the Ethiopian state, namely participation in the transitional government of Ethiopia after the defeat of the Derg in 1991. This lasted for a brief period during which the OLF promoted Oromo culture and the use of the Latin alphabet in the Oromo region within the educational system. However, the alliance was short-lived after disagreements began to emerge over the system of governance and the upcoming election in 1992. The group again returned to its original objective of an independent Oromia, to which the government responded with persecution and mass arrest.

The current system of ethnic federalism has failed to win the hearts of the Oromo people. The system reorganized the country into ethnically divided federal regions and placed power sharing at its core. However, with power concentrated at central government level, where one ethnic group (the Tigre) has predominance, the right of the Oromo to govern their own state is limited. OLF is assumed to mobilize the largest ethnic group in the country, which poses the greatest threat to the federal government. OLF criticize the current government as deceptive, superficial and exploitative, and in a sense similar to the earlier, oppressive Abyssinian powers. The government, in its so-called fight against 'illegal political groups', has used repressive action against many individuals, including large-scale imprisonment, killing and exile.

The Ogaden National Liberation Front (ONLF)

The Ogaden clan is one of the dominant ethnic Somali groups that inhabit the eastern lowland part of Ethiopia. It is the second major group with a distinct identity, and it maintains a long-standing feud with the central rulers (ICG, 2009: 27). The ONLF began with irredentist objectives (the belief of an ethnic group that it belongs not where it presently is but to the 'mother country' to which it aspires to return, in this case to the Republic of Somalia); however, it has come to limit its objective to the right of Ogadens to self-determination and self-rule.

During the early years after the Derg took power from imperial rule, Somalis in the Ogaden area tried to use the instability to further their aim of joining the Republic of Somalia (Lewis, 1989: 574). During the Ogaden War (1977–8), the West Somali Liberation Front (WSLF) was the prominent group fighting against Ethiopian military forces with support from the Republic of Somalia (Møller, 2009: 9). After the defeat of the WSLF by the Ethiopian military force, the group disintegrated and the ONLF was established by members of the WSLF, maintaining wider support and challenging the EPRDF's power since 1994.

Until 1992, Somalis in Ethiopia had never held positions in central government. The Ogaden region is politically neglected and economically under-developed, a policy which was in part designed to prevent the establishment of a base that could provide economic and human resources for ethno-nationalist groups, many of whom identify themselves more with Somalia than with Ethiopia.

Since 1992, the Somali regional government was established with parliamentary representation in the central government. However, the Somali ethnic group remain dissatisfied by the current government system and as a result, the region has been one of the major areas of instability in the country. For instance, the region twice experienced a change of regional leaders and executives within two years after the establishment of the transitional government in 1991.

In 1992, most representatives of the Somali regional parliament were ONLF members. This group was replaced in 1993 by appointed parliamentarians who again did not last long after they began to accuse the federal government of interference in the internal affairs of the region. They voted for secession, a move that led to a severe deterioration in the relationship between the ONLF and the federal government (Markakis, 1996: 568). ONLF insurgency continued during this period. with bomb attacks on hotels, market places, schools and other public areas in Ogaden, the region's capital. The government's response was to use violence and collective punishment, further alienating Ethiopian Somalis (ICG, 2009: 28).

THE EXISTING SYSTEM OF POLITICS AND GOVERNANCE

The current Ethiopian government, comprising a range of different ethnic-based political parties, came to power in 1991, by defeating the Derg regime. With a history of struggle based on ethnic griev-ances, the EPRDF was committed to recognizing the rights of each national or ethnic group in order to address political, economic and cultural inequalities between the different groups in Ethiopia. However, this involved adopting a radical approach.

The EPRDF introduced controversial and contentious policies, including the 'acceptance of Eritrean independence and the reversal of the age-old quest of Ethiopian rulers to centralise the state and integrate a population belonging to more than eighty ethnic groups or nationalities' (Young, 1996: 531). In 1995, the EPRDF formed a federal republic state, the constituents being ethnically divided regional states, as a measure that was deemed to be in recognition of and an answer to the quests of ethnic constituencies, nations and nationalities. The 1994 Constitution ratified the UN Declaration of Human Rights and, most importantly, granted the right of nations to self-determination up to secession in what was a fundamental turning point for Ethiopian politics. The EPRDF also appeared to be supportive of a multi-party political system.

Within this structure, every ethnic group was granted the right 'to speak, to write and to develop its own language; to express, to develop and to promote its culture; and to preserve its history' (Constitution of Federal Republic of Ethiopia, Art 39.2). Furthermore, the consti-tution ratified 'the right to a full measure of self-government that includes the right to establish institutions of government in the territory that it inhabits and to equitable representation in state and federal governments' (Constitution of Federal Republic of Ethiopia, Art 39.3). Enabling groups to preserve 'their cultural and consensus values' is both vital and a stepping-stone to 'long term integration'; thus the move made by the EPRDF government to recognize and support identity groups is vital (Burton, 1990: 140).

The positive benefits of ethnic-based federalism as a system of governance and the ratification of 'self-determination up to secession' are contested by different groups. Advocates of ethnic-based federalism assert that it is the glue that enables multi-ethnic Ethiopia to remain unified with territorial integrity, and the federal system has been promoted as one that could allow and enable the different ethnic groups to govern their own affairs. This form of federalism has also been welcomed by many as the only remedy for 'historic injustice' (ICG, 2009: 23), and as the best way to ensure political stability in the country by creating sufficient political space for the public at large and for multiple parties and organizations established along ethnic or non-ethnic political lines.

The other important factor of support for the current form of governance is the recognition it gives to the rights of ethnic groups to preserve their culture and develop their language. For instance, students in the education system can learn in their own language using curricula that enable children to acquire knowledge of their culture and history. The regions' official languages have become the respective native languages of the regions' peoples; there has been visible improvement in service delivery and access to the state at local levels, and the struggle of people for their cultural development has gained better support (ICG, 2009: 17, 24).

From the start, however, some groups have condemned this form of federalism as designed to weaken national feelings and ultimately to fragment the country. Such groups have directed their accusations most specifically at the Tigrean People's Liberation Front (TPLF), a minority group that still manages to dominate the government. The TPLF is accused of using this divisive system as a malicious means to maintain their power. Furthermore, some groups consider that 'the new regional state boundaries lack historical validity and needlessly endanger the survival of the Ethiopian state' (Alem, 2004: 99). It is clear that the government continues to face challenges with regard to inter-ethnic relations, boundary demarcation, regional cooperation, and the lack of legitimacy of the central government.

CURRENT POLITICAL PITFALLS IN ETHIOPIA

Centralization of power

The current form of federal governance has for the most part failed to achieve the promised results with regard to ensuring an equitable power distribution, peace and stability. For instance, the International Crisis Group (ICG) observed, 'Constitutionally, Ethiopia is a federal polity, but its federal entities are controlled by the strongly centralised EPRDF that predetermines decisions from the prime minister's palace in the capital to remote rural kebelles' (2009: 15).

The major drawback with the current federal system, therefore, is that power is not actually decentralized. Although in principle, the prime objective in adopting federalism is to enable and empower national constituencies for self-governance by diffusing power and decision making downward to local levels, and in other ways to avert ethnic conflicts, nonetheless the regional governments appear to be mere functionalities that implement federal policies and laws rather than represent and defend the interests of the people of their respective regions. It can therefore be asserted that the Ethiopian political system cannot be considered as truly federal, because of the nominal position the regional states have within the political arena.

Discrimination by the government

The political history of the country provides adequate justification for the hypothesis that the control of state power by a single ethnic group, or by a combination of ethnic groups, leads to emergence of grievance, dissatisfaction, rivalry and conflict between ethnic constituencies, and ultimately to unrest and disorder in the nation. In the case of the current political system, it seems that history is repeating itself. Constitutionally, all regional states are equal and the representation of all 'nations and nationalities' is guaranteed. Ensuring equality in this sense presupposes that the state mechanism is impartial. Yet the impartiality of the present state is called into question: 'The TPLF having fought seventeen years of war against the Derg, assumed the "right" to more and even "lifelong" power' (Gebreselassie, 2003: 21).

At regional levels, too, the impartiality of state bodies has been questioned, because in regions with diverse ethnic populations, dominant or majority ethnic groups have political, socio-cultural and economic advantages and dominion over the smaller groups. For example, minority groups are forced by the system and its internal dynamics to adopt the language and cultural elements of dominant groups, thereby acknowledging their power over the smaller groups. It has also been contested that in a country such as Ethiopia, factors like labour migration and mixed parenthood will make 'simplistic deline-ation between ethnicity and territory' complicated, and moreover that the domination of one ethnic group over others produces 'new minorities' in such regional states (ICG, 2009: 23).

The existing dynamics within regions have negatively affected 'settlers' from different ethnic backgrounds and regions; the conflict in Assosa in 2000 is evidence for this, where ethnic Amhara, Oromo and Berta were attacked by the indigenous people of the region. Sometimes such conflicts have taken on the character of ethnic cleansing; 'non-natives' have been chased away in Arussi, Harar and Bale (ICG, 2009: 24). However, inappropriate courses of action appear to substitute for effective solutions; at the national level political leaders advocate heterogeneity, and yet simultaneously at regional level they insist on homogeneity.

These actions were seen as the dawn of another ethnic domination in Ethiopia, and as sowing the seeds of further ethnic tension. The 2005 election revealed latent ethnic tensions when the government and political parties each described the other as a threat to the well-being and security of another particular ethnic group.

Ongoing ethnic conflicts

Various ethnic conflicts have occurred among the constituencies of the country's federal system over the last two decades. Most conflicts have not arisen from the existence of irreconcilable ethnic differences, but from competition over state resources:

> Ethnic conflicts have not disappeared but have been either transferred from the national to the regional, district and kebelle levels or have been contained by the security forces. Relations between ethnic groups have become increasingly competitive, as they vie for control of administrative boundaries and government budgets in addition to land and natural resources.
>
> (ICG, 2009: 25)

Mere recognition of ethnic identities and promoting the values of different groups will not end ethnic competition and conflict, unless the developmental needs of all ethnic groups are met in an equitable and just manner. Although the current government has been promising a lasting answer to the problem, it is very clear that an equitable distribution of resources has not been realized, particularly when government-sponsored parties use regional resource bases more and more to satisfy their patronage. These have given rise to arguments and conflict right from the national parliament level to the lowest localities.

On the other hand, demarcating the regional state between different ethnic groups has proved a challenge for the federal government. Conflicting claims between groups over border areas have led to antagonistic relations in various regions. In 1998, the Guji Oromo and the Gedeo fought each other over Hagere Mariam town. Again in 2006, the Guji Oromo and the Boran Oromo engaged in repeated clashes that included killing, property damage and displacement (ICG, 2009: 25).

The ICG has observed that local politicians and even higher officials of regions have at times incited conflicts between their people and the members of neighbour regions, often due to competition over 'administrative power, land, tax revenue and, potentially, food aid' (ICG, 2009: 24–6).

Ethnicity versus citizenship

The division of the federal constituencies of a country into regions and administrative sections along ethnic lines tends to hinder shared and strong national sentiment. The EPRDF's attempt to enable groups to maintain and develop their identity was seen as a middle ground between the two options: that is, between the imposition of a 'homogeneous' identity, and accepting the demands of secessionist groups. However, the ethnic federal system has encouraged a high level of loyalty by Ethiopians to their own ethnic groups, to the extent that it restricts cooperation and hinders the concept of a shared future. The division of the country along ethnic lines gives much emphasis to the separate identity, leaving less room for 'shared national goals' (Berhe, 2008: 31).

Gebreselassie has noted that 'without national unity, so essential to political stability, it is impossible for constitutionalism to take root' (2003: 32). If adequate emphasis is not given to the enhancement and maintenance of shared national identity, adoption of ethnic-based federalism is more likely to lead to instability and disintegration. In line with this view, the case of Ethiopian federalism seems to have scored less success than it promised, and currently faces a gloomy prospect for the future in terms of national cohesion.

Distribution of economic power

Economic power is vital to the exercise of political power. However, the regional states that comprise the current Ethiopian federal state are economically weak; this constitutes one of the major factors that has made them dependent on central government, and inadequate in active self-governance. In many instances, conflicts between ethnic groups have had their origin in a regional need to gain a stronger economic position, and this need has translated into rivalry and conflict over land, population, tax revenue, and resources such as forests and rivers.

Although most regions have recorded improved economic growth, the perception of inequitable distribution of resources has the capacity to cause ethnic conflict. Economic development is also affected by the positions of exclusivity held by regional state elites. The regional elites make decisions such as:

> distribution and control of economic assets including land, capital, credit, and licenses to operate commercial and financial enterprises so as to benefit their own ethnic constituents. In the process, market rules of competition are either superseded or otherwise manipulated, with the result that members of other ethnic communities are excluded from participation in the local economy.
>
> (Gebreselassie, 2003: 34)

SECESSION AS A SOLUTION

There are currently two major forces, the ONLF and the OLF, that have been active in Ethiopia with the objective of total separation or secession from the country. These forces have been in opposition to the current government system, as they perceive it to be entirely similar to the old, undemocratic, and oppressive governments that ruled the country previously.

Both these forces have engaged in brutal military actions, although the government's response was no better. The ONLF organized and carried out bombings of market places, hotels, buses and trains, in which the only victims were civilians. From their side, the OLF massacred civilians and members of the Ethiopian military forces on various occasions.

These forces chose violent actions as a way to compel the government into accepting their demand for secession. However, the assumption that the establishment of a separate state will answer all economic and political grievances is not well supported. The cases of Ethiopia and Eritrea, the former Yugoslavia and the former Soviet Union are examples where separation was not followed by equality for all ethnic groups gained through the equitable distribution of power and resources. Instead, these countries have faced the emergence of new ethnic-based grievances and secessionist demands.

CONCLUSION

At an institutional level, the current government has attempted to introduce federalism, but it has not fully succeeded in distributing authority and in empowering regional states to meet the needs of their constituencies, and this has resulted in increased insurgency, particularly by the ONLF and OLF. For a federal system to achieve its intended objective, such as reducing secessionist tendencies, 'democratic government' is vital. The government needs to consider more than a constitutional division of power; the free and actual exercise of power by those regions should be ensured.

Attempts to bring about and ensure peace and to end existing hostilities should also involve neutral and mandated actors, such as the African Union. Previous initiatives by the government to negotiate peace have failed due to the asymmetrical power relationship between the government and the ethno-national insurgents. A statement made by the ONLF is worth remembering and considering: 'Any negotiations with Addis Ababa can only take place under the auspices of the international community in a neutral venue with a third neutral party mediator' (*Sudan Tribune*, 2010).

More power must be devolved from the federal government to the regions and to sub-regional levels. Such decentralization ensures checks and balances between the different levels of government and can ensure the accountability of regional government to protect the rights of minority groups. The capacity of regional units to develop their own policies and strategies that reflect contextual and local interests needs to be enhanced. A democratic mechanism that safeguards regional power should be established so that regions feel secure. It is important to open up space for other political parties (both ethnic-based and non-ethnic) to operate legally and within a decentralized and inclusive political set-up. These changes should be targeted not only at the two particular regions where separatist groups operate, but should be applied across all regions. Most importantly, the government must be genuinely committed to a multi-party political system.

Peacebuilding at the institutional level should happen alongside the restoring of relationships. As noted by Francis, 'Whether in situations of latent conflict which have not yet erupted into violence, or in post-violence situations which remain volatile, work is needed to adjust and stabilise relationships' (2002: 36). This could be done through government-level recognition of the unjust and unequal relationships promoted during previous governments, including public discussions that address past stereotypes. Such processes could build trust and cooperation between rival groups and between neighbouring regions as well as within regions; this level of trust could grow into trust of the system itself. The government needs to promote working relationships to reduce differences and to allow the emergence of interests that unite different groups, even when these might require changing the form of the federalism or revising the constitution.

To conclude, the federal system, introduced to avert ethnic conflict and secessionist tendencies, was not able to achieve its goals. The centralization of economic and political power at federal level violates the principle of self-governance and of democracy in general. It is also jeopardized by ethnic favouritism, state partiality, and the absence of a commitment to a national goal. Secessionism still threatens Ethiopia's stability.

PART II

RECONCILIATION AND DEALING WITH THE PAST

PART II

RECONCILIATION OF MAN
CRADLING WITH THE DEAD

4

STATE FAILURE AND CIVIL SOCIETY POTENTIAL: RECONCILIATION IN THE DEMOCRATIC REPUBLIC OF CONGO

Verity Mould

INTRODUCTION

Between 1998 and 2007, the conflict in the Democratic Republic of Congo (DRC) resulted in the deaths of 5.4 million people; a death toll greater than any other conflict since the Second World War (International Rescue Committee, 2006). These figures highlight just one aspect of the severe devastation caused by a prolonged conflict that has ravaged the country's economic and social resources, left millions dead and many more displaced, homeless, malnourished and suffering from disease.

THE COLONIAL ERA TO POST-MOBUTU DEMOCRACY

The DRC's long history of violence, since Belgian rule until the present day, caused Frantz Fanon to remark that 'Africa has the shape of a gun and its trigger is Congo' (Savage and Vanspauwen, 2008: 323). Following the prolific exploitation of both human and natural resources during the colonial period and the subsequent, relatively peaceful move to independence in June 1960, the country fell into political chaos within its first year of independence, and was led for the next five years by a series of weak civilian governments (Savage and Vanspauwen, 2008: 326). On 24 November 1965, Joseph Mobutu, then chief of staff of the army, seized his opportunity and took power in a military coup, surviving as head of the Congolese government under autonomous rule until 1997, and leading a regime characterized by extreme levels of corruption, human rights violations and political repression (Savage, 2006 :3).

After negotiations at the Sovereign National Conference failed in August 1991, further political uncertainty came in 1994, when the effects of the Rwandan genocide spilled over into the DRC. Many of the 1.2 million Hutu refugees who fled to eastern Congo were soon regrouped in refugee camps under the direction of the Interahamwe, the political group largely responsible for deaths during the Rwandan genocide. The leaders of the Interahamwe also recruited Congolese Hutus, forming the Army for the Liberation of Rwanda (ALIR). They carried out attacks along the border against Rwandan and Ugandan forces in Congo, and also launched a counter-attack against the new, Tutsi-led Rwandan government based in Kigali (Savage, 2006: 4). In response, a newly formed coalition between Ugandan and Rwandan forces and Congolese fighters, the Democratic Forces Alliance for the Liberation of Congo-Zaire (AFDL), led by Laurent-Desire Kabila, forced Mobutu finally to surrender power and flee the country. In May 1997, Kabila announced himself as head of the government of the newly named Democratic Republic of Congo, but his style of political leadership failed to involve many of the democratic components that the country's new name would suggest (Havermans, 2000).

Following Kabila's assumption of power, the formally allied Rwandan and Ugandan forces switched to serve their own agendas. The Rwandan, Congolese and Ugandan armed forces, along with numerous rebel groups, then fought each other for power and control of the country's vast mineral resources. The ensuing war, labelled by Borello (2004: iii) as 'Africa's First World War' soon took on a truly international nature when Angolan, Zimbabwean, Chadian and Namibian troops stepped in, in support of Kabila's government.

THE ROAD TO PEACE

A ceasefire in Lusaka in 1999 was followed by the Lusaka Peace Accord. This had little impact however, and the devastating conse-quences of this can partially be seen in the over 3 million deaths that resulted between 1998 and 2002, from continued fighting, malnutrition and disease (International Rescue Committee, 2006).

The turning point came when Laurent Kabila's son, Joseph, assumed the Congolese presidency following the senior Kabila's assassination in January 2001. After four months of false starts, the Inter-Congolese Dialogue, a proposal of the Lusaka Agreement, opened in Sun City in South Africa on 25 February 2002. The Sun City Accord was signed in April 2002, and by the end of the year all stakeholders had signed the Global and Inclusive Agreement. It was here for the first time that the Congolese Government showed its full support for a unified, national reconciliation effort, joining with civil society groups, unarmed opposition, and the warring factions in the process.

THE TRUTH AND RECONCILIATION COMMISSION IN THE DRC

One of the five democracy-supporting institutions established as part of the Global and Inclusive Agreement was the Truth and Reconciliation Commission (TRC). It was through this commission that the government was primarily involved in the reconciliation process.

It is widely agreed that truth seeking has an important and obligatory role in the reconciliation process of any country or region seeking to move on from a period of protracted conflict. Truth commissions are one way of revealing this truth, providing a victim-centred approach that enables wrongs to be identified and acknowledged, and giving victims some form of compensation for the harm caused to them.

The overall mission of the Truth and Reconciliation Commission was to 'establish truth and to promote peace, justice, reparation, forgiveness and reconciliation for sustaining national unity' (Kambala and Savage, 2008: 346). The mandate was twofold; first, through truth-seeking mechanisms, to identify the victims, collaborators and perpetrators of crimes and human rights violations; and second, having established the truth, to promote national unity by 'acknowledging the facts, asking and receiving pardon and providing reparation and rehabilitation for victims' (Davis and Hayner, 2009: 21). The mandate included all crimes committed over the 46-year period between independence in June 1960 and the end of the transition period in 2006.

The TRC was legally established on 30 July 2004, but by August of that year the head of the commission, Bishop Jean-Luc Kuye, without giving any justification, announced that it was not able to investigate human rights violations, but would instead focus on conflict mediation activities (Borello, 2004: 46). In this mediatory role, particularly in the eastern provinces, the TRC was instrumental in collecting victims' complaints, mediating between soldiers of the Forces Armées de la République Démocratique du Congo (FARDC) and Mayi Mayi militia, and facilitating coexistence initiatives between different ethnic groups (Kambala and Savage, 2008: 346). In this way the TRC upheld its mission to 'establish truth and ... promote peace ... and reconciliation for sustaining national unity', but failed to fulfil its specific mandate of investigating political crimes and human rights abuses.

One of the characteristics of truth commissions is the inclusion of some degree of amnesty, and the Congolese TRC was no exception in this. At the Inter-Congolese Dialogue, the parties involved made a power-sharing concession in the form of a Transitional Government of National Unity. However, many of the rebel groups only agreed to the concession upon securing a promised amnesty protection for crimes they had committed during the conflict. For the sake of moving the transition process forward this condition was granted, and in November 2005, the provision was extended to include crimes committed since 1996. This meant, controversially, that those responsible for the assassination of Laurent Kabila were protected by a legal amnesty.

In the case of the DRC, the amnesty was seen as a small price to pay to appease the numerous rebel groups and to start to bring some level of peace to the war-weary country. Many others, however, share Slye's opinion that it is 'one of the most controversial mechanisms contemporary societies have used to address violent pasts' (2000: 170). The controversy surrounding this issue of amnesty will be discussed in the following analysis of why the TRC failed fully to achieve its reconciliatory objectives.

WHY THE TRC FAILED

The work of the Congolese TRC has come under much criticism. It has been labelled a 'stinging failure' (Nyabiringu, quoted in Chaco, 2009) and referred to as a 'truth omission instead of a truth commission' (Yav, 2007).

The formation of the commission was highly politicized from the start, with the eight initial commissioners nominated by members of the parties belonging to the transitional government.

Having committed various atrocities themselves, these commissioners naturally had a vested interest in seeing that the work of the TRC did not succeed. Following pressure from the international community, the commission added 13 new members, but the power still lay firmly in the hands of the appointed political commissioners, and the resulting disunity between commissioners made concrete decisions regarding the operation of the commission very hard to reach (Kasuku, 2010). Various structural barriers meant that the Congolese public failed to engage fully in the work of the TRC. There was very little public ownership, and the conflict survivors were seen solely as beneficiaries rather than participants in the process (Borello, 2004: 40).

Because of the lack of legitimacy and transparency in its design and implementation, the commission was also unable to attract funding from major international donors. These external constraints, coupled with the low level of funding that actually materialized from the Congolese government's promised budget, significantly constrained the commission's capacity to carry out its work across the country (Muiti, quoted in Kahora and Kumakana, 2009).

At the Inter-Congolese Dialogue it was agreed that the pursuit of justice would be an integral part of the work of the TRC. By the end of the conflict, however, the judicial infrastructure had all but collapsed, and according to a survey by Altit and colleagues in May 2004, only around 20 per cent of the population had access to a formal judicial system (quoted in Kambala and Savage, 2008: 336–9). Further condemnation from others such as Kamwimbi (2006), describing the judicial system as corrupt, riddled with tribalism and nepotism, and lacking the necessary impartiality, independence and professionalism to prosecute perpetrators effectively, highlights the lack of support available to the TRC from the country's judicial system.

The blanket nature of the amnesty provision, coupled with the incapacity of the judicial system to carry out trials, meant that there was no credible threat of prosecution and therefore no incentive for perpetrators to engage with the process, rendering its reconciliatory contribution useless. Despite these criticisms, there are others who suggest that the amnesty clause was actually fundamental in advancing the transition process, arguing that the most important goal for the transitional government was the protection and promotion of the fragile peace rather than the more aggressive pursuit of justice. Had the government focused more heavily on the prosecution of perpetrators, the country would very likely still be embroiled in major conflict, as a certain level of amnesty and leniency was necessary to engage the warring parties in the pursuit of peace (Kasuku, 2010). Savage and Vanspauwen emphasize the need to balance the two pursuits sensitively, the need to consider how much truth is needed for victims to gain a sense of justice, but also how much truth the DRC can bear in order to maintain peace (2008: 392).

The chief administrator for the TRC, Kasuku (2010), suggests rather insightfully that the failure of the TRC to uphold its mandate should come as no surprise, proposing instead that the international community's expectations were too high and that they were partly to blame for some of its weaknesses. He proposes that the government never intended to prosecute perpetrators of human rights abuses and that the exceptions to the amnesty clause were included under pressure to please the international community. Instead, he argues that the government chose to act pragmatically to ensure first that the fragile peace was maintained and strengthened before turning to the more aggressive pursuit of justice, suggesting that the TRC was an inappropriate mechanism for furthering reconciliation in the DRC at that time.

WHAT ROLE CAN THE CONGOLESE GOVERNMENT PLAY IN THE RECONCILIATION PROCESS TODAY?

In spite of strongly voiced opposition from leading civil society members concerning the government's conduct in its earlier approach to reconciliation in the DRC, the Congolese population still appears to have faith in its leaders to bring peace, security and justice to their country.

Since the closure of the TRC in 2006, the government's contribution to the reconciliation process has primarily been through negotiations with various rebel factions. The Nairobi peace talks held in 2007 and the Goma conference in 2008 led to a partnership between the Congolese and Rwandan governments to disarm one of the largest rebel groups, and to broker a ceasefire to end the ongoing violence and human rights abuses in the eastern provinces. This ceasefire remains fragile however, and by 23 July 2008, more than 200 people had been killed in the region and 150,000 displaced, with over 2,200 rape cases recorded in North Kivu in June 2008 alone (Trocaire, 2008). The government-led Amani process which emerged from the talks, focusing on the disarmament, demobilization and reintegration (DDR) of armed groups in North and South Kivu, failed to achieve its target. There is still much more work to be done in the DDR with ex-combatants, a process vital to furthering the reconciliation process in the DRC and one in which the Congolese government must continue to play a major role.

One particularly clear role that remains for the government in the reconciliation process is in leading the reform of both the security and judicial sectors. The integration of thousands of rebel soldiers into the national army, and concessions made in giving various rebel leaders high-ranking army positions, has left a highly undisciplined military, which continues to commit crimes and human rights abuses (Davis and Hayner, 2009: 8–9).

Calls for a comprehensive reform of the judicial sector will be equally difficult to meet. President Kabila's spoken commitment to pursuing justice in the DRC has in part been backed up by the government's scheme to train and recruit 2,000 qualified judges as well as initiating a training scheme for lawyers. However, this is somewhat contradictory to the government bill which granted amnesty for 'acts of war' committed in North and South Kivu since 2003 (Kasuku, 2010).

The Congolese government has a vital role to play in securing these conditions, and if these reforms are carried out, it is clear that the government still has the opportunity to play a leading role in the reconciliation process in the DRC. It must act soon, however, to meet the demands of the Congolese public, otherwise its legitimacy and credibility might soon be challenged and the fragile peace might once again be broken.

THE ROLE OF CIVIL SOCIETY ORGANIZATIONS IN THE RECONCILIATION PROCESS BEFORE 2002

In the early 1990s, a number of civil society groups began to document extensively human rights abuses in the DRC, and despite strong opposition from both the government and rebel factions, proved themselves to be a key force in opposing Mobutu's increasingly repressive regime (Davis and Hayner, 2009: 7–8). In the province of North Kivu, an umbrella group brought together more than 60 small regional non-governmental organizations (NGOs), facilitating inter-ethnic dialogue between local communities and bringing the government to a peace conference in Mweso in 1993. The disarmament of troops promised at the conference never materialized, but the work of civil society organizations (CSOs) continued and a national umbrella organization was formed at a meeting of more than 200 civil society representatives in Kinshasa in June 1997. The ensuing war in 1997 hampered civil society efforts, but a new peace campaign was launched in 1999, and with increased international awareness and pressure, the government agreed to hold a national debate on peace later on that year between the government, civil society representatives and the political opposition.

Despite these dialogues and the role of civil society leaders in organizing them, Havermans (2000) still concludes that the full potential of Congolese CSOs at the turn of the century had not been realized, partly because of the susceptibility of such groups to form and divide along ethnic lines. This weakness was made apparent at the Sun City talks in 2002 and, despite the clear unity displayed by the groups in their opposition to Mobutu's dictatorship, the exposure at Sun City showed that they lacked the necessary leadership and guidance to make the transition from mobilizing against to working alongside the government in mutually advancing the process of reconciliation (Masterton, 2006).

THE ROLE OF CIVIL SOCIETY ORGANIZATIONS IN THE RECONCILIATION PROCESS AFTER 2002

Following the criticism at the Sun City talks, civil society leaders took action to address the issues that had been so publicly exposed, and a newly united civil society was behind the initiation of the Goma conference in North Kivu in 2008, bringing the government to one of the worst-affected conflict areas to acknowledge and address the damage for themselves.

Since 2002, the involvement of domestic CSOs expanded within all areas of reconciliation work. Many organizations are involved in trauma counselling, particularly working with women who have been victims of sexual abuse, rape having been used extensively and systematically as a weapon of violence throughout the conflict. Through demobilization, counselling, education and the provision of basic needs and services, other organizations are working to reintegrate child soldiers into communities, especially in the eastern provinces where the forced conscription of child soldiers was particularly widespread.

Many local CSOs play an important role in recording and condemning human rights abuses. This work is not always warmly received by the Kinshasa government however, and the extent of the danger human rights activists face in carrying out their work was brought to the world's attention in June 2010 by the killing of one of Congo's leading human rights activists, Floribert Chebeya.

Other CSOs are able to span the lines of conflict and facilitate communication between enemy groups by holding a unique
position in society. In the DRC, where more than 85 per cent of the
65 million population are Christian, the church has a very strong
voice that the state cannot ignore. A similarly influential group of
domestic CSOs in the DRC is the media. In a country where 54 per
cent of the population listen to the radio daily, this particular form
of media plays a strategically vital role in the reconciliation process
(Vinck et al., 2008: 3). Some radio stations promote reconciliation
by actively disseminating accurate information, resisting hate media
and media manipulation, broadcasting radio programmes focusing
on reconciliation and grassroots issues, hosting listening groups and
carrying out reconciliation activities in local communities. Especially
in many of the DRC's vast expanses of isolated rural areas, these
radio programmes are integral in involving DRC citizens in a process
of unified, national reconciliation.

Many local CSOs are involved in effecting local justice, often
working through centuries-old traditional justice mechanisms. In the
DRC, local mechanisms such as the traditional community court
are used by CSOs to help bring justice at a community level. These
mechanisms bring communities together to engage in dialogue, ritual
and reconciliation through ceremonies involving truth telling, confession, forgiveness and purification rituals. Despite some criticism of
the limitations of these methods and possible bias of some of the
convictions, they provide some level of basic justice to over 80 per
cent of the population, and if well managed, hold great potential for
supporting the national reconciliation process (Kamwimbi, 2008:
361–3).

CASE STUDY OF THE WORK OF CIVIL SOCIETY ORGANIZATIONS IN EASTERN DRC

Compared with the many discussions regarding the reconciliatory
role of both the government and international community in the
DRC, there is very little Anglophone literature that acknowledges
the widespread work of domestic CSOs in the reconciliation process.
In light of this exposed gap in the literature, the author conducted a
survey, collating the views of domestic CSOs working in the east of
the country in a broad range of peace-building activities, including
trauma counselling, DDR, peace training through local seminars
and conferences, women's community projects, peace education and
mediation with the Mai-Mai militia (Mould, 2010).

When asked about the involvement of domestic CSOs in the reconciliation process, respondents all saw this involvement as fundamental, describing such organizations as catalysts of reconciliation and the door to peace in the DRC, acting as advocates for the population to the government, and fighting against impunity, poverty and ignorance. Whilst recognizing the leading role the Congolese government must play in the reconciliation process, for example in judicial sector reform, DDR of ex-combatants, monitoring natural resource extraction and creating jobs, respondents also emphasized the need for the government to listen to the voice of CSOs, which speak with authority on behalf of the Congolese population whose confidence they have gained through persistent grassroots work. Respondents emphasized that without the full inclusion of all members of society (in particular women, civilian conflict victims, ex-combatants and local-level CSOs), the reconciliation process would fail to advance.

The participants all faced obstacles to their work in the form of insufficient financial and physical resources, but more generally, they highlighted the difficulties of pursuing reconciliation within a traumatized population dominated by the language of hate, where people were not always ready to hear the message of peace.

It is clear from this research that the government must take a firm stand in leading the process at a national level, but must also do more to support and resource the work of local CSOs to recognize and fully harness the potential of their reconciliatory contribution.

CONCLUSION

As has been clearly shown in the first part of this chapter, the Congolese government's contribution to the reconciliatory process in the country has been distinctly lacking. Despite following the lead of countries such as South Africa in setting up a TRC, and therefore on paper at least, giving the appearance of having implemented various effective measures to initiate and further the process, in reality the extent of the government's practical involvement was much weaker. Strangled by various political and legal constraints, the TRC proved very ineffective in bringing any kind of reconciliation, and since its closure in 2006, there has been little effort made to renew the involvement of the central authorities in the process.

Rather than suggesting that the government's role should therefore be abandoned, this discussion has conversely called for the government to take a firmer stand and to lead the process from the front. Both the local population and domestic CSOs believe it to be the government's role and duty to do so, although both very heavily emphasize the need for mutual cooperation between the government and the local populations and CSOs themselves, seeing their grass-roots experience as a vital resource to be acknowledged and put to good use by the government in bringing much-needed reconciliation to the Congolese population.

Compared with the extensive literature highlighting the failure of the Congolese government in its reconciliatory involvement, there is very little emphasis placed on the positive involvement of the local population and CSOs. In the regions of the country that are farthest from the Kinshasa-based government, these organizations are in particular leading efforts to bring peace and reconciliation to local communities. Such groups have unique access to local populations and through persistent grassroots efforts have built up solid reputations and firm relationships within the communities, enabling them to carry out various, effective reconciliatory activities at grassroots level. Despite this potential, however, this chapter has highlighted the difficulties such organizations face in carrying out their activities on a daily basis, and it demonstrates the need for the government to acknowledge, support and resource these groups, and to join with them rather than hinder their efforts.

As the work and experiences of the various CSOs shows, reconciliation in the DRC is not merely a dream but is a real possibility in this war-ravaged country. Despite this hope, however, the task ahead remains daunting because of the extreme levels of violence and devastation caused by the various conflicts fought over the last few decades. In order to strengthen this process to combat the destructive desires of a number of rebel groups still carrying out violent attacks in the east of the country, the government must be involved more substantially. With the backing of the state, as well as stronger recognition and support from the international community, we can have faith that the DRC can leave its violent past behind and move forward, through a unified process of reconciliation, to a democratic and peaceful future.

5

REMEMBERING THE PAST AND RECONCILING FOR THE FUTURE: THE ROLE OF INDIGENOUS COMMEMORATIVE PRACTICES IN SIERRA LEONE

Steven Kaindaneh

INTRODUCTION

Scholars have taken a keen interest in the study of war commemoration and its significance in helping survivors of a conflict come to terms with their experiences (Ashplant, Dawson and Roper 2000: 5). However, while much attention has been given to formal and state-sanctioned initiatives, very little scholarly work has examined how ordinary people, especially those in rural African communities, commemorate traumatic events.

The civil war in Sierra Leone (1991–2002) was so traumatic that it can hardly be forgotten by the nation, especially by people who had first-hand experience of it. Consequently, various agencies, ranging from state to rural communities, are constantly involved in remembering it. Formal commemoration initiatives often result in the erection of monuments with plaques, the establishment of museums or the production of historical documents, which are highly visible to the public. Indigenous remembrance practices on the other hand are often not so visible, particularly to strangers and those who may not be familiar with such local cultural processes. These indigenous commemoration practices often rely on oral transmission, low-key rituals and day-to-day interactions between ordinary people. Rather than state-sanctioned formal commemorative processes, rural communities in Sierra Leone frequently rely on such indigenous, informal approaches to remember the past, including the civil war.

This chapter will examine the civil war in Sierra Leone, the extreme violence and destruction that characterized it and how it devastated social cohesion in rural communities. To understand how indigenous commemorative rituals offer the prospect of reconciliation to communities in post-conflict settings, the significance and practice of traditional processes for community life in Sierra Leone will be explored, focusing on the Mende ethnic group in the southern and eastern regions of the country.

Three key indigenous war commemoration practices of the Mendes are particularly relevant here; confession, symbolic cleansing and the performance of rituals in sacred spaces. I will consider how these practices are used to remember the civil war, and how they help survivors cope with the legacies of conflict and violence. This will show that indigenous commemoration rituals contribute to constructing a collective memory of the civil war, to healing survivors and to promoting coexistence among survivors who were divided by the conflict.

The issues discussed here draw heavily on research into how the civil war is remembered in Sierra Leone. Data was collected between 2008 and 2010 using interviews, focus group discussions and observation, and the study was specifically interested in how rural communities were using indigenous remembrance methods to promote coexistence and come to terms with the legacies of the civil war. The study was unique because it explored informal modes of remembrance and their significance in ensuring healing and promoting coexistence in post-conflict communities, thereby providing important learning points for future research into the link between indigenous commemoration practices and reconciliation in communities emerging from repression or violent conflict.

CIVIL WAR IN SIERRA LEONE (1991–2002)

In March 1991, armed men from Liberia attacked Bomaru, a small border town in eastern Sierra Leone. A group calling itself the Revolutionary United Front (RUF), led by a former army corporal, Foday Sankoh, claimed responsibility for the incursion. The RUF was supported by Charles Taylor, a local warlord in Liberia, and by mercenaries from Burkina Faso. According to Foday Sankoh, the aim of the uprising was to liberate Sierra Leoneans from oppression by overthrowing the corrupt and repressive All People's Congress (APC) government and returning the country to a more democratic form of governance (Boas, 2001: 713).

Through coercion, cunning recruitment tactics and an available pool of frustrated youths and street children, Foday Sankoh was able to build a large fighting force, eventually taking control of strategic locations in the country. Government forces could have easily repelled the small force that invaded Bomaru, but this did not happen. Military personnel were demotivated and ill-equipped from years of neglect, because the government had diverted resources meant for national security to equip the Internal Security Unit (ISU). The ISU was a branch of the police, which became the state instrument for protecting APC party officials and their business interests (Humper, 2004: 50). To make matters worse, soldiers were abandoned at the war front by their commanders back in Freetown, who squandered salaries and supplies meant for soldiers at the front. Although the national army was weak and ill equipped, residents in the eastern region believed that a full-scale military response by the APC government would have wiped out the small number of insurgents, thereby curtailing the armed rebellion in that part of the country and eventually crushing the rebellion. Instead of focusing on a robust response, however, J. S. Momoh, the then head of state of Sierra Leone, described the incursion as a plot by APC's political opponents in the southern and eastern regions of the country to destabilize the government (Abraham, 2001: 209).

LEGACY OF THE CIVIL WAR

The civil war in Sierra Leone was characterized by mass destruction and extreme violence. Instead of liberating Sierra Leoneans from oppression and poverty as Foday Sankoh had promised, the aim of the RUF was 'to terrorize the country into submission, into supporting his movement in a trade for mere safety' (Bergner, 2004: 1–2). The long and brutal conflict brought the national economy and individual livelihoods to a standstill, thereby exacerbating poverty across the country. Although the current government is making efforts to improve the social and economic situation in Sierra Leone, the country remains one of the poorest in the world, ranked 158 out of 169 countries in the United Nations Human Development Index (Klugman et al., 2010: 145).

Widespread violence resulted in the death of thousands of Sierra Leoneans and other nationals. The Truth and Reconciliation Commission (TRC) report estimated that 4,500 people lost their lives during the conflict, although independent estimates believe the death toll to be much higher (Conibere et al., 2004: 10). It is also estimated that more than 4,000 people were subjected to amputation of body parts, with the majority of them bleeding to death as a result of poor medical services. When the war ended in 2002, about 1,600 war-related amputees were registered, 78 per cent of them males and the breadwinners of their households (Christodulou, 2004; Conibere et al., 2004, Appendix 5: 5–10). The prevailing insecurity and widespread violence of the civil war resulted in mass displacement which affected more than half of the country's population.

Because of the high levels of trauma, destruction and visible scars, Sierra Leoneans still have vivid memories of their experiences during the civil war. These memories will continue to haunt survivors for a long time to come. But how exactly do survivors in rural communities remember the civil war, and how are its legacies preserved and passed to future generations? How do they manage their war memories and move on with their lives? And finally, how can a community's commemorative rituals offer the prospect of reconciliation after a divisive conflict and the restoration of broken relationships between individuals and within communities?

INDIGENOUS COMMEMORATIVE RITUALS

In most communities around the world, rituals are performed for various reasons such as remembering an important historical event, conducting rites of passage and inaugurating new projects. However, residents in rural communities in the southern and eastern regions of Sierra Leone also use rituals extensively to celebrate success, perform burial and marriage ceremonies, honour people who have contributed to the community, and even welcome the harvest season.

In post-war rural communities in Sierra Leone, commemorative rituals were preceded by elaborate planning which involved preparing sacred sites, inviting other communities and mobilizing resources for entertainment. Based on my observations and from discussions with members of the Mendi ethnic group between 2008 and 2010, particularly with elders and leaders, rituals tend to have several things in common. These include greeting ancestors and reciting their names, confessing wrongdoing and asking for forgiveness, and offering sacrifices to appease ancestors and local deities.

In communities where I witnessed commemorative rituals, most inhabitants gathered at the sacred site in the morning, with traditional leaders and elders in front and close to the inner part of the shrine. The diviner began the celebration with a formal greeting, calling God and ancestors in a loud expression, '*Levei yei yo-ooo ngi bi loe vei*', a Mendi expression meaning 'Almighty God, come down and receive our offering'. In one community, the diviner explained that the purpose of the ceremony was to remember and pay respect to ancestors, to thank them for protection in difficult times and to pray for wisdom to maintain the tradition passed to them by their forefathers. The local historian or storyteller then took over the ceremony and loudly recited the names of ancestors connected with the community, or group of communities that share the shrine. He recounted the deeds of ancestors and their contributions to the community, linking particular ancestors with specific historical events. The historian went on to narrate the history of the group and how they settled in their present location. He used this opportunity to remind people about the civil conflict and the collective war experiences of the community. He went on to mention the names of people who had died during the war, focusing on those who lost their lives in the act of helping others.

According to local leaders, this roll call serves several purposes. Generally, it reminds community members about their past, and more specifically it helps people to remember and honour those men and women in the past who have worked selflessly to establish the community and keep its members together. It enlightens children and young people who may not have heard about their ancestors and their past deeds. Finally, the public pronouncement of names is an invitation to ancestors to be present at the ceremony.

The act of remembering and honouring ancestors is usually followed by an act of collective confession and a request for forgiveness led by the diviner. Confessions involve acknowledging the wrongs done by the community at two levels – first, offences by community members against God and ancestors, and at the second level, wrongs carried out between individuals. Acts of collective confession often end with a plea for ancestors to forgive their living relatives.

In a typical commemorative ceremony, confession and the plea for forgiveness are followed by libation and the offering of sacrifices. Libation is often carried out by the diviner, and involves pouring a strong alcoholic drink and water at the entrance of the shrine for ancestors. Cooked food is then offered to ancestors, and in one community a sheep was slaughtered in the shrine and its blood used as an offering.

As part of the concluding rite, the chief or an elder is invited to address ancestors and to present to them the major issues affecting the community, requesting guidance and the wisdom to solve them. At this point, people also silently meditate on their personal petitions. My interviews with community leaders identified unity, cooperation, general well-being, productive economic ventures, fertility for women and favours from governmental and non-governmental agencies as the most common of petitions.

Of the petition items presented to ancestors, two are particularly significant for social cohesion and coexistence: unity and cooperation, attributes that help to prevent conflict among people who live in close proximity and share the same resources. Chiefs and household heads know that without the social glue of unity and cooperation, life in rural communities would be hard and chaotic. All commemorative rituals end with the diviner offering the final prayers, and then celebration. The end of commemorative ceremonies usually signifies transition to a new and more hopeful era.

Communities always expect a sign from local deities and ancestors to indicate that requests have been heard and will be treated favourably. In the first year when the commemorative ritual was performed in Bomaru after the end of the civil war, one of the things prayed for by the community was fertility among women and for the community to be blessed with children to replace relatives who had died during the conflict. A focus group discussion with the community in 2009 revealed that a few months after the ritual, a higher than average number of women became pregnant, and the community experienced a baby boom the following year which was attributed to this request.[1] In some communities, rainfall on the day of the ritual is their indication that ancestors are pleased and that sacrifices have been accepted. In Ngolahun for instance, the community informed me that heavy rainfall is always a sign from their ancestors, and a youth leader insisted that 'no matter the time of the dry season, it always rains on the day of the ritual'. There is no scientific evidence for these claims, but communities have a strong belief in them.

COMMEMORATING THE PAST:
FORMAL AND INFORMAL PRACTICES

In remembering the civil war in Sierra Leone, and on other occasions where the past being remembered is traumatic in nature, commemoration can serve to heal survivors, helping them come to terms with abuse, loss and broken social networks (Blair and Michel, 2007: 27;

Stephens, 2007: 245). Since commemoration focuses on projecting the past into the present, it could be explained as an educational process aimed at inducting new members into the social group. As demonstrated in the commemorative rituals above, elders provide information about ancestors, the origin of the group and the experiences of the community during the civil war. This is valuable information for new group members, especially young people who may not have heard such historical information.

Commemoration practices can either be formal or informal. Informal commemoration practices, in contrast to formal displays of public remembrance usually initiated by the state or by civil society organizations, take place in the course of everyday interactions by ordinary people. Compared with state-sanctioned practices, informal modes of remembering are not so widely researched, although they have long been identified as key methods of creating and sustaining collective memory (Gongaware, 2003: 488–9). Storytelling, rituals and the use of symbols are major strategies for expressing and sharing representations of the past in rural African communities.

People in rural communities in the southern and eastern regions of Sierra Leone adopt various strategies to come to terms with the legacies of a conflict. Three strategies – confession, symbolic cleansing and restoration of sacred spaces – will be discussed here. These three strategies are important, because in addition to healing hurt and promoting coexistence, they also make a significant contribution to constructing a shared memory of the past, thus helping survivors to remember the past, including the civil war, together.

THREE INDIGENOUS COMMEMORATION PRACTICES OF THE MENDE

Confession or admitting wrongdoing is prevalent in rural communities in the southern and eastern regions of Sierra Leone. Without confession for instance, a healer/diviner may have difficulty understanding the disorder presented by a client, thus making treatment difficult. For disagreements to be resolved effectively, chiefs and elders insist that wrongdoers tell the truth about their actions in the presence of other people. Depending on the nature of the offence, wrongdoers are often encouraged to undergo a process of symbolic washing, to make them clean enough to be reconciled with others and with ancestors.

In Sierra Leone and other West African countries, shrines or sacred spaces are common features of rural settings, and they are usually set aside in demarcated areas for ritual purposes only. Shrines provide spaces for people in rural communities to perform commemorative rituals, communicate with spiritual beings and to offer sacrifices to appease ancestors. In some communities in Sierra Leone, sacred spaces are clearly marked with fences and flags; however, in most communities they are not visibly marked. Apart from local inhabitants or people who can discern hidden symbols in the forest, a stranger can pass by a sacred grove without noticing it.

Confession

When the war ended and displaced people returned home, the high levels of trust that had existed between people before the conflict had been eroded, replaced by fear and suspicion. To address this complex emotional climate and to promote coexistence, some traditional leaders organized open dialogue sessions. These open discussion sessions or mini truth commissions enabled survivors to talk about their war experiences. Compared with the nationally organized truth commission, most survivors found the community-based ones more acceptable, as these were presided over by people they knew and could relate to. These sessions were effective because when elders and traditional leaders in Africa attempt to resolve a disagreement, they focus more on soothing the feelings of disputants, rather than levying accusations of wrongdoing. With the focus on soothing feelings, the possibility of having honest discussions and reaching a compromise that restores relationships is likely to be higher, compared with conflict resolution processes that focus on laying blame and imposing punishment (Malan, 1997: 20). This indigenous conflict resolution approach focuses on both the victim and wrongdoer, setting the stage for a speedy resolution and lasting coexistence. Archbishop Desmond Tutu described the approach as:

> the healing of breaches, the redressing of imbalances and the restoration of broken relationships. This kind of justice seeks to rehabilitate both the victim and the perpetrator, who should be given the opportunity to be reintegrated into the community he or she has injured by his or her offence.
>
> (Tutu, 1999: 51–2)

Confession for healing and reconciliation

In some communities in the southern and eastern regions of the country, open dialogue sessions developed into detailed acts of confession by wrongdoers. Confessions generally revealed the truth about violations, some of which were disturbing for survivors, especially those who were hurt by such violations. Fambul Tok, a national NGO partnering with traditional leaders to ensure reconciliation, provided counselling for communities in order to prepare people for issues that could emerge from confession sessions. In a discussion I had with John Caulker, the director of Forum of Conscience and the national coordinator of Fambul Tok, he noted that although the process of revealing the truth about certain violations during the war was difficult and emotional, and confession sessions were often interrupted by uncontrollable wailing, these emotional outbursts are seen as important indicators of healing and reconciliation (Caulker, 2009). This view was confirmed by staff of another agency, the Bo Peace and Reconciliation Movement (BPRM), who believe that crying during the process of resolving a conflict is an indication that an agreement or resolution is about to be reached. Hassan Feika, director of BPRM, based this conclusion on the following argument:

> Parties to a conflict always maintain positions which are used in arguments to strengthen their case, which may prolong the dispute. However, as people lose their arguments or are prevailed upon by family members and elders to forgo their entrenched positions for the sake of peaceful coexistence, emotions flood in, making some disputants shed tears.
>
> (Feika, 2009)

Through my discussions with community leaders, I learned that confessions helped to reduce rumours and accusations that had previously fuelled tension between people. For victims, knowing the truth about violations and hearing a plea for forgiveness by an offender had a cathartic effect on them. In an interview with Joseph Benji in 2010, he described how, with the truth revealed and the stance of elders to forgive, most victims decided to put violations of the past behind them for the sake of coexistence in the wider community.

The role of public confessions in constructing collective memory

In addition to healing, confessions also bring personal war experiences into the public domain, thereby helping to construct a collective memory of the conflict – a local history of the civil war at community level. However, memories of the civil war generated at this level are based purely on the personal experiences of members of that community; such memories can be in conflict with what other communities and even the state remember about the event. If not managed properly, such area-specific war memories can be misused by people, especially politicians, to become a source of tension.

Through their interaction with rural communities, Fambul Tok experienced another side of public confession. Public confession also acts as a powerful tool for naming and shaming individuals who took part in human rights violations during the conflict. In most rural communities in Sierra Leone, public naming and shaming for wrongdoing smears an individual's name and social status, which itself is considered by local communities as a serious punishment for the offender (Keen, 2005: 302). Solomon Berewa, a former attorney general and vice president in Sierra Leone who supported traditional justice processes, made the following observations in an interview:

> If someone wrongs you ... and he [she] comes forward and owns up to it, that would bring some element of degradation to him [or her] and in the process might chasten him [or her]. It will also bring some element of comfort to the victim.
>
> (Lord, 2000: 58)

Confessions have played various roles in different nations emerging from conflict. While confession in post-apartheid South Africa provided amnesty for perpetrators, in Rwanda it ensured reduced prison terms for individuals charged with genocide (Payne, 2004: 115). In rural communities in southern and eastern Sierra Leone however, the motive for confessions was slightly different; it contributed to reducing tensions and increasing trust between people. In some communities and depending on the nature of the offence, confessions prepared wrongdoers, especially former fighters, for ritual cleansing that facilitated acceptance by and reintegration into their communities.

Symbolic cleansing

Ritual cleansing is common in Africa, and it is often used for healing and for helping survivors come to terms with the legacies of violence or other traumatic experiences (Ranger, 2004: 114; Nolte-Schamm, 2006: 90–1). Cleansing rituals are important components of indigenous conflict resolution systems in Africa, and are highly appreciated by disputants, especially those in rural communities. The process of ritual cleansing and the symbols used are grounded in tradition, which is valued and understood by those who use them (Allen, 2008: 47).

In rural communities in south eastern Sierra Leone, individuals who commit despicable crimes like murder, rape and desecration of sacred places are often considered spiritually unclean and are therefore stigmatized by other community members. In order to be readmitted into the community and be reconciled with others, tradition demands that such individuals undergo a process of ritual cleansing. Although fighters, especially those who committed serious human rights violations such as rape and murder during the civil war, received a blanket amnesty under the Lome Peace Agreement of 1999, some communities suggested that these wrong-doers be cleansed to ensure acceptance and reintegration into their communities.

According to traditional leaders, purification rituals for ex-fighters are conducted by local diviners or herbalists, and involve physically bathing the offender with a view to making the former fighter spiritually clean. Selected herbs believed to have healing and mystical properties are ground into a pulp and mixed with water, which is used to wash the offender. While the wrongdoer is being washed, prayers are chanted to local deities and ancestors to forgive and accept the individual. Once bathed, drinking water is usually offered to the individual to drink and to rub on their chest and face. At this stage, the wrongdoer is considered clean enough to be reconciled with the entire community. The end of cleansing is usually followed by a celebration with food and drink, to symbolize readmission of a family member into society and as a gesture to appreciate leaders and elders for resolving yet another conflict in the history of the community.

The significance of water in ritual cleansing

Water is the most important ingredient in the purification process. While water is generally considered to give and sustain life, rural communities also see it as an important element for maintaining cordial relationships. In Sierra Leone, emotions like anger, greed and difficulty with forgiveness are often associated with the state of an individual's heart. Creole terms like '*bad at*' (bad heart or selfishness), '*wam at*' (hot heart or bad temper) are used all over Sierra Leone, and other local languages also tend to link these qualities with the heart. While water purifies physically, it is also believed to have mystical powers that literally cool the hearts of individuals, thereby reducing negative emotions and improving a person's relationships with others.

Cleansing to deliver from guilt

Apart from rural communities, evangelical or Pentecostal churches also used ritual cleansing extensively in the study area to heal survivors who manifested severe emotional and relationship problems after the civil war. In addition to physical injuries, many survivors suffered psychological disorders as a result of their experiences during the civil war. While some survivors in urban settings benefited from clinical psychotherapy, a large number turned to Pentecostal churches for healing, to deliver them from past guilt or experiences and to be reconciled with God and man. The cleansing process described by Pentecostal churches as deliverance, involved penance and prescribed prayers over a defined period, under the supervision of specially trained deliverance ministers. On completion, it was believed that deliverance gave concerned individuals a sense of being set free from bondage (for example, guilt or shame), which went a long way to improving their relationship with other people.[2]

Restoration of sacred spaces

During the civil war, several sacred places in the southern and eastern regions of the country were violated by armed men. Considering the significance of sacred spaces in the lives of rural communities, leaders addressed the purification, or restoration, of these spaces through ritual cleansing.

Sacred spaces as sites of memory

As explained in an earlier section, shrines are important features of rural communities in Sierra Leone and other West African countries. Communities in the southern and eastern regions of Sierra Leone generally believe that shrines were established by their ancestors, thereby sustaining strong links with the community's past. Sacred spaces are often seen as symbols of the group's collective memory. Considered as the 'spatial seat' of ancestors and local deities, sacred sites are revered and communities are prepared to do all they can to protect them from violation (McIntosh, 2009: 37; Probst, 2007: 203–6). Since a sacred space symbolizes the heritage and identity of a social group, desecrating it could be equated to destroying that group's past and therefore stripping it of its identity (Evaldsson and Wessels, 2003: 64). It is further believed that defiling a shrine will offend ancestors and possibly displace them, subsequently causing the concerned community to forfeit its ancestral protection and favours. Failure to appease angry ancestors will make the concerned community or family vulnerable to a chain of misfortunes.

During the civil war a number of sacred spaces in the region were desecrated by armed men who used them for combat and other purposes. Given the relationship between sacred sites and the identity of communities, and how this relationship is valued, elders worked with their communities to rededicate sites to their original states of sanctity, to enable ancestors to return and to resume commemorative rituals. In the process of restoring these broken links, the community was able to achieve two things; strengthening relationships between individuals who were divided by the conflict, and commemorating the past, including the civil war.

Rehabilitating a social asset like a sacred site requires the involvement of all in the concerned community. Shrine restoration involves repairing both the physical damage and purifying the shrine to make it suitable for ancestors. The purification ritual is conducted by a diviner, and involves sprinkling water mixed with selected herbs in the interior and immediate surroundings of the shrine, literally to wash it to attract ancestors once more.

The diviner wields considerable influence in the community, and is often seen as the only person capable of providing answers to certain challenges facing the community (Alie, 2008: 137). As a Sierra Leonean growing up and working in rural communities, I noted long ago that these particular skills were widely distributed in communities, but it was only in the course of research that I understood the significance of such patterns of distribution. Wide distribution ensures that skills are never concentrated in the hands of one family or an individual, thus making people in rural communities rely on each other for support and ensuring that issues affecting the community are addressed collectively.

Since the skills to repair the physical damage to a shrine and to restore its sanctity require a number of individuals and households, it would be impossible for a community to successfully undertake the restoration if members were in disagreement. From discussions with residents in the research area, I learnt that the Mendes believe that for ancestors to accept sacrifices and respond to requests, communities must approach them as a united and reconciled family. Post-civil war communities were therefore faced with two options: remain divided and break the connection with their ancestors, or reconcile as a family and enjoy their favours. Faced with this dilemma, people had no choice but to put the individual pains of the civil war behind them, in order to reconcile and work together for the benefit of the community.

CONCLUSION: INDIGENOUS COMMEMORATION AND COEXISTENCE

The spread of Christianity and Islam, and the condemnation of traditional rituals by religious leaders, describing them as satanic and unacceptable to God, led to the abandonment of indigenous commemorative practices by many communities.[3]

However, the quest by communities to remember the truth about the civil war and to address its legacies has contributed to the revival of indigenous commemorative practices. After the war, some communities across the southern and eastern regions saw the need to resume commemorative rituals in order to appease ancestors and to 'heal the land of all the ills done to it'.[4] Most of the communities I visited saw the value of making peace with their ancestors as an important strategy for reconciling divided parties in rural communities. On the need to recognize and honour ancestors, a town speaker and community leader in Ngolahun made the following remark during a personal interview in 2009:

> We made a big mistake in the past when we abandoned the rituals and in doing so, we turned our backs on our forefathers. If we are not careful, our children will turn their backs on us while we are still alive. Without our forefathers, we cannot be here today and without them, having a bright future will be impossible. We need to look back on the past, to turn to our ancestors for direction and for peace in our hearts and in the land.

Despite ferocious attacks by Christian and Islamic religious leaders who continue to condemn traditional practices, just as colonial administrators did in the past, some post-conflict rural communities remain determined to restore links with the past and to honour ancestors. Religions however, should be able to support the cultural practices of their adherents, as they are responsible for ensuring the holistic development of people; they should focus not only on the spiritual aspects.

Traditional commemoration practices, including rituals, can enable people and communities in post-conflict settings to address internal divisions and soothe emotions. These practices have contributed to the bringing of former enemies from the civil war together, and have laid the foundation for coexistence that communities now enjoy. With a weak judicial and security system in the immediate post-war years, traditional institutions have generally helped rural Sierra Leoneans to come to terms with the civil war and its legacies more than any other institution in the country. While state institutions were still struggling to help the nation remember eleven years of bitter conflict, rural communities devised strategies in the form of rituals to commemorate the conflict, to heal hurts and to celebrate the resilience of ordinary people and their determination to foster cordial relationships.

NOTES

1   While in Bomaru, I was shown several children between the ages of 6 and 7 years, claimed by the community to be children delivered to replace those who died during the war.

2   Personal communication with a Pentecostal church minister in Bo, May 2009. In Zimbabwe, some communities have similar practices which they refer to as spiritual healing or 'reordering of society after a conflict'. Among these communities, healing is undertaken to restore broken relationships, but they go a step further by getting perpetrators to pay some form of compensation to their victims (Schmidt, 1997: 79–85).

3   Awareness gained from the author's own experience growing up in Sierra Leone. This observation has also been referred to in an unpublished PhD thesis: Prince Sorie Conteh (2008), 'The place of African traditional religion in interreligious encounters in Sierra Leone since the advent of Islam and Christianity' (PhD thesis submitted to the University of South Africa).

4   Peter Gboyawa, Kailahun, May 2009. Peter described the ills as killings during the war, desecration of sacred places, people wrongly claiming what was not theirs, etc.

6

DECOLONIZATION AND RECONCILIATION: THE COLONIAL DILEMMA OF CANADA'S RESIDENTIAL SCHOOL APOLOGY AND RESTITUTION

Patricia Elgersma

INTRODUCTION

In recent decades the Canadian public has heard a number of apologies from various governments and institutions. The apology to Japanese Canadians (1988) and Italian Canadians (1990) for treatment during the Second World War, the Royal Commission on Aboriginal Peoples (RCAP) Statement of Reconciliation (1998) to former residential school occupants, and the apology for the 'Chinese Head Tax' (2006), are just a few examples.

In 2008 the current prime minister, Stephen Harper, added to the trend with his public acknowledgement and apology concerning the Indian residential school system (IRS), a government-led policy between 1874 and 1996, which in conjunction with four major church groups removed indigenous Canadians involuntarily from their homes and sent them to boarding schools where they were forced to learn English and adopt Christianity and Canadian customs. The hope was that residential schools would 'get rid of the Indian problem' by 'killing the Indian in the child' (Ryan, as quoted in Chrisjohn, Young and Maraun, 2006: 61). Harper's apology, which also initiated the Indian Residential Schools Truth

and Reconciliation Commission (TRC), was praised for being a
watershed in Canadian relationships with indigenous people. Not
only had he helped to 'mark an end of the dark period in our
collective history as a nation' (Simon, as quoted in Martin, 2009:
50), the apology was also a key factor in the movement 'towards
healing, reconciliation and resolution of the sad legacy of Indian
Residential Schools' (Harper, as quoted in Martin, 2009: 49). It
finally seemed that non-indigenous Canadians were addressing
the legacies and owning up to the injustices of the residential
schools.

This chapter looks more closely at the apology and at the
TRC, and questions its ability to bring about reconciliation. It
argues that the structure and nature of the current reconciliation
projects are ineffective because they stem from the same structure
and context that led to the formation of residential schools in the
first place. This context is colonial in nature, and simultaneously
reinforces the myth of Canada as a tolerant, benevolent state
while placing the burden of reconciliation solely on indigenous
populations.

I argue that for proper transformation and restitution to occur,
Canadians must engage in a 'decolonizing' process – a process that
requires a more critical, self-reflective, anti-oppressive and anti-
racist approach to relationships with indigenous populations. This
process removes unequal power relationships and accepts responsibility for the way in which the philosophy behind residential
schools continues to affect relationships with indigenous people
today. At the same time non-indigenous Canadians must work
to 're-story' and 're-imagine' history and their relationships with
indigenous Canadians, to find new ways of communicating and
working together that transcend the current power relations and
trends.

The first section of this chapter addresses terms and definitions,
then provides a brief overview of the residential schools and explains
their relevance as a colonial project. It then deconstructs how this
colonial mindset is present in the current apology and TRC, and
the potential problems this creates. Following this, the argument for
'decolonization' will be made, and a new paradigm will be laid out
to explore how non-indigenous Canadians might work to break the
patterns of violence that continue to define their relationship with
indigenous people. Finally, I will propose suggestions for how this
'decolonized' approach could be brought into reconciliation efforts
regarding residential schools.

DEFINITIONS AND TERMS

This chapter is not written from an indigenous perspective and has been conceived in English. This is not to say that it does not have legitimacy; it is to acknowledge that it is limited in both its language and its discourse. Recognizing the limits of such a method, 'indigenous' is used in this chapter to describe all First Nations, Métis and Inuit persons in Canada. Although no legal definition exists, the term First Nations refers to Amerindian peoples in Canada, both those who have been registered with the federal government or with a band that signed a treaty with the Crown (status Indians), and those who have not (non-status Indians). Métis refers to those with mixed European and First Nations parentage, and Inuit refers to culturally similar indigenous peoples inhabiting the Arctic regions of Canada (Shepard, O'Neill and Guenette, 2006). When possible, individual tribes or groups will be referenced.

As stated earlier, this chapter seeks to address colonialism and the colonial mindset within Canada. Colonialism occurs when one people or culture is conquered by another people or culture through destroying and/or weakening the basic social structure in the conquered culture and replacing it with that of the conqueror. The colonial mindset creates the foundation for colonial activity by generating an incommensurable gulf between the dominant group (the colonizers or the settlers) and less powerful group (the colonized or indigenous groups), which simultaneously demonstrates the superior nature of the colonizers while labelling the colonized as 'other' – backwards and inferior. The privileged position of the colonizers relative to 'natives', together with the rationales justifying it, creates a divide between the populations (Green, 2003). As the dichotomy between the two groups widens, the dominant group comes to represent the 'true subjects' of nationhood and the embodiment of the quintessential characteristics and its values, ethics and mores. This 'exalted' status must be continuously reinforced through violent encounters with the 'inferior' group in a manner that appears to bring 'civilization'. Because the dominant group sees itself as superior, these acts of violence are justified as progressive and benevolent because they bring civility and culture to the 'savage'.

RESIDENTIAL SCHOOLS: A BRIEF HISTORY

Residential schools were established as a partnership between the federal government and churches in Canada. The government believed it would be easier and more practical to focus on assimilating and moulding indigenous children, rather than adults, into Christian Canadians. As a result, from the 1870s to the 1980s approximately 150,000 children were forcibly taken away from their homes and shipped to one of more than 130 schools scattered across seven provinces and two territories. The residential school curriculum was based on the assumption that no part of indigenous culture was worth preserving. As Duncan Campbell Scott, the director of the Indian residential school programme from 1913 to 1932, stated:

> I want to get rid of the Indian problem. I do not think as a matter of fact, that this country ought to continuously protect a class of people who are able to stand alone .... Our object is to continue until there is not a single Indian in Canada that has not been absorbed into the body politic, and there is no Indian question, and no Indian Department, that is the whole object of this Bill.
> (as quoted in Mackenzie, 2009: 91)

Within the residential school system, students were severely punished if they were caught speaking their first language or practising their traditions. There were countless cases of sexual, emotional, spiritual and physical abuse. Students lived in substandard conditions and often received a substandard education which made it difficult to function in a Eurocentric 'Canadian' setting. In many cases children returned home no longer able to communicate with or relate to their families. They no longer had the skills to help their families and were ashamed of their heritage. Residential schools robbed indigenous children of their language, their beliefs, their self-respect, their culture, and in some cases their very existence, in a vain attempt to make them more 'Canadian'.

While Canada has not been a traditional colonial nation in that it has not extended its hegemony to other lands and continents, these residential school policies were imbued with the colonial mindset. These practices, which took indigenous populations away from their language, culture and spirituality in order to assimilate them, can only be described as colonial in nature. Beyond this, many of the children were subjected to psychological, physical and sexual abuse in institutions which should have had a duty to protect them. When this is added to the many other policies and practices in Canada towards indigenous populations, practices that included the taking away of indigenous land and resources, laws banning spiritual and traditional practices, and the setting-up of reserves, the only conclusion to be reached is that Canada, despite its virtues, has been as much a colonizer of its own people as other countries have been in their overseas dependencies.

THE COLONIAL MINDSET WITHIN CURRENT
RECONCILIATION ATTEMPTS

One of the results of the colonial mindset is that history is distorted by the colonizers to a myth-like state where certain contributions are overstated, making others invisible. In the case of Canada, the 'official version' of history that has been taught focuses on European settlement and consciousness, leaving the existence of Aboriginal nations prior to the configuration of the contemporary state romanticized, homogenized and largely irrelevant. Additionally, contact with the indigenous population and colonial policies have been brushed over, justified and distorted to comply with the idea of Canada as a peacemaking nation which negotiated treaties with indigenous peoples, made laws and established an Indian policy designed to 'bring to the West the peace, order, and good government that were hallmarks of imperialism and the colonial project of "civilizing savages"' (Regan, 2006). As a result, the legacies and paradigms of the colonial mind continue to structure current policies and trends regarding indigenous populations. This myth making of the colonial mindset satisfies those who do not know, or choose not to know, the fuller historical record, but it does not provide the foundation of information on which to build policy responses to contemporary crises rooted in the colonial past (Green, 2003).

There are several ways in which the legacies of the colonial mindset are still clearly enforced in current Canadian reconciliation attempts with the residential school system. The first is the lack of indigenous language and concepts within the apology and the TRC. Instead, the language of the apology is dominated by Western terms and ideas. A good example of this is the way time is constructed as linear, rather than evoking the indigenous conception of time as circular, wherein the past is alive in the present. This can be seen in Stephen Harper's apology, which acknowledges that wrongs were committed, but contains these within a past exception to the rule. Tied into this linear idea of time is the linking of reconciliation with resolution, a Western term which 'evokes the end of conflict but which is less clear about the extent to which it entails an ongoing relationship or responsibility' (Martin, 2009: 52). Western conceptions of reconciliation focus on forgetting the past and putting it behind in order to move forward, rather than seeing a past that can be alive and worked out in the present. This limits the way in which residential schools are viewed, and confines them to a past chapter that needs to be closed rather than to policies that are very much part of the present.

Another way in which current reconciliation projects are colonially oriented is in their use of structures that are dominated by the Canadian state's notion of reconciliation rather than indigenous beliefs. In fact, at its core, reconciliation is a Western concept with religious connotations rather than an indigenous concept. Although projects such as the Indian Residential School Settlement Agreement and the formation of the TRC are designed to address the devastating legacies of residential schools, their focus is on the level of individual 'survivors' and they are constrained by political and legal realities. Much of the reconciliation process started at a legal level and focused on monetary compensation packages. While these initiatives are important, they fail to incorporate a more indigenous-based approach to trauma that would have focused on the reunification and regeneration of families and communities rather than individuals. The Western model also focused on stories of abuse and victimization rather than stories of resistance and resilience. Finally, it ignored the cultural and spiritual dimensions of survivors' experiences (Corntassel, Chaw-win-is and T'lakwadzi, 2009). When non-indigenous Canadians ask indigenous populations to embrace these Western concepts and structures within the TRC and the apology, they are asking them to adopt the culture that oppressed them in the first place rather than moving beyond a colonial structure.

Second, the apology continues to reiterate this notion that Canada was (and still is) essentially a peaceful and tolerant nation. This can be seen in the emphasis on 'renewal' in current reconciliation projects concerning residential schools, suggesting there was once a harmonious relationship between indigenous people and non-indigenous Canadians that we must return to. As Henderson and Wakeham noted:

> [Western reconciliation] implies that, once upon a time, Indigenous peoples and settlers lived in peace and harmony, working collaboratively towards shared long-term goals, only to have residential schooling (which began with only the best of intentions) rear its ugly head and drive a wedge between Canadians and Indigenous peoples. The job of the Truth and Reconciliation Commission,

like that of a good marital therapist ... is to mend the rift, heal the split, and make the two conjoin again as one.

(Henderson and Wakeham, 2009: 14)

As such the current reconciliation is yet another step in the Canadian story of 'helping the Indian to achieve healing and forgiveness', with the burden and agency of reconciliation on indigenous peoples. This is seen in the wide use of the language of healing and forgiveness, creating a one-sidedness to Canada's attempts to deal with residential schools. Initiatives such as the TRC currently have a more symbolic emphasis on witnessing and healing of indigenous people rather than a justice-based focus which looks at the perpetrators and system that created residential schools. In their reflections on the Forgiveness Summit in 2010, Ray Aldred, Terry LeBlanc and Adrian Jacobs note this contradiction, stating, 'it amazes us that once again it is First Nations people taking the initiative to [forgive] and seek a spiritual solution to the problem of broken relationships' (2010: 4). Rather than focus on reparations and justice, non-indigenous Canadians have turned reconciliation into the responsibility of indigenous people to heal, forgive, and 'get over it' so that the Canadian nation can move forward and progress.

The current reconciliation project can also be seen as colonial because it refuses to include significant reforms to the structure of government that would recognize indigenous people as equal to non-indigenous Canadians. Instead, despite the rhetoric of the TRC and the apology, Canada still continues to be evasive about its responsibility towards its indigenous population. In the first place, Canada has recently refused to sign the United Nations Declaration of the Rights of Indigenous Peoples. In fact, less than one year after the apology Stephen Harper reported to the United Nations that 'Canada has no history of colonialism' (as quoted in Henderson and Wakeham 2009: 1). Additionally, there continues to be a continuous lack of real discourse in mainstream society around the issue of residential schools, leaving it to be referred to as Canada's 'dark secret' and an occluded or repressed form of knowledge amongst the Canadian public. Many Canadians still are unaware that residential schools existed, and most would continue to describe relationships with indigenous populations as peaceful and even overly generous.

Canada has also struggled to recognize the validity of indigenous methodologies and find ways to incorporate these within the Canadian state. Instead, the framework and constitutional heritage of Canada still draws its legitimacy from the authority of the sovereign crown which established the framework for the colonization of the country. Eurocentric cultural values that privilege learning discourses steeped in scientific reason, rationality and objectivity continue to dominate our educational and governmental system. Additionally, the government has failed to recognize the legitimacy of indigenous rights within the nation, ignoring the plethora of problems its colonial history has created, including, to name only a few, problems such as reparations for failed promises to Aboriginal war veterans, the forced relocation of Inuit community members to desolate parts of the High Arctic during the 1950s, appeals for funding for language restoration and outstanding land claims across the country (Henderson and Wakeham 2009: 13).

POTENTIAL ISSUES

Laying the foundations for reconciliation for residential schools within a continued colonial mindset creates several problems for non-indigenous and indigenous Canadians. First, it removes accountability and responsibility from non-indigenous people. This is clearly seen in the way in which the focus of the TRC and the apology is solely on the story of indigenous people, and avoids the story of the perpetrators and a whole understanding of how residential schools were set up, who helped them function, and why the abuse was tolerated. This approach separates what is unjust from the present, narrowing restitution to 'forgiving and forgetting' while brushing aside any deeper discussions of restitution or justice (Islbacher-Fox, as stated in Corntassel et al., 2009). This discourages non-indigenous people from engaging in the reconciliation process, and maintains the status quo rather than making amends.

Because the process of reconciliation continues to be viewed through the prism of a 'colonial mindset' it also continues to create and maintain the dichotomous relationship between the colonizer/colonized that constrains and restricts the potential for reconciliation. As such, non-indigenous Canadians risk becoming, as Alfred and Corntassel have pointed out, 'contemporary colonial shape shifters' who 'continue to erase indigenous histories and senses of place, employing new negotiation strategies and methods that are merely subtler forms of violence than those practised by [their] ancestors' (as quoted in Regan, 2006: 6). There is also a risk that within this colonial dichotomy, indigenous people will continue to be 'othered' – not recognized fully as equal human beings but rather separated because of their differences and patronized as victims rather than survivors. One potential result is that issues or crimes committed will become lost in a veil of euphemism, meaning that the crimes of the past will appear to have been addressed without any actual acknowledgement (Gonzalez, 2008).

Moreover, by not questioning the Canadian state's colonial approach to power, the counterfactual assumptions of cultural superiority latent in colonialism will continue to structure the relationship between the state and Indigenous people. First of all, as Short states, 'any progress made towards justice … will be tolerated by the state only to the extent that it serves, or at least does not oppose, the interest of the state itself' (2005: 267). In this way, indigenous beliefs, ideals and culture will only be considered within the reconciliation process if they coincide with a Western paradigm and narrative. Alternatively, indigenous beliefs have the potential to be romanticized or incorporated into a Western framework in a way that does not fully acknowledge their complexity or spiritual significance.

The assumptions made by a colonial approach also fail to recognize how more complex issues such as second-generation survivors, the complexities of abuse meted out by residential children to each other, and other issues like land rights and dispossession fit into the narrative of residential schools. Instead it limits the entire narrative of indigenous relationships to one chapter, and suggests that the relationship can be mended if there is an apology for that chapter. As a result, current reconciliation initiatives become a political tool for moving on and wiping clean the slate within the non-indigenous mind, disempowering current indigenous pursuits of justice. If the focus of reconciliation is limited to individual 'perpetrators' and 'victims' of residential schools, then reconciliation is easier to achieve. However, if non-indigenous Canadians recognize themselves as 'beneficiaries' of a system created and perpetrated by inequality, it becomes impossible for reconciliation to occur by just addressing residential schools (Regan, 2006). In this way the colonial approach misses significant aspects of the history of residential schools, and ignores the responsibility of non-indigenous Canadians who have benefited and continue to benefit from this colonial system.

Finally, a failure to address the legacy of colonialism and its influence on current attempts of reconciliation means 'every new Indian policy risks echoing the one that governed the residential school system itself: the goal of finally 'get[ting] rid of the Indian problem' (Regan, 2006: 58). By not changing the current power structure, non-indigenous Canadians continue to believe they know what is best for indigenous people, framing policies such as those in the TRC in the language of consultation, negotiation and partnership when the resulting programmes speak the opposite. In this way reconciliation is being offered while harm is still being perpetrated. As Cherokee scholar Ward Churchill said:

> Don't talk to me about 'reconciling' with someone who's stuck a knife in my guts and is still twisting it. 'Heal?' Forgive and forget? Under *those* circumstances? Get real. The only way that's going to happen is if you remove your knife from my belly, accept responsibility for the effects of what you've done – or what you've allowed to be done in your name – and start making consequential, meaningful amends.
>
> (Churchill, 2008)

As a result, the ineffective refrain of reconciliation and the cycles of repentance that it brings with it will continue but without meaning, further breaking down trust and the potential for change.

WHAT IS DECOLONIZATION?

Paulette Regan (2006) describes the process of decolonization as 'unsettling the settler within'. It requires non-indigenous people to take a more critical, self-reflective, anti-oppressive and anti-racist approach to transforming relationships to address violence, not simply resolving disputes within existing colonial structures. Much of the theory behind decolonization comes from the social constructivist paradigm; a holistic, systemic worldview that sees all knowledge and social meaning as derived from social interactions (Shepard et al., 2006). This paradigm encourages the deconstruction of commonly held assumptions and 'truths', prevents the meaning of concepts becoming fixed, self-evident and singular, and allows space for multiple sites of contestation and reimagining (Henderson and Wakeham, 2009). It emphasizes becoming an ally with the colonized, treating them with dignity, and seeing them as equals.

A significant step in decolonization is being honest and coming to terms with the past, and in naming colonial violence. As Chrisjohn, Young and Maraun state, 'a major requirement for undoing what has been done is full recognition of what has been done. Any commitment to "undo" which leaves the "what" unspecified is an empty gesture, and as such is not commitment at all' (2006: 68).

This means that there needs to be a switch in thinking, a rejection of the dominant narrative and a relinquishing of power. It also means opening up to a new paradigm that sees the past within the present. As Trouillot (1995) notes, the authenticity of history lies in its ability to reside in the 'struggles of the present' and to engage people as actors, narrators, witnesses, actors and commentators. If historical injustices are alive in the present it increases responsibility and makes history personal and subjective within alternative stories.

How does decolonization work in practice? First of all, decolonization recognizes that it is not an easy process but is latent with paradoxes, because the colonial mindset is too complex to dismantle fully. As such, any attempt to decolonize will include paradoxes and mistakes because the structures that settlers or colonizers work in will inevitably work 'to reinforce cycles of violence between colonizer and colonized' (Regan, 2006: 276). There are also many risks involved because decolonization is uncomfortable and unsettling and it is easier to keep things the way they are. Part of the challenge, then, is to 'stay the course' and work with these inconsistencies and these risks.

Probably the most important part of personal decolonization is that it needs to be accomplished in the context of human relationships. Decolonization is not a prescriptive set of skills that can be learned, but involves embedding our thoughts and actions in authentic enquiry and respect for the dignity and humanity of others. In other words, decolonization starts at the personal level, through interpersonal relationships with those who have been colonized. As Lederach stated:

> Focus on people and their experience. Seek a genuine and committed relationship rather than results .... Be leery of quick fixes. Respect complexity but do not be paralyzed by it. Think comprehensively about the voices you hear that seem contradictory, both within a person, between people, and across a whole community ... no matter how small, create spaces of connection between them. Never assume you know better or more than those you are with that are struggling with the process. You don't. Do not fear the feeling of being lost. Give it time.
>
> (Lederach, 2005: 53)

Within this respect and recognition of the dignity of others lies respect for the holistic nature and culture of others as well as working to provide space where that dignity and culture can be restored. In this, however, it is important that there is listening and humility. As stated above, relationships within a post-colonial construct can only work if there is an equal sharing of power. This means being open to learn to listen and do things differently.

Personal decolonization also requires creativity and imagination that moves beyond rigid dichotomies in order to open new possibilities for the future. This is accomplished when language and history are recognized as culturally mediated and created. In other words, the definitions of words such as 'reconciliation' or 'justice' are not fixed or self-evident, but can be conceptualized in ways that bring in multiple worldviews. This task is not easy, and requires a complex and often uneasy contestation between different ways of seeing that seem in conflict with each other. The power of creativity and imagination, however, lies in its movement beyond hierarchies and dichotomies, creating space for an enlarged world view that moves away from rigidly fixed terms and ideas to a more fluid and multicultural way of seeing the world.

As the above points out, the road to reconciliation based on decolonization is difficult as it is filled with contradictions and paradoxes. As such, decolonization also requires critical hope. Critical hope is not naive idealism or moral indifference disguised as neutrality, but rather hope grounded in the grittiness of authentic relationship. It is largely accepting personal responsibility and starting at the individual level and finding ways to think and act differently, thereby creating strategies and a critical hope that something different is possible. Imagination and hope makes this job easier, for, as J. Edward Chamberlain states, 'the business of living in the real world depends on living in our imagination' (as quoted in Regan, 2006: 276). In this way transformation, although slow and long, is possible.

APPLYING DECOLONIZATION IN THE CANADIAN CONTEXT

When looking at how to apply decolonization in the context of reconciliation to indigenous populations, we first have to address how to engage non-indigenous Canadians in this process. As seen above, decolonization means losing power, something that the non-indigenous population do not want to dismantle. Decolonization is a daunting and dangerous task. How to begin to undo 300 years of being in power, the blatant stealing of land and culture, and begin to treat indigenous populations as equals rather than 'uncivilized' and 'lesser' citizens? The moral imperative for restorative justice that is created out of decolonization – justice that will include such things as land restoration and reparation – invokes tremendous fear within settler societies. Beyond this, the long and unending process of decolonization does not fit within Western concepts of progress and the Western desire for closure.

Despite these many challenges, decolonization is crucial if Canada wishes to move forward as a nation. Although it may alleviate guilt and continue to give privilege and power to non-indigenous Canadians, the current framework of reconciliation is failing at the most basic level to help those who have been unjustly treated, and is preventing a much richer, multidimensional version of Canada. As Regan points out, 'our persistence in clinging to old colonial myths … keeps us in a state of denial, fear, and guilt … and inhibits our ability to imagine something different …. It is a living testament to the ongoing dysfunction, violence, denial and unequal power relations that characterize Indigenous–Settler relations' (2006: 30, 145). Eventually, the disconnect between the language and the promises of the TRC and the apology and the reality of the colonial system in Canada will make it increasingly difficult to maintain the myth of Canada as tolerant and caring. This is already seen in the fact that, despite the promises of a 'new relationship' between indigenous and non-indigenous populations in Canada, indigenous populations face third-world conditions of poverty, crime, and poor health and housing more than any other group in Canada.

Beyond this, if Canada continues down its current path, reconciliation will not only absolve colonial injustices but will itself be a further injustice. If we do not shift away from the pacifying discourse of reconciliation and begin to reframe people's perceptions of the problem, we will be advancing colonialism, not decolonization. Amends must be made for the crimes that were committed from which all non-indigenous Canadians, old families and recent immigrants alike, have gained their existence as people on this land and citizens of Canada.

Engaging those who are unengaged will not happen immediately. Instead, it starts at the personal level with non-indigenous allies who are committed to decolonization in their own lives. As those engaged in the struggle to dismantle colonial myths, non-indigenous allies have the duty and responsibility to bring decolonization into the mainstream of Canada through social action. Although this may seem daunting, this can be as simple as using privilege to allow Indigenous voices to be heard. Regan further expands how this can be done:

How do we build these decolonizing principles and practices

into our lives more generally at all levels of society? Create transformative learning and teaching possibilities in a variety of formal and informal settings: classrooms, negotiating tables, policy forums, community halls and public history spaces. We can shift our historical consciousness by gaining a deeper under-standing of how myth, ritual and history matter in the work that we do, the classes we teach, the law and policy we make, and the real history of Indigenous–Settler relations that we have denied. We can begin the practical everyday work that will move Settler society from a culture of denial to an ethics of recognition towards a culture of justice and peace. We can link critical reflection and action to vision and hope.

(Regan, 2006: 271)

As Regan shows, decolonization starts at the personal and moves beyond critical reflection to action in ways that continue to decon-struct settler–colonial identities and action at various levels of society.

One step that will be crucial in bringing decolonization into recon-ciliation projects such as the TRC is making the colonial story of Canada more prominent in mainstream Canadian society. Without facing the true history of non-indigenous Canadians as perpetrators of violence, there can be no genuine 'transformative' new relation-ship with indigenous people. As such the TRC would do well to spend time initiating a detailed exploration and study of the settler – the form and functions of the institutions and people who created and sustained the residential school system as well as their current complicity in maintaining the colonial status quo. As Corntassel and colleagues state, 'Settler violence against Indigenous peoples is woven into the fabric of Canadian history in an unbroken thread from past to present that we must now unravel, unsettling our comfortable assumptions about the past' (2009). Gathering the stories of the teachers and church leaders is just as important as gathering the stories of the survivors, because it allows non-indigenous Canadians to turn inward. This also means that initiatives such as the TRC will have to look at the wider colonial history of Canada, including the stories of broken promises, language and cultural loss, and the continuing struggles of indigenous communities in Canada.

Introducing the colonial history of Canada into the dominant discourse can be done in many ways, but it requires creativity and perseverance from non-indigenous allies. In many ways, the story of residential schools is a good place to start because it is a particularly brutal, oppressive and encompassing chapter in the story of Canada's mistreatment of indigenous peoples. Non-indigenous allies need to push for truth-telling efforts in schools, in churches and in the government.

This can be done in two ways. The first is by providing space for indigenous voices to be heard in a way that demonstrates dignity and respect for the equality of their voice. The most obvious way to accomplish this is through a closer look at how various indigenous groups approach reconciliation, and work to enable this to define projects such as the TRC. Another way this could be done is lobbying for classes to be held on indigenous perspectives and knowledge for all government officials, teachers, church leaders, and within universities. Another way could be supporting indigenous arts and advocating funding and space within Canadian society for it to become more prominent. Finally, non-indigenous allies can work creatively with indigenous populations to imagine different realities. When hierarchy is not threatened and cultures are treated as equals there is much to be gained and to learn. This is not to say that that there will not be contradictory narratives, but, as Dorrell states:

> allowing contradictory narratives to co-exist without rushing toward forgiveness or a unifying re-narration could encourage national subjects to reconsider their past and present relation to Indigenous peoples, to reflect on the past abuses carried out in their names, and to consider their current complicity in the oppression of Indigenous peoples.
>
> (Dorrell, 2009: 40)

At the same time, these counter-narratives also continue to increase decolonization through non-indigenous learning, awareness, and recognition.

The second way non-indigenous allies can push for truth telling and decolonization comes through engaging others in their own process of decolonization. This can be done through something as simple as discussions on social networking sites to creating a workshop or a conference. Creative endeavours such as art, theatre, literature and dance are another relatively untapped area for non-indigenous allies to encourage decolonization. A lot of research has gone into how indigenous communities can use the arts to create counter-narratives of Canadian history, but not much emphasis has been placed on the importance of non-indigenous populations doing this as well. When non-indigenous populations open up the myths of Canadian history and confess their part within that history it provides space for others to contemplate their own part in colonialism and do the same.

CONCLUSION

The overarching goal of these initiatives is that eventually, no one can say in Canada that 'they did not know' and hope to be believed. Once settler societies acknowledge injustices and demonstrate contrition, they will begin to create a moral imperative for restorative justice. They can begin to address indigenous populations with equality and open up to creatively find ways in which dignity and freedom can be restored and enough land and power can be returned in order for indigenous populations to be self-sufficient. If the goals of decolonization are justice and peace, then the process to achieve these goals must reflect a basic covenant on the part of both indigenous peoples and settlers to honour each other's existence. This honouring cannot happen when one partner in the relationship is asked to sacrifice their heritage and identity in exchange for peace. As this chapter shows, decolonization is one way in which non-indigenous Canadians can work to ensure that this unequal form of reconciliation is no longer required. Instead, non-indigenous populations can be engaged as allies and move past colonial roles and imperial mindsets that keep current reconciliation projects inadequate and ineffective. It is a formidable task, but, as this chapter outlines, it is an important and necessary one with which to struggle.

PART III

CULTURAL PROCESSES
AND INITIATIVES

7

IS 'INTERRELIGIOUS' SYNONYMOUS WITH 'INTERFAITH'? THE ROLES OF DIALOGUE IN PEACEBUILDING

Sarah E. Bernstein

INTRODUCTION

It is perhaps a truism to say that religion has played a central role in the causation of conflict and maybe less often, a role in peacebuilding. Archbishop Desmond Tutu once stated on a visit to England, 'Religion is like a knife, morally neutral. It is what you do with it' (BBC, 2004). A case in point might be South Africa, where the Dutch Reformed Church was in many ways not just a supporter of apartheid, but indeed led the impetus to create an apartheid state, based on theological underpinnings (Johnston, 1994: 187). On the other hand, many of the leading figures in the Truth and Reconciliation Commission (TRC), such as Tutu himself, were not only religious leaders, their religion served as the central inspiration for their reconciliation work. Likewise, in Northern Ireland, the Protestant and Catholic churches contributed to fanning the flames of conflict, forming theologies and myths that only added to the general level of suspicion and hatred. Later, leaders motivated by religion began to promote initiatives aimed at reconciliation, and many local churches played an important role in fostering dialogue and community cooperation.

As the twenty-first century unfolds, people of different cultures and faiths live in proximity to one another as never before, and religions face the challenge of how they can contribute to peacebuilding rather than to the escalation of conflict. Religious communities are singularly well-organized civil institutions, ideally placed and equipped to undertake a role of fostering understanding and promoting peaceful coexistence between different communities. One forum often adopted is interfaith or interreligious dialogue. Relatively little has been written about the role of interreligious dialogue in peacebuilding. I shall suggest that the field has been further inhibited by a confusion of terms, whereby different types of dialogue, and indeed other activities, are all referred to under the rubric of interfaith or interreligious dialogue. These need to be separated out and analysed if they are to fulfil their potential in conflict prevention and transformation. I will concentrate in this chapter on the three Abrahamic faiths, which have a long history of conflict, but a shorter history of dialogue.

THE EMPHASIS ON RELIGION

What is so special about interfaith and interreligious dialogue? I propose that religion engages people at their deepest level of emotion and intuition, as well as providing a worldview that dictates how people understand the world in which they live. One difference therefore about interreligious work is that once people feel commanded by their faith to engage in this field, this can be a powerful motivator which will help people persevere even in the most difficult times.[1] Beyond this, religions offer a tremendous range of methods and concepts that can add to the dialogue experience. Thus sacred texts and the sharing of ritual and symbol can not only form the meeting point for religious people, providing a window through which the Other can be glimpsed, but also provide inspiration for all participants. They can also provide a 'safe place' in which to engage in a meaningful way, while avoiding direct confrontation on political issues. Interreligious dialogue can engage participants at a deeper spiritual level, in addition to the 'head, heart and hand' (Abu-Nimer, 2001: 689; Abu-Nimer, 2002: 17) of secular dialogue. The spiritual plane provides an additional gateway of access. Religions also offer a wide array of concepts that can offer new possibilities for healing: from forgiveness and compassion to the sanctity of life and the social conscience of the Prophets (Gopin, 2000: 21–3). Thus religion adds both an extra dimension in terms of the level of engagement and meaning of encounter, and a rich resource for methods and concepts that can enrich the dialogue process.

DIALOGUE

I suggest that many activities referred to under the general rubric of dialogue do not in fact embody the defining characteristics of such dialogue. To give some examples, peace negotiations between leaders of different groups who also happen to be of different faiths do not constitute interfaith dialogue. Likewise, problem-solving workshops or other secular conflict resolution programmes that take place between members of different religious groups, but do not relate to religion, are not interfaith dialogue. 'Interfaith cooperation for peace', on the other hand, is an interfaith activity, but is not necessarily a form of dialogue. Similarly, comparative religion courses are not per se a form of dialogue, though they may indeed foster and lead to dialogue between students of different faith backgrounds.

Even within activities between people of different religions, which do relate to and are even based upon religious themes, confusion exists. For example, in a Jewish–Christian–Muslim dialogue I attended in Europe, the Jewish keynote speaker spoke of her attempts to build bridges with local groups of other faiths, cooperating on issues of local concern, such as parking space for services at local places of worship. During the question time following her talk, the first question she was asked related to the possibility of retaining commitment to covenant while affirming other people's contradictory notions of covenant. In other words, a presentation relating to building better relations between groups of different backgrounds was responded to at an entirely different level of dialogue, at a theological level dealing with questions of doctrine and belief.[2]

Specifically, therefore, I propose a distinction between two modes of religious dialogue: what I shall term interfaith dialogue and interreligious dialogue. I shall begin by outlining this distinction, and then continue with further exploration of the differences between the two.

INTERFAITH VERSUS INTERRELIGIOUS

What I refer to here as 'interfaith dialogue' is indeed a dialogue between the faiths. Such dialogue focuses on theology, and its aim is to influence the belief system of the other religion. One example of such interfaith dialogue is the dialogue between Jews and the Catholic Church in the second half of the twentieth century, resulting in Vatican II and other documents that clarify the position of the Church with respect to the Jewish people. Here the aim of the dialogue was to bring about doctrinal changes in the teachings of the Catholic Church, which had led to the dissemination of anti-Semitic attitudes. This type of dialogue takes place between high-level leadership groups examining the truth claims of the different religions, basing itself on study and understanding of religious teachings.

What I shall call 'interreligious dialogue', on the other hand, differs from interfaith dialogue on many levels. Interreligious dialogue takes place between people of different religions whose aim is to build relationships in order to improve inter-communal relations and work together for social change and justice. Taking place mainly at grassroots level, this dialogue can take many different forms, the emphasis being on the fostering of relationships. Table 7.1 summarizes the differences I wish to propose between the two types of dialogue, which I will elaborate upon in the remainder of this chapter.

In the following sections I shall flesh out the distinction I propose between interfaith and interreligious dialogue. The first section will discuss the features of interreligious dialogue; the second section will focus on interfaith dialogue.

Table 7.1 Differences between interreligious and interfaith dialogue

	Interreligious dialogue	Interfaith dialogue
Connection to conflict	Conflict transformation	Conflict prevention
Between	People of different religions	Faiths
Objective	About relationships and attitude change	About changing belief systems
Focus	About inter-communal relations	About theology
Level	Grassroots activity	Between leadership groups
Approach to truth claims	Mitigates truth claims	Examines truth claims
Methods	Based on a wide variety of activities	Based on joint study and learning
Ultimate goal	Social change	Global ethic or celebration of diversity
Limitations	No critical mass	Resistance to change

INTERRELIGIOUS DIALOGUE

Approach to conflict: transformation

Interreligious dialogue is about conflict transformation. The tools of traditional diplomacy are inadequate to deal with the identity-based conflicts that are a feature of the twentieth and twenty-first centuries. 'Lasting peace is impossible without a change of hearts and minds, without a new story to replace the old' (Appleby, 2000: 170). Although some writers suggest that religious leaderships can only help bring about reconciliation after peace is achieved, in fact dialogue can help to build the bridges that can transform conflict (Schneier, 2002 :112). 'Dialogue is the only approach I know that builds trust, mutual respect, friendship and love,' said Rabbi Jonathan Magonet (2003: 9) after more than 30 years of continuing dialogue. In situations of conflict where relationships between the two or more sides have broken down, or never even existed, conflict transformation depends on the building of relationships. Interreligious dialogue fosters the building of relationships between people, nurturing friendship and trust.

Between: people of different faiths

Interreligious, as opposed to interfaith dialogue, takes place between individuals. Relationships are built between individuals, not religious hierarchies, and therefore it is preferable for interreligious dialogue that the participants interact as individuals, not as representatives of a group. Similarly, the focus in interreligious dialogue is on the individual people – their loves and hates, their thoughts, beliefs and feelings – rather than on the religions. Actual religious doctrine is of less significance than personal religious experiences and the practice of religion in daily lives. Thus for example, a women's interreligious dialogue group might discuss the issue of head coverings, concentrating less on the religious sources of the practice, and more on the women's personal experiences and feelings.

Objective: building relationships and changing attitudes

Interreligious dialogue is about rehumanizing the Other (van Tongeren, 1999: 125). The emphasis is therefore on building relationships, and the interpersonal encounter is of more significance than the subject matter under discussion (Kessler, 2003: 26). Faith is an important component of many people's identities and can therefore form a useful meeting point. Exploring their similarities and differences, correcting misconceptions, finding out about each other's lives, all these are ways of building relationships and developing trust between people with different religious beliefs and practices.

In today's world, where unprecedented mixing between people of different religions and ethnicities is accompanied by rising levels of nationalism and racism,[3] dialogue is one of the few ways to 'push attitudes back the other way' (Magonet, 2003: 105). Fisher suggests that the goals of dialogue include changes in the thinking, feeling and behaving of the participants, and it is 'generally hoped that misperceptions will be corrected; attitudes will be improved; positive emotions toward the other side will be kindled or developed and cooperative orientation will begin to emerge or be established' (1999: 88; see also Abu-Nimer, 2001: 688) Abu-Nimer suggests that dialogue can change people's attitudes permanently – building a powerful bridge that will never be broken (2002: 15).

Focus: inter-communal relations

Interreligious dialogue is not only about relationship building between individuals; communities can also build and improve relationships through interreligious dialogue, particularly if such dialogue is accompanied by social action. The British Council of Churches, in its 1981 Guidelines on Dialogue, suggests that people of different faiths can unite in service to the wider community. Dialogue groups offer great scope for the exploration of tensions between religious communities (Sternberg, 1997), which are likely to fester if ignored. Dialogue begins as a way to get to know each other, break down barriers and build confidence so that people can address issues of mutual concern from a basis of trust, and work together to solve problems or take community action. If dialogue is to have a significant role in peacebuilding, it needs to engage whole communities in a process leading to social change.

Level: grassroots

High-level religious leaders are unlikely to be available either physically or emotionally to engage in an ongoing, time-consuming process of dialogue. High-level leaders are also restrained by their position from engaging in open, uninhibited and risky transformative experiences. On the other hand, local religious leaders are in many cases able to reach grassroots communities in ways that political leaders cannot. For these reasons, mid-level religious leaders, educators and community activists are ideal participants in interreligious dialogue.

Whilst more open to transformative experiences, they are also able to influence their communities and thereby effect real change.

Truth claims: mitigation

Interfaith or interreligious dialogue is frequently assumed to involve the comparison of competing 'truth claims' (see e.g. Azumah, 2002: 271–3). Many religions proclaim views about nature and the universe, which are held to be absolute and non-negotiable. It is my contention that comparing competing truth claims is not only unnecessary for creating better interreligious relationships, but can, and frequently does, impede them. Thus, if Irish Protestants and Catholics are to overcome hostilities and work together to build relationships and interreligious cooperation, they would do better to leave issues of communion and salvation to one side, at least until better relations have been established. 'True dialogue, if it is to be productive, must begin with a search for those principles held in common, and a commitment to build on those that bind, not to be blinded by those issues that divide and separate' (Sternberg, 1997: 3).

Liechty proposes the notion of mitigating truth claims, namely that the possible negative outcomes of religious ideas, believed to be God-given and therefore non-negotiable, are lessened or eliminated, while the belief is still upheld. Mitigation seeks to nullify the destructive consequences of a belief, whilst not challenging it directly (2002: 94–5). In essence, this is a technique of conflict avoidance: since competing truth claims can create friction, they are better avoided. The issue of truth claims is a crucial difference between interfaith and interreligious dialogue: where interfaith dialogue tackles competing truth claims head on, interreligious dialogue often avoids or mitigates these issues, which hinder the building of better inter-communal relations.

Methods

There are any number of methods that can be used in inter-religious dialogue. Any activity that contributes to the creation of more complex, multiple identities that allow the building of bridges across the divide: women with women, people of faith with people of faith, citizen with citizen, human with human. It would seem that a significant difference between those whose faith allows no room for the Other, and those who can lead a richly fulfilled religious life and yet respect other religious traditions, is a multiplicity of healthy identities which prevent over-identifying with any one group (Gopin, 2000: 32). As Shakdiel suggests, dialogue is a meeting of multi-dimensional human beings (1991: 48). Any method that can connect people on a variety of levels will be beneficial to the interreligious dialogue process – whether conversation or cooking, text study or T-shirt making, singing or story-telling.

Ultimate goal: social change

The ultimate goal of interreligious dialogue is social change. Dialogue alone can change people's hearts and minds, but unless those people then work together for social justice, dialogue can only make a limited contribution to peacebuilding. Through social action, dialogue partners can not only bring about real change in their own lives, but can also provide pressure for the political change that must come about to create peace. Dialogue is not a substitute for social action, but builds the relationships that create the desire to act together for peace and justice (Gopin, 2002: 44; Abu-Nimer, 2002: 15–16). Through dialogue, the hope is that all participants will be filled with creative energy towards social action. 'At the end of the day, it is mere men and women who change the world, whether for good or for ill' (Sternberg, 1997: 3). Dialogue can give them the will to join the struggle for a better world.

Limitations

There are two core limitations regarding the role that interreligious dialogue can play in peacebuilding. First, dialogue is of necessity a small-scale, intimate, time-consuming activity. Relationships do not develop overnight, and often groups must meet regularly over a course of months, if not years, to overcome their anxieties and preconceptions, and achieve real trust. As I have said above, it is essentially a grassroots activity. It is therefore difficult to reach a critical mass of people through dialogue.

Second, the people most likely to participate in dialogue are those for whom religion plays a less important role in their lives, or who are religiously liberal. This means that dialogue is often said to occur amongst the 'converted' – those who are already open to the Other and convinced of the need for relationship building and equality. One project that attempted to address all these issues was the Voices for Religious Reconciliation programme of the Interreligious Coordinating Council in Israel, which brought together mid-level mainstream religious leaders for intensive, ongoing dialogue, with a commitment on the part of all the leaders to bring their communities into the process in the second year. In this way, the project tried to spread the impact of the dialogue to whole communities. Other such ideas and projects must be developed if interreligious dialogue is to play a significant role in peacebuilding.

INTERFAITH DIALOGUE

Having analysed the nature of interreligious dialogue, it is time now to turn our attention to interfaith dialogue, in order to understand the differences between the two.

Approach to conflict: prevention

If interreligious dialogue can play a role in conflict transformation, interfaith dialogue can and must contribute to conflict prevention. Unless religions can make peace with each other, religion will always spark conflict and violence. Hans Kung states that there can be 'No peace among the nations without peace among the religions; No peace among the religions without dialogue between the religions' (2002: xvii).

In this statement, made as part of an initiative to promote the development of a 'global ethic', I understand Kung to be referring to dialogue among the religions aimed at doctrinal change in the religions themselves, not just the building of better relations amongst the adherents to different religions. As long as religions are exclusive or inclusive,[4] this will remain a major cause for hostility between people of different faiths (Kasimow, 2003: 9).

Between: faiths

Whereas interreligious dialogue occurs between individuals, participants in interfaith dialogue represent their faiths and speak on behalf of their faiths. Thus in the dialogue which led to the changes in doctrine of the Catholic Church, the Catholic participants represented the Church, not themselves.[5] Participants speak not only about their own personal religious experience, but also about the general precepts and practices of their faith. Faith communities must learn how to respect each other as equal partners with equal validity. Otherwise the violent aggression, exploitation and intolerance that have been sanctified in the claims to absolute validity of all the religions will dominate.

Objective: changing belief systems

The objective of interfaith dialogue relevant to conflict prevention is that of bringing about changes in religious belief systems,
to transform them from exclusivist and inclusivist positions into
pluralist and accepting ones. 'It is clear that unless and until some
rethinking of the religious traditions takes place, the use and abuse of
revelation to perpetuate hatred and violence will continue' (Azumah,
2002: 275). Rabbi Tony Bayfield (2003: 25), in an interreligious
indictment in response to the events of September 11, suggested
that Judaism, Christianity and Islam are guilty of failing to confront
the challenges of their own scriptures. It will never be possible to
separate religion and national or ethnic identity, and religion is not
going away. It is therefore imperative to bring to the fore the moral
and religious interpretations that foster coexistence and peace, as
opposed to conflict and violence (Appleby, 2000: 76).

In order to do this, the inbuilt potential for destructiveness that is
endemic within the religions themselves must first be acknowledged
(Magonet, 2003: 68), and then creatively changed. Values of forgiveness and reconciliation must be emphasized and given priority over
revenge and the nourishing of grievances (Appleby, 2000: 171).
Religious traditions are, at least to a certain extent, dynamic and
open to change (Gopin, 2000: 19), through theological debate both
with other religions and within the religious group itself. While
progress has been made in the development of a positive Christian
theology towards the Jews, much remains to be done to create a
positive theology towards Islam in particular (Young, 2002: 69)
and the other religions in general. The other religions also have to
work to create more positive theologies about other faiths. Once a
pluralist or acceptance model has been adopted, other theological
problems fall away: the problem of mission, which has played such a
central role in religious violence through history, becomes irrelevant
once other religions are accepted as part of God's plan. Religions
must come to see that while God is universal, religions are particular.
'Religion is the translation of God into a particular language' (Sacks,
2002: 55).[6]

Focus: theology

Interfaith dialogue is therefore about theology, not about relationships. If religions are to promote peace rather than conflict, they must
work to become more pluralist or accepting.[7] The acceptance model
put forward by Knitter proposes that this can come about through

comparing and contrasting the insights and perspectives offered by different religious orientations in conversation, or dialogue, with one's own (Knitter, 1985: 35). This dialogue will clearly concentrate on the theology of the different religions.

Level: senior leadership

Whereas interreligious dialogue is more suited to grassroots and mid-level leadership, interfaith dialogue is of more importance to leadership groups within the religious hierarchies (where such exist). This is because in many religions, doctrinal change can only officially come from the top, and therefore if the aim is to change the actual religious belief systems, top-level leadership must be engaged in the process. In many religions, the importance of authoritative leadership cannot be overestimated (Gopin, 2002: 20). The pattern may often be that official representatives, where these exist, take part in such dialogue. Religious leaders are responsible for interpreting today's reality in the light of sacred tradition, and for determining a course of action for their communities (Appleby, 2000: 40,56). This leads to constant change, whether acknowledged or not. This process of change needs to take the form of a hermeneutic shift, reworking the sense of religious identity to make room for the Other within the religious tradition. It may therefore be true that for the many religious groups with no official hierarchy, much internal dialogue within the faith will be crucial to the process of theological change.

Truth claims: examination

Comparing truth claims when attempting to build relationships is not helpful. In interfaith dialogue, however, where theological change is the goal, competing truth claims lie at the very heart of the problem. The process of comparing truths is of course, dangerous and delicate, as truth claims lie at the very core of religious belief and are often held with passion. Yet if the religions are to foster peace and harmony between themselves, they must find a way to live with each other.

It took the Holocaust to stir the beginnings of real Jewish–Christian dialogue. Many Christians asked themselves how the Holocaust could have happened in a culture formed and shaped by Christian ideas. The world cannot allow religions to wait for such a calamity to happen again before they engage in a genuine process of self-examination and change. Two different directions have been proposed for developing interfaith harmony – a global ethic and the celebration of diversity. Although these might superficially seem to be contradictory possibilities, closer study will show that they in fact overlap.

Celebration of diversity or a global ethic

For the 1993 Parliament of World Religions, Professor Hans Kung was asked to prepare a draft *Declaration Toward a Global Ethic* (Kung, 1993). Kung argued that in order to deal with global problems – drugs, organized crime, terrorism and the environment – a global ethic is needed. This would not, he suggested, be a replacement for specific religious teachings, but a 'necessary minimum of common values, standards and basic attitudes which can be affirmed by all religions despite their dogmatic differences, and can also be supported by non-believers' (Kung, 2003: 12). Although this global ethic received much support amongst liberal religious leaders, it may threaten fundamentalist leaders precisely at their most sensitive point. If fundamentalism is a reaction to the modern, secular world, an attempt to 'arrest the erosion of religious identity' (Appleby, 2000: 86), then any universal initiative will inevitably meet with resistance and opposition. Thus the idea of a global ethic is unlikely to appeal to fundamentalist leaders.

A second suggestion is to promote a 'celebration of diversity'. Although the global ethic does indeed refer to this idea, its presentation differs significantly. Here the idea is not to build an entire ethical system that everyone can embrace, but rather to encourage all religions to adopt a more positive stance towards difference as being part of the divine plan.

Limitations

The limitations of interfaith dialogue seem clear. Changing belief systems is a laboriously slow, if not impossible task. Theologies are not flexible and open to change. Rather, they are remarkable in their rigidity and perseverance across generations. Even when changes are considered and even adopted at the top level of leadership, such changes are slow in the extreme to filter down to grassroots leaders. In addition, religions differ in their approaches both to theology and hierarchy. There is no central Jewish or Muslim body that can adopt changes on behalf of all adherents to the faith. Similarly, what Christians mean by theology does not really correspond to anything in the Jewish or Muslim world. Theological dialogue can therefore be complicated between Christians and members of the other Abrahamic faiths.

It would seem that there is no easy answer to this problem. Perhaps the route towards religious pluralism must be a slow process of reinterpretation, or the adoption of particular existing interpretations over others. Expecting religious authorities to abandon or radically depart from existing beliefs is unrealistic. Instead, more open interpretations must be explored and encouraged in the hope of affecting a gradual process of change. Another possibility is to foster greater humility, such as that demonstrated by Monsignor Sambi, the Pope's former representative in Jerusalem. When asked how Christians should understand Islam, he asked the question why, if Jesus brings salvation, God allows so many people to follow other faiths. He went on to say, 'I am not God and I cannot give you an answer in his name' (Dowd, 2004). Such humility and the recognition that humans cannot *know* the ways of God would greatly improve the current situation.

CONCLUSION

Both interfaith and interreligious dialogue have important roles to play in peacemaking and peacebuilding. Interreligious dialogue can play a central role in the building of relationships, a vital part of conflict transformation. Interfaith dialogue must play its part in conflict prevention, by finding a path to the celebration of diversity. These two forms of dialogue are distinct: they play different roles, have different goals and employ different methods. Interreligious dialogue is a tool for conflict transformation. Taking place between individuals of different religions, it concentrates on building relationships and changing attitudes, in order to improve inter-communal relations. A grassroots activity, it preferably avoids or mitigates truth claims. Interreligious dialogue can involve a wide variety of activities, including but not limited to text study and discussion. Its ultimate goal is to bring about social change. Interfaith dialogue, on the other hand, is a tool aimed at conflict prevention. Religions' absolute truths have been the source of much conflict and violence. Interfaith dialogue aims to change belief systems, examining theological claims and attempting to make room for the Other. It involves leadership groups and is based on joint study and learning. Its ultimate goal must be the celebration of diversity.

The distinction I attempt to make in this chapter is plainly not absolute. Clearly, understanding other religions must be part of interreligious dialogue, just as the creation of relationships will be important to interfaith dialogue. I believe, however, that this distinction may be helpful, both in academic and in practical spheres. When the interfaith and the interreligious become confused, the dialogue only suffers, and little progress is made towards either conflict prevention or transformation.

NOTES

1   My own experience in the field also seems to indicate that of the few ongoing dialogue groups that survived the onset of the second Intifada in Israel/Palestine, many were interreligious.
2   Interreligious Dialogue in Situations of Conflict II – 31st Student Conference of Jews, Christians and Muslims, 15–19 March, 2004, Germany.
3   Bin Talal (1996) quotes the statistic of the European Values Survey, which found that significant numbers of Europeans think that a neighbour's practice of Judaism or Islam is more alarming than adultery or drug abuse.
4   Exclusivist view: one and only one religious position is true and superior to all others.
    Inclusivist view: one religion is superior; all other religions are valid but only because they unknowingly contain unacknowledged truth within them.
5   For other religious groups, with no formal 'church', this can be more complicated.
6   Interestingly, after the publication of this book by the chief rabbi of Britain, following pressure from the Jewish ultra-orthodox wing, this third chapter on religious diversity was heavily revised and a second edition was published with substantial changes.
7   Pluralist view: all religions are valid, none superior to others. Acceptance model: the religious traditions of the world are different and we have to accept these differences (Wiggins, 2003: 34).

8

THE ROLE OF HEALTH IN BUILDING PEACE: THE CASE OF AFGHANISTAN

Wossenyelesh Kifle

INTRODUCTION

In the war zones of contemporary intrastate conflicts, the health of the population is severely affected by accompanying humanitarian crises and complex problems that often result in excessive morbidity and mortality amongst civilians. The primary causes of these are direct killing, injuries and the disruption of economic and social systems that lead to food shortage, infectious disease, damage to health facilities and to the forced mass displacement of the population.

Health is not only adversely affected by conflict; it is also inextricably linked to peace, human security and development. Good health enables people to exercise their choice, pursue social opportunities and plan for the future. In contrast, illness, avoidable death and health inequality resulting from violent conflict create enormous grief and lead to economic and other development catastrophes, and insecurity at the individual and collective community levels (Commission for Human Security, 2003: 96).

In the midst of many conflicts, the health sector has played a significant role in humanitarian responses to complex emergencies, contributing to the protection of life and alleviation of human suffering (Arya, 2007: 369–72). There is also a growing awareness that health sector initiatives have the potential to make meaningful contributions to building trust, cooperation and sustainable peace in conflict regions. Addressing the health needs that lie behind some of the root causes of conflict can help to alleviate the symptoms.

This chapter evaluates the role of health in peacebuilding, analysing post-Taliban health interventions in Afghanistan as a case study. It argues that the health sector has actors, potential resources and unique characteristics that can be used for peacebuilding. Moreover, health intervention in a post-conflict environment can improve government legitimacy and serve as an overriding goal to create opportunities for conflict resolution or reconciliation, which can contribute to sustainable peacebuilding.

This chapter will highlight the impacts of the conflict in Afghanistan on health, and will examine post-war health intervention attempts to address the health problems in Afghanistan. Next, the rationale behind the role of health for peace will be discussed, enabling post-war health interventions in Afghanistan to be analysed through a 'peace lens' in line with the pre-existing assumption of the role of health in peacebuilding.

Afghanistan is selected as a case study for two reasons. First, the nature of the Afghan conflict has some similarities to complex conflicts going on elsewhere in the world. Second, multi-type and multi-level health sector actors are participating in Afghanistan post-war health sector reconstruction. Both these reasons offer the opportunity for lessons to be learned by others; they also mean that Afghanistan is a useful environment in which to assess the role of the health sector in peacebuilding, and to help understand the challenges.

BRIEF OVERVIEW OF THE CONFLICT

Since the invasion by the Soviet Union in 1979, Afghanistan has experienced decades of unrest. Over 30 years of violent conflict have affected the very foundations of society. More than 3 million Afghans are refugees in different parts of the world, and millions have been forced into internal displacement and impoverishment (UNHCR, 2012). Thousands of civilians have been killed and injured in the midst of long-standing conflict. One study estimates 2,777 killed and 4,347 injured as a direct result of violence in 2010 alone (Chesse, 2012: 3).

Moreover, significant parts of Afghanistan have been identified as heavily mined, and the death rate from mine accidents prior to 2002 was 150–300 people per month (UNDP, 2002: 13). The total number of land mine survivors in Afghanistan is unknown; in 2006 it was estimated at 60,000 (Landmine and Cluster Munition Monitor, 2010). In 2009, the Landmine and Cluster Munition Monitor identified 859 new casualties from mines and the explosive remnants of war.

Following the Soviet Union withdrawal in 1989, the Taliban government came to power in the mid-1990s. The Taliban administered most parts of Afghanistan according to Islamic law, until they were brought down by United States forces in 2001 (Swanström and Cornell, 2005: 1–2). Currently a new modern Islamic government is being built, with presidential elections held in 2004 and 2009 (Independent Election Commission of Afghanistan, 2009). However, in Afghanistan, the informal cultural and tribal structures still hold immense power, and in parts of the country constant low-intensity and sporadic high-intensity violent conflicts remain (NATO, 2009; International Crisis Group, 2009). In addition, ethnic divisions, warlords, the opium trade and smuggling remain long-standing problems in Afghanistan (Swanström and Cornell, 2005: 6–9). These multi-layered and complex problems make the Afghan conflict extremely difficult to resolve, and pose great challenges to building a strong central government and a functional health care system.

THE AFGHAN HEALTH CARE SYSTEM

The lack of a strong centralized government and the effects of protracted violent conflict have almost destroyed the pre-existing health care system, which was already extremely weak. Consequently, health care service delivery is fragmented and the population experiences extremely poor health. Amongst the most serious health problems in Afghanistan are chronic malnutrition and infectious diseases such as tuberculosis (Strong, Wali and Sondorp, 2005: 10). Health indicators during the immediate post-Taliban period showed that maternal mortality rates and those of the under-fives were the worst of already poor levels in the region (DFID, 2004: 4). Moreover, women are disproportionally affected by weak and inadequate health care because of gender segregation and restrictions imposed by local traditions, such as the restriction on women receiving medical care from male providers, restriction on movement, and attitudes that discriminate against women (IRIN, 2009).

In 2000, a survey showed that one third of Afghan health facilities were found to be severely damaged; more than 70 per cent of this damage was from the conflict. The survey identified a total of approximately 11,285 health professionals, including doctors, nurses, midwives and assistants, of which only 208 were women. About 40 per cent of primary health care facilities did not have women health providers (MSH and HANDS, 2002: 21–37; Thompson, Gutlove and Russell, 2003: 3).

HEALTH INTERVENTIONS IN POST-WAR AFGHANISTAN

Both prior to 1979, and during the Soviet occupation, the Afghan health system was mainly hospital-centred and city-based. During the Taliban period, the existing health care system deteriorated and health service provision by non-governmental organizations (NGOs) expanded. These NGOs became the main providers of health services (DFID, 2004: 4), managing over 80 per cent of all facilities by the time of the fall of the Taliban in 2001 (HealthNet TOP, 2008).

Shortly after Afghanistan's interim government was installed by the Bonn Agreement in December 2001, the Afghan Ministry of Health was revived with a new team of leaders. However, this new Ministry was faced with the worst health indicators in the world:

• inequitable health care distribution
• uncoordinated health intervention by various NGOs
• poor and damaged health care facilities
• inadequate access to health services particularly for the rural poor
• an insufficient number of health care professionals (DFID, 2004: 6–7).

To meet the vast challenges with the limited capacity of the newly formed ministerial team, the Ministry of Health began to work with international and local partners, such as the United States Agency for International Development (USAID), the European Commission (EC), and the World Bank (WB), as well as with various international and local NGOs and United Nations agencies (DFID, 2004: 6; Strong et al., 2005: 18–20). Some of these partners provided financial and technical support for the Ministry of Health, and others were involved in direct service implementation.

In cooperation with its partners, the Ministry of Health drafted a new public health policy strategy, whose key aim was to deliver a basic package of health services through local government and NGOs, in a manner equitable for all Afghans. This policy document prioritized and standardized the basic package that should be available in all parts of Afghanistan, and suggested the resources needed to achieve the required level of health services. The policy document retained the leadership and financial and service implementation monitoring responsibilities for the Ministry of Health, and subcontracted most aspects of the basic package of delivery to non-state actors. This was designed with financial and technical support from international organizations (AMOH, 2005: 1–3; Waldman, Strong and Wali, 2006: 4–6).

Although technical support is available from the international community, and expatriate staff are deployed across all departments to build the management capacity of the Ministry of Health, the Afghan health system still suffers from a lack of capacity and skilled professionals, particularly at the provincial level. Despite attempts to build the capacity of provincial offices in recent years, capacity-building initiatives have largely been concentrated at the centre. Furthermore, most of the time these initiatives are implemented in a way that fosters dependency (DIFD, 2004: 10; Waldman et al., 2006: 8–9).

Because the state-based health care system has very limited capacity, almost all health care service delivery is implemented by non-state actors under a performance-based contracting scheme. This strategy was based on strong recommendations by major donors and after the Ministry of Health realized that it was not able to provide a service at the level and speed deemed necessary to address the poor health care status of Afghans. Hence, at the moment more than 70 per cent of the population receive their primary health service from NGOs, and only 5 per cent receive such services from the public sector. The Ministry of Health however, is responsible for the delivery of essential, hospital-based services (WHO, 2010: 7–8).

The missions and strategies of the health programmes of the different NGOs working in Afghanistan, either through the subcontracting scheme or through parallel programmes, vary according to the policies of the organizations and their donors. Donors themselves differ in their approaches towards implementing the health service delivery contracting scheme, which reflect the overall financing and administrative policy to which the donor country must adhere (Waldman et al., 2006: 13). Some prefer to work through or in coordination with the Ministry of Health, while others channel funds and sign agreements directly with non-state health service providers. The diversity of this overall approach can create problems with implementation, but the various organizations are nonetheless making considerable contributions to addressing the complex health care demands of Afghans, even under difficult circumstances (DFID, 2004: 9–10).

Thus, the new Afghan government's official health policy aims to standardize the level of health care facilities available, and ensure at least minimum standards are met. Where implemented properly this strategy has brought coherent and unified priorities to the Afghan health care system; it has facilitated decisions and established a clear direction for the health system between the government and its partners (AMOH, 2005: 1–2). However, challenges remain because of a lack of coordination and lack of harmonization in the implementation of the policy.

THE CONNECTION BETWEEN HEALTH AND PEACEBUILDING

This section explores the health sector and its potential contribution to peacebuilding, as well as its limitations.

The potential resources of the health sector for peacebuilding

The health sector has some unique characteristics that can provide a point of entry for peace work. First, health is people-centred. It addresses the daily survival needs of individuals and contributes to the physical, social and psychological well-being of people and their communities. Second, health is a universal concern and a fundamental human right (WHO, 2002). Third, health problems in one part of the world affect health conditions in another; disease can travel beyond political and geographical boundaries, and health problems have a spill-over effect on to other human security and development issues. These make it less controversial for both donors and recipient countries to allow health-related support into a country at times of conflict, and enables health sector actors to gain access to conflict areas. More importantly, health care actors can win the hearts and minds of the community and persuade both governments and the international community to offer support and cooperation. Health care actors can therefore use these entry points to integrate health and peace issues within a conflict environment.

Health sector organizations, governmental or non-governmental, have entry points at varying levels of influence; health sector actors can therefore potentially take part in peacebuilding work at these different levels, from grassroots intervention to international diplomacy, advocacy and negotiation. Additionally, the networks that exist within the health sector for reporting and controlling diseases, for example through journals and conferences, can be used for swift communication and cooperation at these different levels (MacQueen, 2008).

Health care workers are often the primary contact for victims of conflict and conflict-affected communities; health professionals have the knowledge and skills of diagnosis and healing for many of the physical and mental health conditions common to conflict areas. Knowledge of epidemiology, health promotion and education within public health science enables health workers to quantify and disseminate information on mortality and morbidity from injuries, disease, malnutrition, reproductive health problems and mental health in war-affected zones (Murray et al., 2002). Such evidence is based on scientifically quantifiable grounds and as such, is likely to be received with credibility and with recognition by the general public and by politicians. These, together with the medical principles of confidentiality, altruism, impartiality, as well as the traditional legitimacy and respect for health professionals, can be used as additional assets to enable health care actors to engage in peace work (MacQueen and Santa-Barbara, 2000; Buhmann, 2007 :60).

However, despite these assets, health professionals may not have the skills necessary for peace work. They may not have adequate knowledge of the basic concepts of peace, conflict, conflict resolution and peacebuilding. In addition, they may lack the skills of negotiation, communication, mediation and conflict analysis, and may lack a culturally sensitive approach (Arya, 2007: 381–2). Therefore, to engage in peace work effectively and for maximum success, they need to learn and develop these knowledge and skills, enabling them to take account of the social, political and economic context of health, and see this through the lenses of peace and conflict.

Possible ways for health to contribute to peace work

Using the potential resources and opportunities described above, the health sector can contribute to peacebuilding; through improving the health care system governments can (re-)establish their legitimacy (Rushton, 2005; Eldon, Waddington and Hadi, 2008: 20–5). This assumption reflects the common understanding that addressing security, good governance and good public service delivery by governments, particularly in the health and education sectors, is the key to building government legitimacy, and the most effective way to bring lasting and sustainable peace in fragile post-conflict states (UN, 2007: 9, Maass and Mepham, 2004: 13).

In addition, poor health, disease and gross health inequalities contribute to or fuel violent conflict, due to their effect on the social, economic and political institutions of the community. When large parts of the population suffer from various diseases, this impacts on the economy and on governance (Peterson and Shellman, 2006; Solana, 2006: 10–11). This in turn leads the government to violate people's right to health care, and encourages the government to direct health programmes disproportionately to certain parts of the community, which further aggravates social tensions and conflict. This can be exploited by ethnic, religious and other elites for their own interests (Solana, 2006: 10–11). Therefore, through improving the health care system and addressing health inequalities, governments can reduce alienation within society. This may help to visibly demonstrate a government's commitment to upholding their socio-political responsibility and to maintain long-term peace (Rushton, 2005; Eldon et al., 2008: 14–18).

The second way for the health sector to contribute to peace is by deliberately integrating peacebuilding issues into health initiatives. This approach is based on the assumption that as health is vital to everyone, health care workers can use health as an overriding goal or a meeting point to bring the conflicting parties together and create opportunities for peace. This strategy was formally accepted at the 51st World Health Assembly as a feature of health for everyone in the twenty-first century (WHO, 2011). It has been implemented by the WHO and by several other health sector agencies in different conflict areas under different working titles. A frequently mentioned example of the use of health as an overriding goal was the ceasefire agreement of El Salvador to enable the annual immunization of children from 1985 to 1992. The health of children was proposed as a priority goal of the conflicting parties, which resulted in the brokering of 'Days of tranquillity', allowing children throughout the country to be immunized (Santa-Barbara and Arya, 2008; Arya, 2007: 373–4).

The two approaches described above use different mechanisms but demonstrate how health intervention can contribute to lasting peace, over and above the provision of health services. Combining the two can enable health professionals to identify their skills and the opportunities to work for peace as well as for health, in the progressive dynamics of conflict.

CAN HEALTH INTERVENTIONS EXACERBATE CONFLICT?

Health interventions in conflict zones do not always contribute to peace. Health initiatives, in attempting to do good, may sometimes facilitate and support the conflict system. Any assistance given in the context of violent conflict becomes part of that context and thus also part of the conflict (Anderson, 1999). Hence, the positive intentions of health work might produce a negative peacebuilding outcome, which in turn affects the health intervention. Health programmes which collaborate with the existing power structures may support a corrupt and oppressive system and undermine the local community (Anderson, 1999; Arya, 2007: 369). Additionally, in situations of violent conflict, the dual loyalty of health professionals working in the military and other military-affiliated groups may jeopardize their perceived professional loyalty and legitimacy. Occasionally, against the rules of medical ethics, health professionals pass patient information to a third party for non-medical reasons. This creates suspicion towards health and humanitarian workers in many conflict zones and poses considerable risk to health workers (Arya, 2008).

Significant amounts of funding that enter conflict areas through international health organizations may create problems for the local health system. High salaries within NGOs disrupt the professional labour market and drain highly skilled and experienced workers from local government health care systems. This affects poor health care delivery systems in conflict zones, which further aggravates the conflict and reduces the legitimacy of the government. Furthermore, the way health services are provided in a conflict zone may aggravate tensions and polarization within the community. Health interventions that prioritize the most affected and address the emergency needs of particular communities or groups may leave others feeling excluded. Competition for resources and funds between organizations may further exacerbate suspicions within the conflicted community (Anderson, 1999; Arya, 2007: 369). Unless health programmes are very familiar with the conflict context, health work could fuel the conflict.

EXAMINING POST-WAR INTERVENTIONS THROUGH A PEACE LENS

An efficient and equitable health service for sustainable peace

In the reconstruction of Afghanistan, significant emphasis is placed by much of the international community on improving the new government's capacity to exercise its authority and deliver effective public services to its people (Government of Canada, 2008). As an important public sector, health received priority attention in the post-Taliban reconstruction of Afghanistan. This is critical for Afghanistan, as the health sector has been severely damaged by long-standing conflict, and the population suffers from various diseases, health inequality and the worst health conditions. Even though Afghanistan's enormous health problems are the consequences of violent conflict, at some level they are also a contributing factor to the violence. Unequal treatment of women and denying women's rights and access to health and education were among the issues that the Taliban government was condemned for by the international community (PHR, 1998; US Department of State, 2001). In one post-conflict needs assessment, Afghan civilians described health as a priority need along with security and food (Ipsos and ICRC, 2009). Thus, addressing health needs, providing an equitable health care service, and empowering the Ministry of Health and the government as a whole, can significantly contribute to Afghan reconstruction and sustainable peacebuilding.

In the reconstruction of the Afghan health sector, considerable emphasis is given to building the capacity of the Ministry of Health, both technically and financially, which is starting to show some positive results. Some changes to the major health indicators of the population have also been observed. Restructuring and strengthening the Ministry of Health and creating a policy document to guide health intervention at the early stages have created a foundation for building a sustainable health care system in Afghanistan. The policy document also provides an official guide for prioritizing and coordinating the delivery of all post-conflict health care services.

The Ministry of Health is responsible for coordinating and evaluating all health care funding and service delivery in the country, which provides an opportunity to exercise leadership and a management role under the financial support and technical guidance of international expertise. However, the implementation is problematic; the Ministry lacks the infrastructure and skilled and experienced professionals at all levels. In most cases, local and international NGOs have better infrastructures, resources and skilled workers than the Ministry, particularly at the provincial level. This undermines the government health sector, both in the eyes of the general public and the various implementing partners, which jeopardizes the potential to build trust in the government sector and increase its legitimacy.

Furthermore, because most capacity building for reconstruction is concentrated centrally, this is creating dependency, rather than building sustainable local capacity (World Bank, 2007: 1–2). This reduces the opportunity to build capacity at the provincial level, and challenges the coordination and decentralization of health services to ensure equitable access. This is exacerbated by the lack of security in some rural areas of Afghanistan.

Because of the limited capacity of the state health sector in Afghanistan, almost all basic health care services are delivered by non-state actors. This is a critical, emergency response to the poor health status of the population, but one that must be implemented in line with a policy that aims to build a sustainable state health service. In practice however, donors and NGOs often implement services according to their own internal requirements and their donor country policy. This causes disharmony, duplication of efforts, differing accountability and lack of coordination. Moreover, this form of health intervention lacks uniformity in service delivery to community groups, which has negative consequences for the ethnically divided communities of Afghanistan. Donors and practitioners must identify and respond to these discrepancies to establish a sustainable health care system.

Despite these many challenges, some improvements are being recorded in the overall health of Afghans and in the capacity of the Ministry of Health. However, the health care system still depends on external support, both financial and technical. Rebuilding the Afghan health care system to the level where it provides an adequate and equitable service, and no longer relies on external support, might take some time due to the complex and multifaceted problems already discussed. Further, this directly relates to the improvement of overall social, economic and political conditions in Afghanistan, which still suffer from poverty, challenges associated with governance, corruption and the lack of security in parts of the country (Governance and Social Development Resource Centre, 2006).

Integrating peacebuilding initiatives in health interventions

The health sector can also contribute to peace through integrating a peacebuilding agenda within health interventions. This approach involves multi-type, non-governmental health care actors, and uses various health care assets for peacebuilding. In Afghanistan, local and international NGOs are contributing a great deal to the improvement of the health care system. However, these organizations approach conflict in different ways, like other relief agencies. Most view conflict as an external negative force to be avoided, and prefer not to interfere if they choose to remain in the region of conflict. Some organizations include conflict-sensitive policies within their programmes to avoid exacerbating the conflict, but only a very few organizations incorporate conflict reduction and peacebuilding agendas in their programmes (Goodhand, 2001: 30–2; Atmar and Goodhand, 2002: 40–6). However, considering the number of NGOs in Afghanistan and the resources owned by this group, their involvement in peacebuilding will contribute a great deal to building sustainable health services and peace in Afghanistan.

Some health sector organizations are working to integrate health and peace programmes in Afghanistan, although there are very few of them. The International Committee of the Red Cross (ICRC) for example, in providing care to victims of mines and other explosive remnants, advocates limiting the production and use of weapons through gathering images of victims and collecting data on injuries caused by explosives remnants in Afghanistan (ICRC, 2008). Similar interventions by health care sectors elsewhere in the world have contributed a great deal to raising public awareness about the damage caused by weapons (Santa-Barbara and Arya, 2008; Arya, 2007: 370–1). At the same time, the ICRC is impartial in its treatment of victims from different community groups, and despite divisions within the community, this sends a message to the community that every human life is equal, and it may contribute to creating a culture of care within the divided community.

In addition, the ICRC works to prevent damage to the civilian population by advocating international humanitarian law within the police, judiciary, military and other government sectors (ICRC, 2008). This is important in conflict-affected and fragile states such as Afghanistan, where the principle of justice and other key institutions may be affected by discriminatory practices, corruption or abuse of power by officials, and exhibit a failure to protect human rights, thereby exacerbating or even triggering violence and instability. Lawyers, police officers and civil society groups may lack the capacity to address civilian needs, hence this intervention by the ICRC may significantly contribute to addressing civilian needs, protecting them from human rights violations and institutional abuse and violence (United Nations, 2006; Governance and Social Development Resource Centre, 2006).

McMaster University (Ontario, Canada) led a research programme on the relationship between health and peacebuilding in Afghanistan. This integrated a peacebuilding agenda within health initiatives, and health professionals from McMaster University designed a story-based peace education project to address mental health as well as peacebuilding issues in collaboration with the Afghan education sector, which considered the significance of mental health problems in Afghanistan that result from the stress of long-term violent conflict, as well as addressing the need for peace education. The mental health component of the McMaster University project intends to facilitate living together under difficult conditions, coping with mental health problems and healing at the individual and society level, which may contribute to building cooperation, tolerance and reconciliation between different groups in Afghanistan. Similar programmes implemented in Croatia showed moderate success in coping with ethnic diversity and associated antipathy among children (Santa Barbara, 2008). More importantly, the peace education part of the project delivered through the school curriculum with its themes of reconciliation, ethnic tolerance, conflict resolution and resistance to armed activity, may plant the seeds of a culture of peace and non-violence amongst Afghan children, who can be the window of hope for Afghanistan's sustainable peace and stability.

These examples demonstrate that health and peace interventions, if properly designed and implemented in partnership with the local community, may contribute to post-war peacebuilding in Afghanistan.

Nonetheless, the work of NGOs is not without criticism from the Afghan public and government:

- The high salaries and living standards among NGO employees in Afghanistan are criticized for creating elitism and draining already scarce human resources away from the Ministry of Health.
- Particularly in the provincial areas, NGOs have better resources and capacity than government institutions, which undermines the authority and credibility of Afghan government institutions in the eyes of the public.
- The lack of clear distinction between civilian NGO workers, the military and groups affiliated to the military, creates confusion particularly among rural communities.

This raises questions about the impartiality and neutrality of NGOs and may also have contributed to the recent rise in the number of attacks targeting NGO health and humanitarian workers in Afghanistan (Rubenstein, 2010). Nevertheless, health organizations that are not working to incorporate peacebuilding in their health programmes are missing a real chance to alleviate the root causes of the conflict and contribute to sustainable peacebuilding, as well as improving the health of the population.

CONCLUSION

The complex nature of contemporary violent conflict demands that peacebuilding interventions be multi-level and multi-track, and health should be the priority in post-conflict and post-war reconstruction programmes. However, poor and fragile post-conflict governments may not have the capacity to respond adequately to the challenges of post-conflict health care needs, hence financial, technical and other capacity building support by donors, international and local NGOs is mandatory in such countries, including Afghanistan. Improving and rebuilding the Afghan health care system requires that emergency health care needs are addressed, at the same time as a sustainable and equitable state-based health care system is being established. This will enable the government to demonstrate a commitment to fulfil its socio-political responsibility, and (re-)establish its legitimacy. Therefore, rebuilding and achieving a sustainable health care system may contribute to peacebuilding by helping to establish legitimate government, as well as encouraging the spill-over effect of the improved health of the population on to security and other development issues. It is appropriate therefore for multiple donors and NGOs to invest in health care system reconstruction and capacity building. However, support and capacity-building attempts by NGOs can target only short-term needs, and can be implemented in a way that creates dependency on external support; this may weaken the capacity of state-based institutions, and discredit the authority and legitimacy of the state.

Building a sustainable health care system is a long-term process, and may take longer in complex environments like Afghanistan. Improving the health care system can only be effective along with an improvement in security and other socio-political conditions in the country. Hence, it demands a continued and integrated effort from donors, NGOs, government institutions and communities.

NGOs are important in alleviating and addressing emergency health care needs and in building the health care system in Afghanistan. However, they can also contribute to sustainable peacebuilding by integrating a short to long-term peacebuilding agenda into their health initiatives. Using their health intervention as an entry point, they can build cooperation, reconciliation and trust within the community – an approach which is being implemented in Afghanistan and in other places in the world and is proving able to make a considerable contribution to wider conflict prevention and peacebuilding efforts beyond improving health problems.

Nonetheless, many health sector organizations working in Afghanistan do not integrate conflict resolution and peacebuilding agendas within their health interventions; although some have started developing conflict-sensitive policies in their programmes, only a small number integrate peacebuilding in their health initiatives. However, considering the considerable resources and opportunities to which they have access, NGOs may do much more than 'do no harm' to peacebuilding, while improving the health of the population more effectively.

Whichever approach is used, post-conflict health is a priority, and improving the health care system and the status of health itself is crucial in building sustainable peace. Usually the health impact of conflict will be felt for many years after the violent conflict is over, and so without addressing the health care needs and without building an effective health care system, attaining sustainable peace is impossible. Similarly health sector actors working in conflict and post-conflict zones attempting to address health care needs while ignoring conflict factors, will only be able to alleviate the symptoms, as these needs cannot be met within a violent and hostile environment. Consequently, looking at health through the lenses of conflict and peace is essential when addressing health care in zones of conflict.

PART IV

CHALLENGES TO PEACEBUILDING AND RECONCILIATION

9

THE NEW ECONOMY OF TERROR: MOTIVATIONS AND DRIVING FORCES BEHIND CONTEMPORARY ISLAMIST INSURGENCIES

Peter Keay

INTRODUCTION

In *Modern Jihad,* Loretta Napoleoni approaches armed insurgency and terrorism from a novel and different perspective, asserting that there is a 'new economy of terror'; namely that it is not possible to view modern Islamist (or other armed) movements without acknowledging their dependence on specific financial factors that may be the real drivers behind the groups. She pointedly ignores the more conventional approaches of focusing on religious and cultural differences, and claims that Islamist groups are driven more by real economic forces in the Muslim world. She claims:

> Money is terrorism's lifeline. Economics, not politics or ideology, is the armed struggle's universal engine. This is the unexpected and disconcerting scenario unveiled by an economic analysis of modern terrorism.
>
> (Napoleoni, 2003c)

Napoleoni's research is extraordinarily thorough. Her claims that the rise of violent Islamic extremism is based not on religious fervour but on the desire for financial gain and a wish to separate the Muslim world from the Western economic system, together with opposition to corrupt Arab governments, are bold. Does her analysis however replace or simply complement the more traditional viewpoint of religious motivation? What in fact does it say about the way the Muslim faith and its traditional, assertive but non-violent jihad is being hijacked in justification of a new wave of terrorism?

BACKGROUND

'We are terrorists; yes we are terrorists, because it is our faith.' This statement by Palestinian extremist Abu Mahaz to CNN in 1993 (Napoleoni 2003a: 3) goes to the heart of the argument surrounding contemporary religious extremism and terrorism and the search for an explanation about its motivation. It highlights a direct link between religion and religious violence. Samuel Huntingdon, in his seminal essay, claims in even more controversial, perhaps apocalyptic terms, that there is an impending 'clash of civilisations' (Huntingdon, 2004). Viewed from a post-11 September perspective and amidst the hyperbole of the 'war on terror', which is littered with pedantic interpretations and deliberate misinterpretations of 'fundamentalism', 'jihad' and 'Islamist', looking into the above themes is a minefield of definition, cultural diversity and political correctness.

Has the nature of religion-based political violence changed since 11 September 2001? In a fatwa, or religious ruling, issued in 1998, Osama bin Laden and other signatories declared war on the United States and its allies. But it also warned Muslim states of the consequences of cooperating with the 'infidels'. The fatwa contains many references to the Quran and claims holy justification for extreme violence. Three years later these words were brought home to the public in the most horrific act of terrorism – and justified in the name of God. So what was the real motivation? What drove 19 men to hijack planes and fly them into buildings? Is their motivation important, or are they pawns in a wider war that has more to do with resurgent Muslim power and identity? *The Economist* noted in an editorial piece published within days of the terrorist attacks, 'such arguments [as motivation and methods] will form the debates of a new era' (*Economist*, 2001).

However we should not just focus on the terrorism of al-Qaeda and its affiliates. Islamism does not exclusively comprise those who have taken up the 1998 call to arms. There is also a non-violent but potentially extremist Islamic activism on the rise. There are well-established Islamist insurgencies throughout Africa and Central and Southeast Asia. Terrorist attacks in Western Europe by groups claiming religious motivation and affiliation to al-Qaeda speak to the claim that 'fanatical' or 'radical' Islam is on the rise. Rising Muslim populations in European countries are alienated and disenfranchised. Has the focus on al-Qaeda created the perception of a link between a resurgent Islam and terrorism? Does the resurgence of the Taleban in Afghanistan and its gains in Pakistan, or the rise of Islamist groups in, for example, Somalia tell us that there is no stronger motivation than religion? Or is there an alternative view of the rise of this more politically assertive Islam – a view that is based more on an analysis of the financial drivers of these movements and their interdependence with the world economy?

JIHAD AND THE RISE OF INSURGENT ISLAMISM

Jihad

The political scientist Gilles Kepel (2003) writes that in the aftermath of the 11 September attacks, 'the term Jihad has gained currency in a number of European languages'. In the years since Kepel first wrote those words, the term has become loaded with the rhetoric of the Bush administration's 'war on terror'. The literal meaning of jihad may be seen as 'struggle' or 'effort', with a deeper meaning than just holy war. Muslims use the word jihad to describe three different kinds of struggle:

- the internal struggle to live out the Muslim faith as well as possible
- the struggle to build a good Muslim society
- holy war: the struggle to defend Islam, with force if necessary.

David Waines, along with many modern writers, asserts that the main meaning of jihad is the 'internal personal struggle in the faith' (Woodhead, 2001: 188). However, there are so many references to jihad as a military struggle in Islamic writings that it would be incorrect to claim that the interpretation of jihad as holy war is wrong. It would also be incorrect to claim that radical or militant Islamic views in any way represent the majority of Muslims. As Lloyd Ridgeon notes, 'It is probably the case that universalism represents a minority view and that the views of [radical thinkers] have arguably been adopted because of the corners into which they [believers] have been forced' (in Schmidt-Leukel, 2004: 176). Ridgeon also explains the views of non-universalists but concludes that their voices all too often go unheard and 'it is the anger and animosity of the universalists that receive media attention' (Schmidt-Leukel, 2004: 150). It is not my intention here to give an overview of Islam through the ages or make any linkage that the spread of Islam was accompanied by decades of military conquest – this can be said of other religions also. However, in order to understand the modern Islamic insurgency it is necessary to look at the reasons and ideology behind the resurgence of Islamism over the last 30 to 40 years.

A number of beliefs and assumptions lie at the heart of the Islamic political revival, perhaps most importantly that the Muslim world is in a state of decline caused by not living according to Islam, and could be rectified therefore by a return to Islam in personal and public life, ensuring the restoration of Islamic identity, values and power. At the heart of Islam is faith: a comprehensive way of life as stipulated in the Quran and embodied in Sharia law. It follows, therefore, that for Muslim governments to be true, acceptable and representative, Sharia law must be (re-)introduced to establish a socially just state and society.

Islam on the rise

While the majority of Islamic activists seek to bring about such change from within society, a small but significant radical minority believe they are carrying out God's will in their use of violent means. This extremist minority further believes that because rulers in the Muslim world are authoritarian and anti-Islamic, violent change is necessary and that the activists have the responsibility and the authority to change governments in this way. These radical movements often believe that Islam and the West are engaged in an ongoing battle that reaches back to the early days of Islam; they blame the West for its support of un-Islamic or unjust regimes and its biased support for Israel in the face of the displacement and suffering of the Palestinian people. Thus, violence against such governments and their representatives is regarded as legitimate self-defence (ICG, 2005).

Modern Islamic insurgencies are for the most part Sunni; Sunni Muslims make up approximately 90 per cent of the Muslim world. (Although it cannot be listed in the developmental phases of Sunni Islamism, in terms of ideology, motivation, inspiration, funding and recruitment, the Shiite Iranian Revolution in 1979 also has to be mentioned here.) Contemporary Islamist insurgencies can be broken down into distinct phases (ICG, 2005: 15):

- the emergence of a radical jihadist tendency in Egypt in the 1970s and 1980s, based on the thoughts of the Egyptian academic Sayyid Qutb, himself inspired by the writings of the Indian Muslim/Pakistani journalist and politician Abul Ala Mawdudi
- the 'mobilization' of fighters from across the Muslim world to combat the Soviet presence in Afghanistan in the 1980s
- the long-running but ultimately unsuccessful insurgencies against un-Islamic regimes, for example in Algeria and Egypt
- the terrorism spearheaded by al-Qaeda against the West since the mid-1990s.

Radical ideology

Abul Ala Mawdudi's call in the 1930s for a universal jihad to counter Western domination and the decrease in influence of Islam as a religion marks a turning point. As the influential religious historian Karen Armstrong notes: 'Never before had *jihad* figured so centrally in official Islamic discourse' (2001: 239). Mawdudi (1903–1979) believed the Muslim community's decline resulted from practising a form of Islam corrupted by non-Islamic ideas and culture. He reminded Muslims that Islam is not simply a religion, but a complete social system that guides and controls every aspect of life including government. He believed tolerating non-Muslim rule and non-Islamic concepts and systems was an insult to God. Therefore, according to him, the only path to pure Islam would be through the establishment of Islamic states. Mawdudi argued the only practical way to accomplish Islamic rule was through jihad, which he explained as the following:

> Islam is a militant ideology and programme that seeks to alter the social order of the whole world and rebuild it in conformity with its own tenets and ideals. 'Muslim' is the title of that International Militant Party organized by Islam to carry into effect its militant programme. And 'Jihad' refers to that militant struggle and utmost exertion which the Islamic Party brings into play to achieve this objective. ... Islam wishes to destroy all States and Governments anywhere on the face of the earth that are opposed to the ideology and programme of Islam regardless of the country or the Nation which rules it.... It must be evident to you from this discussion that the objective of Islamic 'Jihad' is to eliminate the rule of an un-Islamic system and establish in its stead an Islamic system of State rule. Islam does not intend to confine this revolution to a single State or

a few countries; the aim of Islam is to bring about a universal revolution.

(Mawdudi, 1980)

Hassan al Banna (1905–1949) was the main architect and founder of the Muslim Brotherhood in Egypt. He believed in the same broad concepts as Mawdudi, but did not outline an operational method for taking power. As proposed by Barbara Zollner, his legacy was reminding Muslims that the Quran says jihad against non-believers is an obligation of all Muslims (2008: 13). The idea of jihad to spread Islam and to establish the Islamic state was then expanded by his contemporary Sayyid Qutb (1906–1966). Qutb is regarded by some as the founding father and leading theoretician of the contemporary radical movement. Qutb became one of the leading spokesmen and thinkers of the Muslim Brotherhood, advocating the use of violence to establish Islamic rule. In direct contrast to al Banna, Qutb developed a top-down approach that focused on replacing non-Islamic rulers and governments. In prison in Egypt he took the basic tenets of the Muslim Brotherhood and formed a new Islamic ideology, one that justified the use of violence in any form, thus inspiring future generations.

Qutb refined Mawdudi's argument that the Muslim world was in a state of *jahiliyah* (ignorance) where man's way had replaced God's way. According to Qutb, since *jahiliyah* and Islam cannot coexist, offensive jihad was necessary to destroy *jahiliyah* society and bring the entire world to Islam. Until *jahiliyah* is defeated, he argued, all true Muslims have a personal obligation to wage offensive jihad. When Qutb added offensive jihad to the widely accepted concept of defensive jihad, he broke with mainstream Islam:

Those who say that Islamic Jihad was merely for the defence of the 'homeland of Islam' diminish the greatness of the Islamic way of life and consider it less important [than] their 'homeland.' … However, [Islamic community] defence is not the ultimate objective of the Islamic movement of jihad but it is a means of establishing the Divine authority within it so that it becomes the headquarters for the movement of Islam, which is then to be carried throughout the earth to the whole of mankind.

(Qutb, 2006: 71)

In addition to offensive jihad, Sayyid Qutb used the Islamic concept of *takfir* (denunciation or excommunication of apostates), providing a legal loophole around the prohibition of killing another Muslim, making it in fact a religious obligation. This concept lies at the very heart of the justification used for the extreme violence of al-Qaeda and other Islamist terrorist movements since the late 1990s. Ayman al-Zawahiri, Osama bin Laden's key lieutenant, credits Qutb's execution and the legacy of his Islamist thought for inspiring modern jihadists (Calvert, 2007: 234).

AL-QAEDA AND THE 11 SEPTEMBER ATTACKS

The terrorist attacks of 11 September 2001 mark a turning point in the development of radical Islam. The hijacked planes which flew into the twin towers of the World Trade Center in New York City and the Pentagon in Washington can be seen as a call to arms, daring the Western powers to respond, and providing a signal to millions of Muslims around the world that the world had changed; that Western hegemony was no longer to be tolerated, that it was possible to change the course of history and world politics by massive violence in the name of God. Kepel calls the attacks a provocation, 'albeit a provocation of gigantic proportions' (Kepel, 2003: 4). The attacks provoked a response and formed the basis of American and Western response to terrorism for the rest of the decade. The attacks of 11 September also provided inspiration for thousands or even millions of people who dreamed of an end to Western hegemony and its supposed suppression of Islam.

The 11 September attacks were effective also in terms of the cost–benefit analysis. In *Modern Jihad*, Napoleoni posits that, excluding compensation payments, the attacks cost as little as $500,000, in contrast to the estimated $135 billion cost in property loss, clean-up and federal bail-outs (2003a: 179). Importantly the attacks came to define assertive Islamism, casting a shadow over non-violent fundamentalist views.

EXTENT AND AREAS OF ISLAMIC INSURGENCY

This section provides an overview of the current areas where there is an ongoing Islamist insurgency. Although in the context of the 'war on terror' led by the United States, there have been many claims that there is a worldwide Islamist insurgency, it is countered that al-Qaeda, the only organization or network that purports to have an overarching coordination role, is simply a group of followers of

Osama bin Laden, who provides inspiration and possibly funding for other affiliates. Nevertheless, modern Islamist insurgencies cannot be viewed outside the context of the 11 September attacks or the fatwa issued by bin Laden and his main lieutenants in 1998. The fatwa itself called for the establishment of an Islamic caliphate in Egypt, to be used in a subsequent phase as a staging post for launching jihad against the West.

The picture suggests a much more complex situation than the simplistic concept of 'global Islamist insurgency' controlled by al-Qaeda as propounded by some. Rather, it points to separate and distinct insurgencies around the world, which are more prevalent in some regions, and are linked by some common thematic elements. They may follow general ideological or strategic approaches that conform to the pronouncements of al-Qaeda, and they share a common tactical style and propaganda. Adapted from *Countering Global Insurgency* (Kilcullen 2004: 5–6), the main areas of Islamist insurgency are as follows:

- *North America and Western Europe.* The United States is most prominent as the scene of the 11 September terrorist attacks; in Spain, the May 2004 Madrid train bombing; in the United Kingdom, the July 2005 Underground and bus bombings.
- *Muslim Northwest Africa.* The area has seen major terrorist bombings in Casablanca, Morocco, ongoing Islamist insurgencies in Algeria and Morocco, and terrorist attacks in Tunisia.
- *Greater Middle East.* The area including Turkey, Syria, Jordan, Lebanon, Israel/Palestine, Egypt, the Arabian Peninsula and Iran is by far the most active. There are ongoing Islamist insurgencies in Iraq, Jordan, Egypt, Saudi Arabia, Yemen, Turkey, Lebanon and Israel/Palestine. There is a separate pattern of Shi'a terrorism and insurgency across this region.
- *East Africa.* Kenya and Tanzania suffered simultaneous terrorist bombings of US embassies in August 1998, coordinated from a base in the Sudan, which has an ongoing Islamist insurgency against Christian and Animist Sudanese. Kenya suffered an additional attack in 2002. The ongoing threat of violent Islamism in Somalia is very real.
- *The North Caucasus.* There is an ongoing insurgency or threat of insurgency in Chechnya, Dagestan and Ingushetia against the Russian forces deployed in the area.
- *South and Central Asia.* The Declaration of War of 23 February 1998 was co-signed by leaders from Afghanistan, Pakistan and

Bangladesh. Afghanistan was controlled by the Taleban and was the main al-Qaeda sanctuary until October 2001. Pakistan itself has been experiencing an intensifying Islamist insurgency. The republics of former Soviet Central Asia and the Xinjiang Uighur region of China have also seen Islamist terrorist activity and low-level insurgency.

- *Southeast Asia.* There are ongoing Islamist insurgencies in Indonesia, the Philippines and Thailand, with substantial terrorist activity in these countries and in Singapore, Malaysia and Cambodia. There is also a broader pattern of Islamic militancy, Muslim separatist insurgent movements, and sectarian conflict. The principal terrorist grouping in the theatre is Jemaah Islamiyah, which operates across the entire region and beyond, advocating a pan-Islamic agenda.

Kilcullen makes the point that apart from the 11 September attacks, Madrid and London, all terrorist attacks have taken place where there is an ongoing Islamist insurgency (2004: 6).

THE NEW ECONOMY OF TERROR

The section above demonstrates the extent of Islamist insurgent activity around the world, as well as the ideology and/or motivation behind the insurgency. The propaganda of the 'global war on terror' spoke of a 'global insurgency' and 'al-Qaeda and its affiliates'. More recent research has suggested that, given terrorism is simply a tactic, different parameters should be used to analyse and therefore difference tactics used to fight Islamist violence. Napoleoni suggests a different approach. She states that, '[Islamist violence] is, as any revolutionary force, an economic engine, fuelled by a very special source of energy, the Modern Jihad' (2003a: 154). As a driver of Islamist violence, she excludes politics and ideology. She claims that over the last ten to twelve years the 'new economy of terror' has merged with the international illegal and criminal economy, together generating an annual turnover of $1.5 trillion (approximately £0.9 trillion), which is roughly equivalent to 5 per cent of the entire world's gross domestic product. In her analysis of the economic role of armed organizations since the end of the Second World War, Napoleoni identifies three major evolutionary transitions: state sponsorship, privatization and globalization.

According to her overview, state sponsorship was a familiar feature of the cold war, when the United States and the Soviet Union fought wars by proxy along the periphery of their spheres of influence, using armed groups fully funded by each of them. The next stage, the privatization of terrorism, took place in the late 1970s and early 1980s, when terrorist organizations such as the Palestine Liberation Organization (PLO) and the Irish Republican Army (IRA) succeeded in financing themselves. In the 1990s, seeking to increase their independence, terrorist groups widened their economic horizon. When the deregulation of international markets broke down financial and economic barriers, they took advantage of economic liberalization, and terror groups thus became transnational, fully globalized entities, raising money and carrying out violent attacks across international borders.

Napoleoni suggests that it is ironic that the new economy of terror is a product of globalization, particularly of the globalization that emerged after the fall of the Berlin Wall. Globalization allowed non-state entities to promote a variety of liberal causes, social changes and economic advancement, but also facilitated the networking of terrorist movements such as al-Qaeda and the growing sophistication of the 'terror economy'. Napoleoni also puts forward the thesis that armed Muslim groups are trying to accomplish a sort of reversal of the Crusades, 'the oppressed Muslim masses are encouraged to take up arms against the corrupted, Muslim, oligarchic rulers and their backers, the West' (2003a: 149).

However, she posits that an economic analysis downplays the role of religion, relegating it to a mere means of recruitment while focusing on the growing tension between a dominant Western capitalist system and a resentful and growing Muslim population, hemmed in by corruption and deceit. Napoleoni continues: 'What we are witnessing today, therefore, goes well beyond the motivations of single Islamist armed groups: it is a clash between two economic systems – one dominant – the West, and the other insurgent – Islam' (2003c). In conclusion, she writes:

> Thus the Modern Jihad is a brew made up of a mixture of Islamist revolutionary ideology, Muslim search for identity and socio-economic aspirations. As such it feeds into the network of terror economies created by armed groups attempting to achieve self-sufficiency: the smuggling of drugs and narcotics, the partnership with crime, the transfer of wealth from rich Muslim charitable organizations, money laundering, etc. It is the desire and the possibility of becoming part of such a network and at the same time the willingness of the network to embrace all

Islamic state-shells that contributes to the proliferation of the Modern Jihad.

(Napoleoni, 2003a: 157)

In partial support of this theory, Peter Bergen also describes post-11 September Islamist jihadists in corporate terms – as creating a 'franchised business model with centralized corporate support and autonomous regional divisions (2002: 56). In an article for the *Wall Street Journal,* novelist Martin Amis speaks of the 'new structure' of terrorism, and posits that the forces driving new radical Islamist violence go well beyond religion and are now more to do with alienation, the thirst for power and the quest for fame (2008). Citing the different approaches but convergent views of the international experts Professors John Gray and Philip Bobbitt, Amis in part supports Napoleoni's theory that the new strain of violent Islamism is a direct product of globalization. Amis argues:

> Al Qaedaism, for them, is an epiphenomenon – a secondary effect. It is the dark child of globalization. It is the mimic of modernity: devolved, decentralized, privatized, outsourced and networked. According to Mr. Bobbitt, al Qaeda not only reflects the market state: it is a market state. Globalization created great wealth and also great vulnerability; it created a space, or a dimension. Thus the epiphenomenon is not about religion; it is about human opportunism and the will to power.
>
> (Amis, 2008)

In deliberately provocative terms, he continues:

> There are several reasons for hoping that international terrorism isn't about religion – not least of them the immense onerousness, the near-impossibility, now, of maintaining a discourse that makes distinctions between groups of human beings. Al Qaedaism may well evolve into not being about religion, about Islam. But one's faculties insist that it is not about religion yet.
>
> (Amis, 2008)

It is clear that as terrorist groups evolve, they become dependent on the economy around them. The gambling and prostitution rackets controlled by the IRA, the narco-terrorism of the Revolutionary Armed Forces of Columbia (FARC) and the kidnapping activities of Sendero Luminoso in Peru, are all examples of the privatization of terror. Napoleoni goes into great detail about how terror groups fund themselves and how, since globalization, they have become dependent on the international financial system. She argues that globalization itself created the conditions that have allowed such massive terrorist atrocities to take place. She suggests that the Western perception of the aims of Islamist groups – the destruction of the state of Israel and its Western imperialist allies – is skewed. The real target is 'the House of Saud and [other regimes] that block the formation of pure Islamist states' (2003a: 204). The statistics on al-Qaeda attacks would seem to bear out this argument. A RAND Corporation report states that of the 69 terrorist attacks between 1994 and 2007 claimed by al-Qaeda, only the attacks in New York, Washington, Madrid and London took place outside a Muslim state (Jones and Libicki, 2008: 187–96).

CONCLUSION

The renowned writer on modern terrorism Walter Laqueur talks of a 'growing fanaticism', and claims that 'much of today's terrorist violence is rooted in fanaticism' (1998: 48). Napoleoni tries to go beyond the sensational. She provides in *Modern Jihad* an extremely thorough and sober analysis of the financial underpinning of, and linkages within and between, terrorist groups. She downplays the primary driving role of religion in Islamist and other movements, and shifts it to a more economic focus. By her own admission, her approach is geared towards finding ways of combating terrorism, rather than understanding the motivation behind the rise of Islamism. Yet there is no doubt that there is a connection. Her conclusions here in some way contribute to the perceived linkage between the rise of Islamism and the rise of terrorism committed in the name of Islam. There is certainly resentment in the Islamic world against the West. Radical views may be becoming more popular, but extremist views, expounding violence, remain on the fringe. The French/Algerian journalist Mohamed Sifaoui writes:

> If the majority of Muslims were not moderate, Islamists would have destroyed the Western world a long time ago. Despite its technological lead, its nuclear power, and all its armies, the Western world would never be able to face an Islamist world entirely convinced by the terrorist cause. One billion people supporting al-Qaeda would reduce the rest of the world to ashes.

Islam contains violent texts that need not be applicable today. Islam is a religion of moderation.

(Sifaoui, 2008: 16)

Napoleoni's analysis determines that today's violent extremist Islamist groups are embedded in the international economic system and that in order to counter them, their financial structures should be targeted. While this is no doubt true, it is perhaps simplistic to relegate the role of religion to that of 'recruiting tool'. The non-Muslim world cannot afford to discount or downplay the role religion plays in the desires and aims of the Muslim world – not just the demands of the armed extremists. Napoleoni argues that the war against groups such as al-Qaida stems from a clash of economic systems, not of religions.

Raymond Ibrahim, writing in the *Middle East Review of International Affairs*, states that:

The current battle at hand may ostensibly revolve around those grievances [intervention in Iraq and Afghanistan, presence in Saudi Arabia, interference in the Islamic world's affairs, US support for Israel over a 'just' settlement to the Palestinian question]; but the forthcoming war will ultimately be about militarily establishing Islamic supremacy over the entire globe.

(Ibrahim, 2008)

This language is evocative of the propaganda of the 'war on terror' and bin Laden's 1998 fatwa. 'Waging war', 'military means' and such terms have widened the gap between Muslim and non-Muslim populations. There is a fundamental schism between the Muslim and non-Muslim world. More important than ever are organizations such as the Foundation for Dialogue among Civilizations and the Alliance of Civilizations Forum. Bin Laden's 'declaration of war' has attempted to hijack the wider Islamic agenda, contributing to the false impression that al-Qaeda somehow represents Islamism or Islamic activism.

Modern Jihad does not supersede a more conventional focus on religious motivation for jihad, but complements it and provides very serious ideas for combating aspects, in particular financial aspects, of armed insurgency that may have previously been overlooked. Napoleoni's analysis starkly highlights the way that modern processes, in particular the consequences of globalization, have contributed to a rise in super-violent Islamist insurgency. In particular she highlights the ability of al-Qaeda and post-11 September terrorist groups claiming affiliation to conduct terrorist operations with global reach.

Between 2001 and 2009, the US administration of George W. Bush appeared to equate political Islam with extremism and terrorism, and certainly did not attempt to take into account the real grievances of the Muslim world, at least in their perception. The administration's over-simplified rhetoric, combined with a catastrophic failure to address core issues and grievances such as the Palestinian question, has left a lasting impression. The administration of Barack Obama has done a good deal already to reach out to the Muslim world to try to rectify past mistakes. More than anything *Modern Jihad* highlights the very serious risk that those who would consider themselves to be the real jihadists – Muslims struggling to assert themselves peacefully within their faith – are drowned out by the sea of violence being committed in their name.

10

THE QUESTION OF HOME: REFUGEES AND PEACE IN THE ISRAEL–PALESTINE CONFLICT

Abigail Bainbridge

INTRODUCTION

In 2001, Edward Said stated:

> The issue, in the by now notorious peace process, finally has come down to one issue, which has been at the heart of Palestinians depredations since 1948: the fate of the refugees who were displaced in 1948, again in 1967 and again in 1982.
>
> (Said, 2001: 1)

This chapter will explore how the status of Palestinian refugees in the Middle East, specifically those in Lebanon, Jordan and Syria, must be addressed to ensure the sustainability of the Palestinian–Israeli peace process.

After a brief introduction to the Palestinian refugee issue, I will examine the Palestinian–Israeli peace process and the situation currently faced by Palestinian refugees in the Middle East. Analysing the current status of refugees within the ongoing process, the chapter will question how their status must be addressed if the peace process is to be sustainable. Finally, this analysis will serve to understand how a peace process can be sustainable if the official status of the refugees is addressed, but the wider concept of providing justice for those in exile is not.

The origin of the Palestinian refugee issue lies in the 1948 Arab–Israeli war. According to Sayigh (2007: 99–100), Palestinians now fall into three broad groupings. The first are those who remained within the three-quarters of Palestine controlled by the Israelis, approximately 60,000 people. The second, and largest group of around 1 million people, are those who remained in, or fled to, the areas of Mandate Palestine that were not under Israel's control, areas which became known as the Gaza Strip and West Bank. The third group are the approximately 300,000 refugees who fled to neighbouring Middle Eastern countries or in some cases, even farther afield.

Those in the third grouping, specifically those who fled to Lebanon, Jordan and Syria, arrived in their countries of exile in general with little more than the items they had been able to grab as they left their homes and found shelter in refugee camps. To this day, more than 60 years later, the United Nations Relief and Works Agency for Palestine Refugees in the Near East (UNRWA) continues to administer 58 recognized refugee camps throughout the three countries, as well as in the Occupied Palestinian Territories of Gaza and the West Bank, providing basic health, relief, education and infrastructural support to the inhabitants of the camps. The Agency defines those under its remit as people and their descendants, whose 'normal place of residence was Palestine during the period 1st June to 15th May 1948 and who lost both homes and means of livelihood as a result of the 1948 conflict' (www.unrwa.org/about).

The reception offered to refugees in the three countries and subsequent attitudes towards them continue to vary significantly. In Jordan and Syria the host governments have facilitated some integration, while the situation in Lebanon has produced only limited integration. Moreover, refugees in Lebanon have been exposed to and involved in the many internal conflicts that have ravaged the country since the mid-1950s.

Regardless of their experience since exile, it remains the case for the refugees in all three countries that they are unable to return to their family homes, a situation which does not currently appear as if it will change. In addition to the unlikelihood that they will gain their international right to return (or the right to compensation), the Palestinian refugees are the component of the Palestinian–Israeli issue that continues to be a significant bone of contention in the peace process.

THE PALESTINIAN–ISRAELI PEACE PROCESS AND PALESTINIAN REFUGEES IN THE MIDDLE EAST

A comprehensive discussion involving the peace process could include the entire Palestinian community, including refugees and non-refugees in the Occupied Palestinian Territories (OPT), refugees in Middle Eastern countries, and Palestinians of the wider diaspora. However, because the status of these groups greatly differs, and therefore they impact on the peace process in very different ways, only refugees living in exile in Syria, Jordan and Lebanon will be discussed.

This section will focus on quantifying why the peace process in question is the development of a two-state solution to the conflict, based on pre-1967 borders, and how Palestinian refugees in Lebanon, Syria and Jordan feature within this.[1] It will then identify, in relation to the refugees, the areas of weakness within the process that mean that until now despite considerable international pressure, the peace process has not been able to develop a sustainable momentum.

Resolution of the Palestinian–Israeli conflict through the two-state solution

The Palestinian–Israeli conflict has now entered its seventh decade, during which time there has been a considerable amount of conflict in many forms. To this day, factions, political parties and sectors of both communities believe they are engaged in a struggle that will ultimately see them 'win' control of all of the land of Mandate Palestine.[2] However, while victory on either side might yet happen, this would undoubtedly be a military victory that would leave one side under the control of the victor. If this were to occur, it can be argued that the result would not be a sustainable peace, but a continued protraction of the conflict, with one side fighting to maintain their gains and the other engaging in conflict for political and military control.

The manifestation of the Palestinian–Israeli peace process as it currently stands and is understood by the international community, is the Road Map for Peace, based on the development of two independent states along 1967 borders, which will acknowledge and then allow the implementation of the Palestinian right to self-determination, ensuring that this is a just process allowing for the creation of a viable Palestinian state alongside Israel (Carter 2006: 213).

The concept of the two-state solution was officially accepted by the Palestinian Liberation Organization (PLO) in November 1988,

with the first meaningful agreement between Israel and the PLO
being the Oslo Accords of September 1993 (Slater, 2001: 176). Prior
to Oslo was the Madrid Conference of 1991, which many consider
the first breakthrough in the process, as for the first time it brought
together Arab states and Israel to discuss the development of a
two-state solution. The Declaration of Principles, signed at Oslo in
1993, was not in itself a peace agreement, 'but an agreement that the
parties were ready to work for a peaceful and processural solution to
their long-time conflict' (Schulz and Hammer, 2003: 142).

Given the current Israeli reluctance to halt the building of Jewish
settlements in the OPT, supported by the reluctance of the United
States to enforce this (as was seen recently with their veto of a related
UN resolution), given the continued division between Hamas in the
Gaza Strip and the Palestinian Authority in the West Bank, and with
the tide of protests in the Arab world that began at the beginning
of 2011, a peace process that began in the 1980s seems of very
little relevance in the reality of early 2011. However, the two-state
solution continues to form the basis of the official peace process and
therefore is the focus of this discussion.

Palestinian refugees as official components of the peace process

The issue of Palestinian refugees in exile (in addition to those
displaced within Israel and the OPT) has been officially addressed in
international law with the acceptance of the United Nations General
Assembly Resolution 194 (III) (referred to as Resolution 194) on
11 December 1948 (Parsons, 1997: 232). Since this time, the rights
of Palestinian refugees with regards to any peace process have been
defined by the right of return to their place of origin, and the right
to welfare until they return. When the PLO officially accepted the
two-state solution in November 1988, it was maintained that the
development of such a solution was based on the understanding
that there would be a symbolic return to Israel, combined with a
large-scale international economic compensation of the refugees,
and resettlement with a focus on the Arab region.

Resolution 194 has been affirmed annually since 1948, and
allows Palestinians the right of return or to compensation (Massad,
2001: 107). UNRWA was created in 1949 and continues to provide
basic relief, health, education, housing and infrastructure services
to refugees. However, since the official process began at Oslo, the
issue of refugees, as well as the status of Jerusalem and the Israeli
settlements in the OPT, has been postponed until negotiations
for the final settlement (Slater, 2001: 177), originally planned for

May 1999, but for which the process has still not achieved a sustainable momentum.

Recent events of the 'Arab Awakening', particularly the election of new governments in Egypt and Tunisia with a majority of Islamist parties, may alter the power dynamics in the Middle East, especially in relation to peace agreements with Israel. In addition to continued settlement building by Israel, it may well be that the development of a sustainable momentum for the peace process is not possible in the foreseeable future. Moreover, recent comments by the president of the Palestinian Authority, Mahmoud Abbas, indicate that he might not stand for re-election. Nonetheless, while these events may alter the direction of the peace process, refugees in Lebanon, Syria and Jordan will still remain an integral component of any process that may emerge in the future.

The Arab Spring encouraged people to use nonviolent tactics to achieve their national and civil rights. In an act of remarkable courage, thousands of Palestinian refugees from Syria and Lebanon crossed the heavily protected border with Israel on 15 May 2011, to commemorate Nakba day (Catastrophe day). This action highlighted the plight of the refugees and showed that the Arab regimes do not have the legitimacy and the authority to decide their fate. This action provided hope for them in their demand for participation in the peace process and the right to return (Cook, 2011).

Practical impact of the status of Palestinian refugees on the peace process

To date, the peace process has not brought the refugees any closer, either to return or to a resolution of their final status.

As the Palestinian refugee population grows in the Middle East countries that UNRWA operates in – apart from the OPT – some of the youngest are now fourth or even fifth-generation refugees.[3] As noted earlier, conditions in the three main countries of exile differ greatly. In Syria and Jordan, Palestinians have largely been integrated into society (Khashan, 1994: 2). However, Palestinian refugees in Lebanon continue to suffer as a result of their exclusion from the peace process, in terms of their living conditions and access to rights. The impact of this on their daily lives is exacerbated by the fact that there is no single agency with a mandate to work to secure their rights. Consequently, Palestinians in Lebanon have become engaged in many conflicts; in the early days of the diaspora directly with the state of Israel, in the Lebanese civil war, and recently in replicating the division between Hamas and the PLO in Gaza and the West Bank within their community in Lebanon. The results of such attempts to gain control over their situation through asserting identity and striving for power demonstrate what can happen if refugees are excluded from the peace process.

Consequently, even though the issue of the status of refugees both is enshrined in international law and has been addressed (however nominally) within the peace process, it remains effectively 'on hold' until the process has progressed further. This has implications not only for the Palestinian–Israeli peace process but also for peace throughout the Middle East, especially in Lebanon. Therefore, for the peace process to be sustainable, must it address the status of the refugees in exile in Lebanon, Syria and Jordan?

Sustainability and the Palestinian–Israeli peace process

In order to address the crux of the issue, conclusions need to be drawn on what exactly constitutes a 'sustainable' peace process, and whether it is necessary that this include working towards resolving the status of the refugees.

DEVELOPING A SUSTAINABLE PEACE PROCESS

There are many elements that can contribute to a sustainable peace process, including, but not limited to, contextualization beyond the immediate conflict zone, mediation and compromise (with a focus on the 'sticking points'), and restoration of 'normality' (Ramsbotham, Woodhouse and Miall, 2005: 183). This section will expand on these components, and will determine whether they exist within the Palestinian–Israeli peace process and whether the process is thus sustainable as it stands.

If the Palestinian–Israeli peace process is to be sustainable, the conflict resolution process must be contextualized within the wider region in which the conflict is situated, not just within the countries experiencing the conflict itself (Ramsbotham et al., 2005: 183). This means not only working on developing the two-state solution, but incorporating within this process the wider context of the refugees in Lebanon, Syria and Jordan. For instance, in the case of the refugees in Lebanon, omitting the right of return from the ongoing dialogue impacts not only on the refugees in exile there, but also on Lebanese attitudes to the refugees. While there are other factors such as the continued Israeli occupation of the Sheba'a farms area, such an omission can increase the rhetoric between the two nation states and the potential for conflict between Lebanon and Israel.

Furthermore, in order to develop a sustainable peace process it is important that both sides identify areas of mediation and compromise. It could be argued that Palestinians must accept that they are approaching any discussion related to peace from the perspective of having 'lost' most violent conflicts and most diplomatic discussions since 1948. While it must be recognized that compromise is necessary on both sides, it is clear that at least for the foreseeable future, if the peace process is to progress, Palestinians must acknowledge that they, along with the Israelis, may have to make the more drastic concessions. One concession may turn out to be the omission of the status of refugees from the peace process in an effort to move forward, given the reality that their status so far has been ignored, and that the refugees currently have a very limited political outreach and impact.

The right of return

On paper, the question of the right of return has been dealt with by an agreement to put it on hold until the peace process progresses. However, given the need to contextualize the process, it can be argued that this issue does need to be addressed again, if the process is to be sustainable. Whilst compromises on both sides will have to be made, it is perhaps necessary for both sides to re-evaluate the concessions that have been made previously, and to acknowledge that mediation is needed over the issue of the right of return.

The third factor in developing a sustainable peace process is the need to demonstrate how a return to relative normality (that is, the cessation of the violence) is a more attractive proposition to all parties than a continuation of the conflict. This requires recognition of the status and living standards of those suffering in the conflict, and ensuring that by engaging in the peace process their situation will improve.

The status and living standards of refugees must be restored to an acceptable level within the post-war society. While they remain displaced and excluded from 'normal' life, not only is there no peace or justice for them, but also the refugees will remain a source of social and political tension and pressure. The ideal of 'return' may or may not be a realistic or desirable option, but on the other hand there may be no long-term home for them within the host society. Although both in human and political terms the status and needs of refugees is of great significance, this is one of the most difficult aspects of implementation in any post-settlement context.

With the omission of the Palestinian refugees from the peace process until it progresses, and the uncertainty over how they may be incorporated into any process in the future, there is currently no prospect that their conditions will improve to allow them to return to a state of 'normality'. This means that there is very little incentive for them to contribute to ensuring the sustainability of the peace process.

Nonetheless, based on the analysis of what constitutes a sustainable peace process, it follows that the Palestinian–Israeli peace process must include the status of all Palestinian refugees in the Lebanon, Syria and Jordan.

Annual ratification of UN Resolution 194

As the status of refugees is one of the issues on hold until the final negotiation stage, it has so far not hindered the peace process, and will not become an obstacle as long as the issue continues to be recognized, if not yet acted upon. In a sense then, the current peace process is at the moment sufficient with regard to refugees.

While it is important that alternative possibilities regarding the status of Palestinian refugees should be identified, currently the only hope for a sustainable peace on the table is the two-state solution. It may be sufficient that Resolution 194 continues to be re-ratified annually with the agreement that the status of the refugees be addressed at a later stage. However there is still the question of where this leaves Palestinian refugees in the meantime.

Integration in the host country

This means that Palestinian refugees will remain in their countries of exile for the foreseeable future. While it can be claimed that their status is being delayed in order to ensure the sustainability of the peace process, the question of integration of the refugees within their host countries may still have ramifications not only for the Palestinian–Israeli peace process itself, but also for regional stability. Within both the national and refugee populations of Syria, Lebanon and Jordan there is a great deal of suspicion regarding the issue of integration. The term is generally used in connection with the long-held suspicion that the international community intends to solve the refugee problem by incorporating Palestinian refugees within their host countries (Weighill, 1997: 306–7).

Resistance to integration is especially prevalent within Lebanon, where the history of the Palestinians engaging in violent conflict, and the suspicion held by Christians that the presence of a large number of mainly Sunni Muslims will upset the precarious sectarian balance, mean that 'Lebanon will not accept any agreement on the Palestine problem that does not include the right of return to their homeland' (Khashan, 1994: 4).

A balance must be found between delaying agreement about the status of the Palestinian refugees in order to allow the Palestinian–Israeli peace process to progress in a sustainable manner, and reassuring the refugees themselves and those in their host nations that the issue has not been completely sidelined.

Consequently, the status of the Palestinian refugees in Lebanon, Syria and Jordan has not yet been sufficiently addressed within the current peace process to ensure sustainability, especially in relation to potential regional conflict. Moreover, some groups have legitimate reasons to demand to be stakeholders in a process after years of oppression and discrimination (Jarstad, 2008: 22), and it is only by ensuring that the status of the refugees is addressed that those in exile will feel that the conditions that caused them to flee in the first place have at least to some extent been remedied (Wallensteen, 2007: 150).

HOW TO ADDRESS THE STATUS OF REFUGEES IN THE PEACE PROCESS?

The previous section concluded that for the peace process to be sustainable it must address the issue of Palestinian refugees. However, the next question to ask is, how must their status be addressed for the process to be sustainable? As Lederach states, 'We must not limit our lenses to only the highest level of political actors and the peace negotiations they forge' (2001: 843).

This final section will examine whether it is sufficient that the status of refugees is officially addressed under international law, or whether more needs to be done in order to ensure that the peace process can be genuinely sustainable. One area in which more effort could be focused relates to the needs of Palestinian refugees and non-refugees in believing that their perception of justice will be served.

Through international law

It could be argued that the status of Palestinian refugees has been addressed in the only way it can be, namely through Resolution

194, and that this is sufficient contribution to a sustainable peace process. This is for two main reasons; first, because Resolution 194 covers refugees under international law, and second because, as Slater states, 'It is increasingly clear that the right-of-return issue is far more symbolic than a real obstacle to a settlement' (2001: 196).

However, in the eyes of many Palestinian refugees, Slater's statement is part of the problem. Since the shift in focus to the West Bank and Gaza away from the refugees in neighbouring countries, especially from Lebanon after the PLO lost its sphere of influence in the country following the 1982 war (Osberg, 2009), it has become obvious that the right of return may indeed be symbolic for wealthy Palestinians of the diaspora and for some of those living in the areas that became the OPT. However, for the refugees living in exile both inside and outside the OPT, it remains much more than a symbolic statement. Rather it is an imperative right that must be addressed through the negotiations of a final settlement. As Sayigh states, the Palestinians 'know well that most of their villages have been erased or turned into Israeli settlements, but this knowledge does not sever their ties with the land, it politicizes them' (2007: 3). As seen above, the practical implications of relying on the international community to uphold international law in relation to Resolution 194 are complicated by the continued lack of will on each side of the conflict to address the issue effectively during the various stages of the peace process. This leaves refugees with a growing feeling of disillusionment and abandonment.

Therefore, if it is not enough to address the status of refugees solely through existing UN resolutions, how else must the status of the Palestinian refugees be addressed to ensure it contributes to a sustainable peace process? Along with the possibility of a new or amended Resolution 194, the status of refugees in their countries of exile could be addressed and improved.

The responsibilities of host countries

If all Palestinian refugees were afforded the same rights in their host countries regardless of their geographical location, thereby improving their living conditions, ensuring consistency, and enabling them to develop a sense of improved normality, there would arguably be less resistance to progressing the peace process as it stands, even if the issue of right of return was not immediately addressed. This would provide the possibility for the peace process to move forward and to develop the sustainability that would then facilitate the capacity of all to address the issue of refugees at a later stage.

Such an approach, however, might be resisted both by Palestinian refugees themselves as well as the governments and populations of their host nations. As Rosemary Hollis stated, 'Lebanon wants to get rid of them, Jordan wants compensation for hosting them, Syria wants its own peace process and the refugees feel caught up in a process over which they have no control' (ICG, 2004: 21). While the majority of these stakeholders would not necessarily be involved in the development of the peace process and therefore have a limited potential to stall it, their potential to disrupt the process from the sidelines through both violent and non-violent means is great. For the peace process to remain sustainable, the legal and final status of refugees would have to be formally addressed as a major component.

There are those who believe that 'the return of the refugees is practically feasible and even desirable for permanent peace to prevail' (Massad, 2001: 114). This may require amending the practical implementation of Resolution 194, while maintaining its spirit. If governments of host countries recognize that the peace process can move forward with the right of return still enshrined in the process and the issue of refugees being addressed at a later point, they may be willing to provide concessions to the status of refugees in their countries in the intervening period. This in itself will increase the chances that the peace process will be able to develop peacefully and in a sustainable manner.

Therefore, not only must the status of Palestinian refugees be addressed if the Palestinian–Israeli peace process is to progress, it must be addressed more comprehensively and with a wider long-term vision. There will have to be some form of reconciliation between Palestinian refugees and those they deem responsible for their exile to ensure even the glimmer of concessions is considered. If Palestinian refugees do not feel the peace process provides them with justice for their exile, then the peace process will not be sustainable.

This is especially true given that, 'for all Palestinians the right of return is sacred. It is built into their psyche' (Abu-Sitter, 2001: 195). This is especially true for refugees in exile, who believe that through Resolution 194 they will receive justice for their initial displacement and continued exile. If Resolution 194 were to be amended, refugees would have to gain their 'justice' in another manner.

Providing justice

For Palestinian refugees, the question therefore is what must be done to counterbalance any changes to Resolution 194 that will nonetheless ensure they still receive due justice for their exile. As a starting point, a key consideration is the reality that justice can indeed be sought. However, as the 'losers' of the conflict, Palestinian refugees currently lack political bargaining power.

Even arriving at a concept for potential justice is complicated for Palestinian refugees, because not only did they lose their homeland in 1948, since then they have failed to win any concessions from the state of Israel. In addition, through a process of gradual erosion they have subsequently lost any relative power they originally had, especially since the political representation of Palestinians returned to the West Bank and Gaza, further alienating the refugee populations in Jordan, Syria and Lebanon. As Assefa states, 'Where one side has clearly won over the other, it is more difficult to influence the reconciliation process to incorporate either forgiveness or accountability as the situation might require' (2005: 641). Refugees from any conflict need to recognize the legitimacy of the post-war rule of law, while the victors need to recognize that if peace is ever to be achieved, those who 'lost' must have access to compensation, reparation and structural adjustments (Ramsbotham et al., 2005: 236). It is only by both sides recognizing this that there is any chance at 'distributive justice'; addressing the 'structural and systemic injustices such as political and economic discrimination and inequalities of distribution that are frequently underlying causes of conflict' (Mani, 2002: 3–11; Ramsbotham et al., 2005: 235).

Three steps to justice

Lederach states that there are three stages to achieving justice, and it is the assertion here that the practical steps to address the status of the Palestinian refugees need to focus on this (2001: 852–3). Lederach's first stage is to achieve accountability; 'something to be done to account for and prevent the inhuman treatment and suffering that destroys families and communities'. Palestinian refugees need to feel that those who perpetrated both the cause and continuation of their exile should accept accountability. Until now this has not been forthcoming from Israel, because of the concern that if they accept responsibility for the initial displacement of Palestinians, they must also accept the full right of return. Moreover, it is not only the Israelis who need to accept some accountability for the plight of the Palestinians, also greater responsibility should be demanded of the Arab states, host governments and the international community for the 'continuation' of their plight.

Lederach's second stage is recompense, 'the perpetrator should not only be held accountable but should also "pay" to restore in some form what has been lost by those who lost it' (2001: 852–3). Palestinians should at least be able to claim economic compensation for what they have lost. This would more likely than not have to be a claim from the current Israeli government, and could only happen after stage one has been completed. While it is currently impossible to envisage the peace process progressing this way in relation to the refugees, it can be argued that if the process is to be sustainable the refugees have to be included in it, and in a different way than they are now. However, after decades of suffering, it will be hard to agree on adequate compensation.

The third and final stage that Lederach proposes is equality and fairness, meaning that a peace process needs to do more than end open violence, it also needs to 'adequately increase access to resources, participation and protection of rights' (2001: 852–3). In relation to the case study being discussed here, the scale of violent conflict on the levels seen in 1967, 1973 and 1982 has decreased. However, the continued lack of progress in terms of real, sustainable peace has been hampered, among many other issues, by Palestinian refugees continuing to feel marginalized in relation to the peace process. This is an issue that should be addressed more by the Palestinian Authority, which is the only political representative of the Palestinian population in the peace process. In many ways it has been their policy of concentrating on the West Bank and Gaza, and allowing the issue of refugees to be sidelined at Oslo, that means refugees are nowhere near to achieving stage three.

It should also be noted that those who advocate a system of obtaining justice for Palestinian refugees do not maintain that access to resources, participation and protection of rights need to be within 'Palestine'. As mentioned previously, it could mean improving the situation where they are, at least socially and economically, meaning that they would accept that the practical right of return will be addressed further along in the peace process. Arguably, this is where the role of the international community comes in; enabling joint efforts to improve current conditions while working towards a final settlement of some sort might be successful. 'It is therefore crucial that the international community provide sustained assistance throughout the peace process (Ball, 1996: 613).

CONCLUSION

The answer to the question of whether or not the status of Palestinian refugees in Lebanon, Jordan, Syria and the OPT must be addressed in order for the Palestinian–Israeli peace process to be sustainable, is clearly in the affirmative, because for any peace process to be sustainable all major stakeholders must be included.

In order to develop a *sustainable* peace process, there needs to be contextualization of the wider issues at stake within the process, identification of areas for mediation and compromise, and a clear demonstration to the stakeholders that engaging in the process will lead to an improved 'normalization' of their daily lives.

It is imperative therefore that Palestinian refugees who have been living in exile in these countries must be recognized as stakeholders in the process, and their situation be included in the development of a peace process that can only be sustainable if the refugees and their needs are taken into consideration. Only then is there the possibility of developing a sustainable peace process that will, it is hoped, one day lead to the creation of two viable states, a Palestinian and Israeli one, living side by side along the pre-1967 borders.

Although the status of refugees is enshrined in international law through UN Resolution 194, major issues nonetheless arise when the practicality of how the status is to be addressed is broached. If the peace process is to be sustainable in the long term, both the refugees themselves and their host nations need to support and engage with the process, but in its current state this is not the case.

The crux of the argument is that a sustainable peace process demands not only that the status of refugees be addressed, but that it is addressed in a manner that refugees themselves accept, which is only possible if the process provides them with the satisfaction that justice has been served for refugees who have endured more than 60 years of exile from their homeland. This has to be balanced not only within the wider context of the peace process and the reality of a conflict with far-reaching regional and international implications, but also with both sides of the conflict recognizing that concessions will have to be made by each of them.

This begs the question of whether or not Palestinian refugees will ever be able to engage in such a process, because at some point there will have to be a level of forgiveness, not only with regards to the Israeli state, but also in relation to Palestinian leadership, the Arab world and the international community for the injustices the refugees have suffered. Therefore, for the Palestinian–Israeli peace process to be sustainable, will the status of the refugees have to be addressed through serving them with justice to allow them to forgive, or must they first forgive before justice can be served?

NOTES

1   The refugees in these three countries constitute the largest group outside Palestine, and the United Nations mandates the United Nations Relief and Works Agency for Palestine Refugees in the Near East to meet the basic needs of them, in addition to those refugees in the OPT.

2   In 1922 Britain was granted the Palestine mandate by the League of Nations, which was based on the principle of self-determination and on the provisional recognition of the Palestinian people as an independent nation (Gilmour, 1980: 38).

3   According to UNRWA (www.un.org/unrwa/publications), as of June 2008 there are 4.6 million Palestinian refugees registered as living in its area of operations, of which 2.8 million live in Syria, Jordan and Lebanon. Of these, almost 700,000 continue to live in one of the 32 official refugee camps that UNRWA administers (ibid).

11

HAMAS: BETWEEN MILITARISM AND GOVERNANCE

Ibrahim Natil

INTRODUCTION

Hamas's success in the Palestinian national elections of 2006 marked a significant milestone in the movement's strategic transition from militarism and resistance to political governance, which reflected a significant shift in the focus and activities of the movement.

The purpose of this chapter is to show how this dramatic transformation was possible, and to explore the roots and rationale of the transformation, examining its effects on the Palestinian political scene, and the resulting fragmentation of Palestinian society into two political and ideological – as well as geographic – entities in the Gaza Strip and the West Bank.

In order to predict the prospects for reconciliation between Fatah and Hamas, the chapter explores the impact of the events of the Arab Spring, and the significance of the signing of a reconciliation agreement by the two rivals following Egyptian mediation efforts in 2011.

This chapter is partly based on my own observations, as a Palestinian living and working in Gaza during the lead-up to the Palestinian elections of 2006. The chapter reflects analysis from a series of interviews held in Gaza with influential figures, including politicians and decision makers from both Fatah and Hamas.

THE BIRTH OF HAMAS

By the beginning of the 1980s, the senior leadership of the Palestinian Muslim Brotherhood (MB) in the Gaza Strip was facing significant pressure from a group of young leaders who had graduated from Egyptian universities. Several of these members of the younger generation, led by Sheikh Fathi Shqaki, challenged the approach of the older generation of the MB in the Gaza Strip, who believed their principal task was to effect change through *tarbyiah* (education) and *dawa* (outreach) with individuals, particularly the younger generation, and across the wider community in Palestine, and maintained that the task of rescuing Palestine lay with an external power. Shqaki, however, believed that the MB should focus not solely on social and grassroots activities; it must use military resistance against the Israeli occupation forces and against Israeli settlers (Tamimi, 2007: 45).

Inspired by Iranian Islamic revolution ideology, Shqaki and his close friend Abed Aziz Owda, who had been expelled from the MB, began mobilizing others to join their new group – Islamic Jihad – in 1979. The ranks of young cadres of the MB were attracted to the military activities and ideology of Islamic Jihad, and demanded that the senior leadership of the MB in the Gaza Strip should prepare for military action. To sustain the unity of their movement, the MB had to find an answer that would appease these young leaders. At a conference in Jordan in 1983, the MB endorsed the Palestinian delegation's proposal to establish a 'special committee' for Palestine as a section within the Jordanian office. The task of this committee was to provide financial and logistical support to train fighters from the Gaza Strip in Jordan (Tamimi, 2007: 43–4).

This strategic shift from a focus on social work to political and armed resistance was taken by the MB abroad and refined in the Occupied Palestinian Territories (OPT) by Sheikh Ahmed Yasin, the political and spiritual leader of Hamas. Sheikh Yasin established two paramilitary wings, Al-Majd and Al-Mujahideen, to monitor and punish collaborators, and to attack Israelis. In 1984, Israel arrested Sheikh Yasin and sentenced him to 13 years' imprisonment, accusing him of storing weapons to use against Israeli forces and settlers, but he was released ten months later in a prisoner exchange between Israel and the Popular Front for Palestine. Yasin continued conducting activities in secret until the outbreak of the first intifada ('uprising') in the OPT in December 1987. Along with six colleagues from the MB in Gaza, Yasin established Hamas (the Islamic Resistance Movement), which replaced the MB, to take part in the intifada and to resist Israeli occupation (Abu Amr, 1994: 35–53).

HAMAS DURING THE FIRST INTIFADA (1987–93)

As part of this strategic shift to combine political and armed struggle, Hamas organized a number of events and strikes to demonstrate its strength as a resistance movement against Israeli occupation. In a charter published on 18 August 1988, Hamas called for a synthesis of nationalism and Islamism in Palestine, envisioning in its charter that the Palestinian state would be run according to Sharia law. Hamas's charter stated that Palestinians should not cede one inch of land to Israel, and that jihad, or 'resistance', for the liberation of Palestine was the religious duty of all Muslims (Hamas, 1988).

Hamas's emergence as a resistance movement threatened the hegemony of the Palestine Liberation Organization (PLO), which saw itself as the sole representative of the Palestinian people. During the Palestinian–Israeli peace process, which began in 1991 and was outlined in the Oslo Agreement signed in Washington in 1993 to establish a Palestinian Authority (PA) in the Gaza Strip, political and ideological rifts between Hamas and the PLO intensified (Rigby, 2010: 59).

HAMAS AND THE PALESTINIAN AUTHORITY (1994–2000)

In 1994, as a result of the Oslo Agreement, most of the PLO's security apparatus and political structure moved from exile in Tunisia and Algeria to the Gaza Strip, to lay the foundations of the Palestinian Authority. This new political structure threatened the ideology of Hamas and its expansion, encouraging Hamas to form an alliance with other Islamist, secular and nationalist groups based in Damascus that also opposed the establishment of the Palestinian Authority. This alliance declared that the intifada against Israeli occupation would continue until the liberation of Palestine. Hamas considered the Agreement a strategic threat to Hamas's sociopolitical existence and to its influence in Palestinian society, and confirmed that it would launch a series of attacks against Israeli targets in an attempt to halt the peace process. As Mousa Abu Marzouk, the chairman of Hamas's political office, stated, 'Military activity is permanent' (Mishal and Sela, 2000: 66, 67).

Hamas's commitment to armed struggle against Israel was strengthened by the massacre of 29 Palestinian worshippers by a Jewish Israeli settler in Hebron in 1994. Hamas carried out its threats of suicide bombings in Israeli cities in 1994 and 1995. The Palestinian Authority considered Hamas's strategy of violence and suicide bombings to be against Palestinian interests, and put in place security measures that included freezing Hamas's bank accounts and imprisoning Hamas members, thereby undermining the movement's important social and political institutions. Nonetheless, Hamas vowed to continue its strategy of jihad against Israeli occupation (Schanzer, 2008: 42–3).

Politically, the Palestinian Authority sought to legitimize self-rule and gain support for the peace process with Israel, by organizing the first historic legislative and presidential elections in Palestine on 20 January 1996. Hamas was determined to delegitimize the Palestinian Authority, and so did not participate in these elections. The outcome of the Oslo Agreement – which Hamas believed solely served Israel's interests – was the exacerbation of fierce divisions between the various Palestinian political factions.

From 1996 to 2000, Hamas adopted a new strategy that moved away from violent confrontation towards a focus on social work, religious education and outreach. Nonetheless, the movement had to function underground to avoid any possible crackdown from the Palestinian Authority and from Israel, which were collaborating together against Hamas (Roy, 2011: 91).

HAMAS AND THE SECOND INTIFADA (2000–04)

In 2000, the failure of the peace process led to a state of tension and violence, which intensified following the visit of the Israeli right-wing opposition leader Ariel Sharon to Harm Al Shareef, the holy site for Muslims in Jerusalem. Sharon's visit triggered the outbreak of the second intifada, whose violence quickly spread to the OPT. Israel responded with extreme force, resulting in a high number of Palestinian civilian casualties; Palestinian militant groups responded in turn with small-scale bombings and shootings against Israeli forces (Rigby, 2010: 63).

This transformed the popular uprising into a military one, despite a clear imbalance of military power between Israel and the Palestinian militants. Israel systematically destroyed buildings and the infrastructure of the Palestinian Authority's security forces, in response to their support of the militants of the intifada, thus weakening the Palestinian Authority and its security forces, and allowing Hamas militants involved in the uprising to strengthen their position and to begin challenging the legitimacy of PA security forces. The continuing deterioration of the Palestinian economy increased the value and status of Hamas's social and welfare services. Islamic charities within Hamas responded to the needs of Palestinians and established a number of local subcommittees that provided essential social relief and financial support to large numbers of people struggling to sustain themselves throughout the continuing cycles of violence.

One such cycle of violence occurred in response to the assassination of Sheikh Ahmed Yasin by the Israeli Air Force on 22 March 2004. He had been the symbol of Hamas in the OPT, and the leader able to bridge the radical and moderate ideologies within Hamas; his assassination left the movement with a leadership vacuum. At the time of Sheikh Yasin's assassination, President Arafat was still confined by Israeli forces to his compound in the West Bank city of Ramallah, where he remained until he was moved to Paris, where he died on 11 November 2004 (Roy, 2011: 191–207).

Despite the chaos and lawlessness in Palestinian society, Arafat's power and responsibilities transferred seamlessly to his successor Mahmoud Abbas (also known as Abu Mazen). The dramatic events of the second uprising and the escalation of violence, seemingly without any hope for peace, left the Palestinian people in chaos. This increased the power of the militant groups and of Hamas, mainly at the expense of the legitimacy of the Palestinian Authority, particularly after Israel's disengagement from the Gaza Strip on 12 September 2005. Hamas claimed that the Israeli 'withdrawal' from Gaza had come about as a result of its resistance and efforts to liberate the Strip (Roy, 2011: 191–207).

HAMAS AS A POLITICAL PLAYER

Following the death of Arafat, Hamas took the decision to participate in the second Palestinian national elections to the Legislative Council of 2006. Arafat had represented a degree of legitimacy for the Palestinian political system, post-Oslo, but his death left the Palestinians in a transitional phase of leadership that lacked legitimacy and popular support.

As noted in the Introduction, I conducted research, including interviews, in Gaza during the period leading up to the elections. I suggest that Arafat's death gave Hamas an opportunity to seek domestic and possibly international legitimacy. Hamas's chances of victory in these elections were much greater with the Fatah party fragmented and weaker after Arafat's death, and Hamas grasped the chance to achieve a strong result in the elections, whilst Fatah struggled with internal divisions. Arafat had presented a major obstacle to Hamas's full successful participation, and to its capacity to influence Palestinian politics. Hamas could not have succeeded in challenging the symbolism of Arafat's leadership. It could be argued that Hamas understood that, without Arafat's capacity to unify all the elements of the Fatah movement as well as the PLO under his authority, the Palestinian national movement had become weaker and internally divided.

HAMAS'S TRANSFORMATION TO POLITICAL VICTOR

 In addition to the fundamental changes in the Palestinian political arena described above that occurred after Arafat's death, there were a number of other reasons behind Hamas's decision to participate in the electoral and political process, as described below.

Failure of the peace process

The failure of the peace process between Israel and the PLO, and thus the PLO's failure to achieve its national goal of achieving a viable Palestinian state, enabled Hamas to become a significant political military force and to threaten PLO power. The collapse of the peace process had also been the main cause of the renewed spiral of violence, which had increased the power and expansion of militant groups at the cost of the Palestinian Authority. Hamas participated in the violent uprising, building military power and increasing its political influence on the streets of Palestine in order to resist Israeli occupation. This elevated the image of Hamas in the popular consciousness of Palestinians. The failure of the peace process and the outbreak of the second intifada appeared to signify the end of Oslo Agreement.

Hamas's image

The failure of the peace process and Hamas's growing strength contributed greatly to the weakening of the Palestinian Authority, and to its increasingly poor image in the eyes of Palestinians. Many Palestinians did not trust the PA leadership because of poor govern-ance and the corruption of some leaders, while Hamas's image was more popular amongst Palestinians, who now saw the movement as a viable alternative to the Palestinian Authority. This increasingly powerful image encouraged Hamas to run in the municipal elections of the Palestinian Authority in 2004 and 2005.

Municipal elections

Hamas's subsequent decision to participate in the Palestinian national elections was encouraged by the movement's success in the municipal elections. This significant victory, which came fairly easily, strengthened Hamas's image on the streets and gave the movement a chance to test its political weight and power against the Palestinian Authority, and against other national movement forces (Milton-Edwards and Farrell, 2010: 245–7).

Israeli withdrawal

Much more importantly, Hamas's decision to participate received a new impetus after the unilateral Israeli withdrawal from the Gaza Strip in 2005, under the terms of the 'disengagement plan'. Hamas repeatedly claimed that the withdrawal was a victory for its resistance. According to a senior Hamas founder and future member of the Palestinian Legislative Council, Abed Fatah Dokhan, Hamas promoted the idea that it alone was responsible for expelling Israelis from the Gaza Strip, while the Fatah-led Palestinian Authority had simply collaborated with the Israelis (Dokhan, 2008). However, despite the withdrawal, the Gaza Strip was still occupied by Israel, which maintained control of the borders, airspace, territorial waters, and the movement of goods and persons from and into Gaza.

Palestinian national dialogue

Hamas's participation in the elections also came about as the result of a comprehensive dialogue convened by Egypt in 2005, between all the Palestinian political factions. The dialogue concluded with an emphasis on the need to conduct municipal and legislative elections in the Palestinian Territories and to reform the PLO. During the dialogue, Hamas demonstrated a degree of political realism and pragmatism when it asked for a reformed PLO to be an umbrella for all factions, so that Hamas might join the Palestinian political system after Arab states had rejected Hamas's claim to be recognized as the alternative to the PLO (Tamimi, 2007: 212).

Hamas's decision to take part in the political process on one hand and to continue with resistance on the other demonstrated the internal tension within the movement's strategy of 'resistance and political participation', as senior Hamas figure Ghazi Hamad stated, 'We cannot drop the resistance against occupation, because our territories are under the occupation' (quoted in Warner, 2006).

I think Hamas considered itself part of the political reality and sought long-term political participation and power sharing. It aimed to translate its popular support into institutional power. This change became a reality when Hamas won the national elections to the Palestinian Legislative Council, with 74 seats compared with Fatah's 45 seats, according to the Palestinian Central Election Commission. These surprising results represented a major shift in the Palestinian political landscape, which had been dominated by the secular nationalist Fatah faction and the PLO for 40 years.

HOW WAS HAMAS'S VICTORY SECURED?

At the elections which I observed while living in Gaza, Hamas's victory did not come as a surprise for four key reasons:

- Hamas used religious and social figures to influence specific constituencies such as academics, trade unionists and teachers, which gave Hamas an advantage over the secular Fatah movement. Hamas also used a religious platform with rhetoric and slogans to disseminate the movement's political programme. Meanwhile, Fatah was unable to convince the electorate of its capacity to achieve its political goal of an independent Palestinian state through ongoing negotiations with Israel.
- As my interviews demonstrated, Hamas had put its success in providing social welfare and its anti-corruption image to good use, as prior to the elections, the movement had used a social network to promote its image as a competent movement able to respond effectively to the needs of poor people in the Gaza Strip and the West Bank.
- Hamas selected locally and nationally respected, reputable person- alities to be included in its 'Change and Reform' list of candidates. By contrast, Fatah provided a list that included several candidates with poor reputations who had faced accusations of corruption.
- Fatah was suffering from internal division, as mentioned earlier. The movement's younger generation was marginalized by the older generation that dominated its Central Committee, and this impacted negatively on Fatah's election preparation. More than 70 well-known figures from Fatah ran in the elections as independents, after rejecting the list of nominated representa- tives prepared by the Fatah leadership. This divided the Fatah movement, which as a consequence lost thousands of votes in the Gaza Strip and the West Bank. Meanwhile, Hamas members and supporters were more focused and disciplined in their

commitment to securing the vote for their candidates (Milton-Edwards and Farrell, 2010: 249–59).

THE HAMAS GOVERNMENT

The Palestinian president, Mahmoud Abbas, directed the Hamas leader in Gaza, Ismail Hania, to form the first Hamas-led government, despite Israel's refusal to negotiate with the Palestinian administration if its members included armed 'terrorist groups' such as Hamas. Hamas therefore sought to lead a coalition government drawn from all factions, including from its rival Fatah. However, Fatah and other national factions refused to participate in any political union because Hamas was reluctant to compromise on its political positions. Hamas considered the international conditions unfair, and its subsequent political programme of 'Change and Reform' did not address any of the international community's demands. Hamas also saw rejection by other factions to enter into a coalition as an attempt to isolate the movement: a 'let them go it alone' strategy engineered by Fatah described by Abed Fatah Dokhan as designed to ensure that 'President Abbas could exploit his mandate and undermine the power of any Hamas-led government' (Dokhan, 2008).

However, it was not clear how Hamas could respond in the face of Israel's refusal to have any contact with the newly elected government. Hamas had to liaise with Israel in order to ensure the basic needs of the Palestinian people were met – the daily flow of electricity, food, water and health supplies – and this required direct coordination with Israeli military command. Israel immediately stopped transferring tax revenue from imports and exports to the Hamas government (tax revenue from the West Bank and Gaza estimated at US$60 million per month was collected by Israel and constituted a major source of the Palestinian budget for the payment of salaries and delivery of public services). As the result of the freezing of tax revenue, both internal and external pressure on Hamas increased, particularly when the lack of revenue meant suspending the salaries of roughly 150,000 civil servant employees. In 2006, the United States firmly supported the Israeli position and cancelled its US$368 million annual direct aid to the Palestinian Authority. Added to this, Hamas's government had inherited US$1.2 billion in debt to local banks from its Fatah predecessor, as well as unpaid bills to Palestinian suppliers and Israeli utility companies (Milton-Edwards and Farrell, 2010: 262–7).

The loss of these revenues led to the decision of 73,000 security staff from the Fatah-run security forces to reject Hamas-led government policies, and the refusal by Fatah personnel to cooperate with the Hamas government. In April 2006, Hamas exploited the situation by transforming all 3,000 members of its Executive Security force into the de facto security forces for Gaza. Hamas deployed its force in this way in the fear that Fatah security forces might attempt a coup to remove Hamas. Hamas had never trusted PA security forces, and accused them of hostility towards its members and of collaborating with Israel (Dokhan, 2008).

Establishing this new Hamas force designed to protect the government did not help to restore law and order; the fragile security situation escalated, and amidst a state of security chaos in the Gaza Strip, a number of attacks were carried out against public institutions and officials. In May 2006, Hamas's government rejected President Abbas's orders and deployed its forces, which resulted in the death of a 19-year-old man in clashes between Hamas forces and the Palestinian Authority's security agency in Gaza City, according to the Palestinian Centre for Human Rights.

The following month, Hamas's military wing, Az Al Deen Al Qassam, and two other militant groups launched an operation against Israeli military posts along the border of the Gaza Strip and Israel, kidnapping an Israeli soldier, killing two soldiers and injuring more. I was in Gaza Strip when Israel immediately conducted a large-scale operation in the Gaza Strip, closing the entry and exit points, and detained most of Hamas's ministers and parliamentarians in the West Bank. As a result, the Palestinian legislature was paralysed. Having closed all channels between the Gaza Strip and the rest of the world, Israeli forces then bombarded Gaza's infrastructure of bridges and main roads, as well as the only power plant of the Gaza Strip, leaving the Palestinian people in darkness for days. I lived and witnessed these hard days.

In 2007, the economic and security situation in Gaza deteriorated drastically, with the Gaza Strip on the brink of civil war, when Hamas militants attacked the presidential armoured convoy in the centre of Gaza in an attempt to capture weapons destined for PA forces. Hamas feared that the Palestinian Authority and Fatah would use these weapons against the Hamas government, enabling Fatah militants to oust Hamas. Egypt's mediation efforts failed to achieve a truce between Hamas and Fatah, and clashes caused further division within Palestinian society and threatened the existence of the Palestinian Authority (Palestinian Strategic Report, 2007).

After Egypt failed to negotiate an agreement, it was clear that a stronger third party would have to intervene. The Saudi King Abdullah Ben Abedalaziz initiated the Mecca Dialogue sessions between Hamas and Fatah, which began on 6 February 2007. The Saudi King used his influence on the two rivals to reach an agreement, choosing the holy shrine of Mecca with its significance for Muslims all over the world, to force the movements to reach a consensus. The Saudis helped the two parties to resolve their security and political differences and to compose a national unity government, with the signing of a Reconciliation Document called the Mecca Agreement on 8 February 2007. The agreement received great popular support from the Palestinian people, who came out onto the streets to celebrate. The agreement was designed to create a national unity government reflecting the spectrum of political factions in Palestine (Palestinian Strategic Report, 2007).

NATIONAL UNITY GOVERNMENT

This new national, unity government came into being in 2007, but lasted barely a year. It was led by Hamas and its leader Ismail Hania, and based purely on political affiliation; it included eleven Hamas ministers, nine Fatah ministers and four independents. However, the various political factions in the government all had differing interests and agendas and were simply not prepared for the huge challenges caused by the international boycott. It had become impossible for this or any Palestinian government to survive without at least some international cooperation.

In addition to these challenges, Hamas was also concerned about the appointment of Mohammed Dahlan as the security chief of the Palestinian Authority. Dahlan was a leading figure in Fatah and known for his close links with Israel and the United States. Concern about his appointment increased after the United States appointed General Keith Dayton to strengthen the presidential guard under Dahlan's responsibility. Hamas insisted that there was still a conspiracy to undermine the national unity government, the Mecca Agreement, and Hamas's forces. As Abed Fatah Dokhan declared:

> The Palestinian Authority plotted a plan to attack Hamas and topple its government by late June 2007.... Hamas intended to use its power to protect Palestinian democracy based on the results of the elections. The Palestinian President issued a number of decrees to control all aspects of the Palestinian governance.

The Palestinian President's decrees made the Hamas' government powerless and valueless.

(Dokhan, 2008)

Based on this view, on 14 June 2007, Hamas took pre-emptive action against the forces of the Palestinian Authority. This action led to the collapse of the Palestinian Authority's civil and military institutions. Hamas imposed its own Islamic government in the Gaza Strip, and its military takeover divided Palestinian society into two distinct identities, two authorities and two governments: one governed by the Fatah movement in the West Bank and one governed by Hamas in the Gaza Strip. After the shock of Hamas's takeover, it was clear that Fatah would not enter into any direct dialogue with Hamas or respond positively to Hamas's calls for reconciliation. As Dr Yousef Rizka, the Hamas Minister for Information said:

> There will be no national reconciliation in the time of the Palestinian President Mahmud Abbas. The President saw Hamas' Gaza takeover as a personal stab against him. Hamas' government in Gaza will continue despite the international and regional boycott and challenges.
>
> (Rizka, 2008)

Both sides had reached a state of even deeper mistrust, and there was no prospect of dialogue between them.

THE ISLAMIST GOVERNMENT OF HAMAS IN GAZA

Following the collapse of the short-lived unity government, Hamas established itself as the Islamist government for Gaza. Hamas was in need of both national and international legitimacy, and from its status as a democratically elected government, took measures against Fatah military groups and against clans that supported Fatah. In an attempt to reduce the threat to their authority posed by these military groups and clans, Hamas forces confiscated their weapons, killed a number of Fatah members, and imprisoned others (Schanzer, 2008: 108).

Meanwhile internationally, Hamas sought recognition through diplomatic channels and dialogue with Western countries that had refused to recognize its authority. To encourage the West to agree to a dialogue, Hamas freed the kidnapped BBC journalist Alan Johnston, who had been in captivity for four months after being kidnapped in

March 2007 by the Army of Islam. Hamas used its military power against the Army of Islam, which was linked to the Dogmush clan. This group had been involved with Hamas in the earlier kidnapping of the Israeli soldier Gilad Shalit in June 2006 (Milton-Edwards and Farrell, 2010: 292).

However, the release of the British journalist did not achieve instant success for Hamas at official diplomatic levels, although it did improve the image of Hamas. Although Western countries remained reluctant to engage in any direct dialogue with Hamas, the movement intended to show that it could impose law and order as a responsible government, hoping that this would also lead to international acceptance of the movement as the recognized representative of the Palestinians. In short, Hamas wanted to prove to all that it had the capacity to succeed where Fatah had failed; to fight lawlessness and to use its forces for state building and resistance in Gaza.

Hamas's apparent capacity to continue governing the Gaza Strip while dealing with a number of threats caused the Palestinian Authority concern for its own support base and for the possibility of its return to Gaza in the future. The Palestinian Authority and President Abbas continued to apply a policy aimed at undermining Hamas politically. The Palestinian Authority continued to challenge its governance by calling for early elections, a demand that Hamas rejected. The Palestinian Authority also sought to emphasize its disengagement with Hamas by asking for an international peace conference to restart negotiations with Israel over final status agreements, in an attempt to demonstrate to the Palestinian people that Hamas represented an obstacle to peace and economic development. The Palestinian Authority was determined to demonstrate that Hamas could not improve the lives of Palestinians while it continued to promote unrealistic political programmes (Schanzer, 2008: 155–60).

Eighteen months after its military takeover, Hamas had still not shown any political flexibility towards the Palestinian Authority, nor had it made any gestures or concessions to Egyptian mediation efforts to end the Hamas–Fatah conflict. Hamas did not soften its position towards Egypt as a moderator with any attempt to release a captive Israeli soldier, and Egyptian mediation efforts were unable to secure the renewal of the Israeli–Hamas *tahdyiah* (period of calmness), which expired on 19 December 2008. Hamas refused to renew the *tahdyiah* while the siege of the Gaza Strip was still imposed by Israel, and while the Gazan population was suffering extreme hardship amidst a severe shortage of essential foodstuffs and basic supplies. Hamas's popularity began to decline because of the deterioration of social, economic and health conditions in Gaza (Milton-Edwards and Farrell, 2010: 297–8).

On 27 December 2008, Israel bombed Hamas military compounds over the Gaza Strip in a military campaign called 'Operation Cast Lead'. The campaign caused a high number of casualties amongst Hamas members and civilians in the Gaza Strip. Israeli military operations left more than 1,300 people dead, over 5,000 wounded, and 2,400 buildings in Gaza were destroyed. The operation increased the suffering of the Gazan population for years to come (Levy, 2010: introduction ix).

At the end of the war, Palestine was still deeply divided, with two authorities in the West Bank and Gaza. Hamas was, however, still a political player despite Israel's efforts to undermine its governance and the fact that forming a unity government remained at a stalemate. Nor had the Israeli military operation achieved a single one of its goals, which were to prevent Hamas launching rockets, ensure the release of the Israeli soldier Gilad Shalit, and topple the government of Hamas, in the context of fighting a terrorist organisation as classified by the international community. The political division within Palestine, the impasse in Palestinian politics and the suffering of Palestinians in the Gaza Strip continue to this day.

CONCLUSION

The Palestinian elections propelled Hamas through its transition from a militarist movement to a political authority, although the movement has not yet fully transformed itself into a political authority, because it is too concerned about losing its popular support. Hamas tried to implement its own brand of politics based on a combined strategy of resistance and governance, but the movement was unable to exercise this strategy while continuing to be rejected by the international community, Israel and the Palestinian Authority. Hamas itself rejected international demands to be a full player in the peace process between Israel and the PLO, a decision that created a genuine crisis for Hamas.

Instead, Hamas took the radical step of settling its political differences with Fatah using weapons and violence, which led to the collapse of the Palestinian Authority. The Hamas military takeover divided Palestinian society into two distinct entities politically, geographically and economically. Hamas's takeover did not create peace and economic prosperity for the Palestinian people, nor did it unify the Palestinian Authority, and the division led to a war in the Gaza Strip that cost the lives of innocent people. The war was a key element of Israel's coercive policy; it maintained the division of the Palestinian people, thus serving Israel's interests.

Prospects for reconciliation

On 27 April 2011, Hamas and Fatah responded positively to regional changes in the Middle East and North Africa and to calls within Palestinian society for reconciliation and for the formation of a unity government, when they signed an agreement of reconciliation. This agreement was supposed to end the division between the two rivals, and concluded with the formation of an interim government of independent professionals and 'technocrats', to last for a period of one year from implementation, with the responsibility to ensure that national elections are held at the end of the 12 months.

By enabling Hamas to retain a major part of its existing governance, the reconciliation agreement allows Hamas to offer an incentive to its constituencies; for example, it is likely that the majority of Hamas employees and security officers will keep their positions. The agreement grants Hamas full participation in political decision making through the interim committee, which includes the current PLO executive structure, the independents and Islamic Jihad.

This agreement poses a challenge to Israel, the United States and the European Union, which have all shunned Hamas as a terrorist organization. The agreement was influenced by the mass street protests of the Arab Spring, and the end of dictatorship regimes in Arab countries, giving the hope of change after years of impasse. This has emphasized commonalities between Hamas and Fatah, as both parties feel threatened by the changing dynamics in the region.

However, the reconciliation process between Hamas and Fatah remains in its infancy. There is still a long process ahead, and a number of challenges still remain:

- Israel does not accept the Palestinian reconciliation between Hamas and Fatah, as Palestinian division serves Israel's interest. Israel has warned that it will not deal with the next government if it includes independent members supported by Hamas.
- The United States does not accept Hamas's inclusion in the Palestinian political system as long as Hamas does not recognize Israel. The United States might lead international pressure to boycott the Palestinian government.

- A few members of Hamas and Fatah do not accept the agreement and they might pose a threat to it.
- Some families and clans that suffered and lost members during clashes between Hamas and Fatah might pose further threats.

Despite the challenges facing the reconciliation, there is still strong hope for success this time, given the regional changes, popular support for the agreement by Palestinians, the need and willingness of both parties, and the support of international civil society groups. Arab financial support will strengthen and contribute to the sustainability of the reconciliation process. Palestinians are desperate to implement the reconciliation agreement after five years of disastrous social and political consequences for society at large. The agreement also represents new hope for political participation and social change in the OPT, when Hamas will participate in a political system based on democracy, non-violence, good governance and respect for human rights.

The agreement provides a positive step towards Hamas's engagement in the peace process, even if only indirectly at this stage. The reconciliation process will also allow Hamas to participate in efforts to ensure the Palestinian state gains international recognition. If the Palestinian state gains international recognition, Hamas will find itself in a stronger, more integrated position politically.

Hamas now explicitly supports a Palestinian state within the 1967 borders, which is an implicit recognition of Israel's existence. Hamas is much closer to Fatah's political programme, and it has offered to play a more constructive role in Palestinian politics, and to be open to other regional and Western powers, even though it refuses to negotiate directly with Israel. It can be argued that Hamas is likely to deliver a more constructive political role in state building and in governance, following the model of the moderate religiously driven Turkish Justice and Development Party (AKP).

Consequently, I believe it is essential to provide Hamas with space to manoeuvre within the political system, rather than to exclude Hamas from it. Hamas must be given a status similar to Israel's religious political parties, which are included within Israeli political democracy. In democratic countries, religious parties that contribute to their societies are better off playing in a narrow space within the political system through democracy and public accountability, than if they were excluded from the system. Within the political system, they are required to be accountable and responsible for their actions. If they were excluded from the political system, they might use violence to achieve their goals.

If no Palestinian state emerges in 2012, the signs are that Hamas will still play a peaceful and constructive role through political participation, in accordance with the changes in the region and within Palestinian society at large. As Hamas has already experienced a number of tough lessons from its governance of the Gaza Strip and from the division of Palestinian society after its military takeover, it is now able to consider this role. Following this difficult experience of governing the Gaza Strip, I believe Hamas will take future decisions in coordination with Palestinian groups in general, and with the new regime of Egypt in particular, and will not take any unilateral steps to influence Palestinian politics, in war or in peace.

12

RETURNING HOME TOWARDS A NEW FUTURE: NEPAL'S REINTEGRATION PROGRAMME FOR FORMER CHILD SOLDIERS

Dilli Binadi

BACKGROUND

From 1996–2006, Nepal experienced a decade of armed conflict between the government and the Communist Party of Nepal-Maoists (hereafter the Maoists). During the conflict, children were deployed in various military activities, including as combatants, by the conflicting parties. Along with others, children were deeply affected by the conflict and their rights were comprehensively violated. Even after the peace deal, the effective release, return and reintegration of former child soldiers, often referred to as 'children associated with armed forces and armed groups' or CAAFAG, did not happen according to the provision outlined in the 2006 Comprehensive Peace Agreement and the Agreement on Monitoring of the Management of Arms and Armies.

Since 2000, many children's rights' organizations, including the United Nations, international non-governmental organizations (INGOs) and non-governmental organizations (NGOs), have been working on the issue of child soldiers in Nepal. This chapter examines the reintegration of children associated with armed forces and armed groups in Nepal, in particular from 2005 to 2009. It explores how children were used during Nepal's ten-year insurgency, and then analyses the strengths and weaknesses of Nepal's child soldier reintegration programme, arguing that reintegration in Nepal must tackle the root causes of enrolment and offer viable livelihood alternatives. The chapter argues that a community-based approach to reintegration must be adopted in order to reduce the stigmatization children face when returning home.

THE TEN-YEAR INSURGENCY

From constitutional power to a people's revolution

The history of modern Nepal began in the mid-eighteenth century when the King of Gorkha, Prithivi Narayan Shah, unified tiny states to form the country of Nepal. In 1846, autocratic family rule imposed on the country by Jung Bahadur Rana shifted power from the king to the prime minister and made the position hereditary. The people's revolution in 1950 brought an end to Rana family rule, and Nepal experienced a multi-party democracy. Despite a period of autocratic government imposed by King Mahendra in 1962, multi-party democracy was reintroduced in 1990 and lasted until 1996. During this period of transition, Nepal experienced unrest within the population and an increasing level of corruption by politicians (Karki and Seddon, 2003: 14).

The demands of the Maoists

The Maoists, a hardline communist party whose aim was to establish a classless society and to replace Nepal's constitutional monarchy with a republic, put forward a 40-point demand to the government on 4 February 1996, giving the government an ultimatum of 13 days to fulfil their demands (Riaz and Basu, 2007: 133). Their demands included reform in the social, economic and political spheres 'with the proclaimed aim of establishing a new democratic socio-economic system and state' (Karki and Seddon, 2003: 22). The most sensitive demands of the Maoists related to the abolition of royal privileges, the declaration of Nepal as a secular state and the drafting of a new constitution for the country through a constituent assembly. On 13 February 1996, after blaming the government for not adhering to its demands, the Maoists began armed conflict against the government, which lasted for ten years until the conflict formally ended on 21 November 2006, with the signing of the Comprehensive Peace Agreement (CPA) by the government of Nepal and the Maoists (Riaz and Basu, 2007: 133).

Between 1996 and 2001, the Maoists carried out a series of

attacks on government offices and infrastructure, including on financial institutions, in order to raise funds. They captured land from powerful landlords and distributed this to small peasants and landless people in the rural part of the country. They ran campaigns against gambling and against the production and consumption of alcohol to gain sympathy and increase support for the party. In 1998, early attempts to settle the conflict peacefully through peace talks had failed due to lack of consensus between the Maoists, other political parties and the king, over the agenda proposed by the Maoists. The failure of the talks further intensified the conflict, and insurgents instigated the worst violence and disruption that Nepal had experienced in its entire history (Muni, 2003: 37). Within two to three years of the 'People's War', the impact of the conflict was widespread throughout the country.

The end of the monarchy?

On 1 February 2005, King Gyanendra assumed executive authority, citing the inability of the civilian government to resolve the conflict, and declared a state of emergency in Nepal. Many leaders of the major political parties were taken into custody and King Gyanendra imposed severe restrictions on civil liberties. Consequently, the conflict dynamics between the king, the political parties and the Maoists developed into a conflict of two parties: the political parties and the Maoists, against the king. With support from the Maoists, an alliance of seven political parties led protests throughout Nepal against the monarchy and against the civil war. In April 2006, after 19 days of intense protest, King Gyanendra was forced to relinquish direct rule. The alliance of seven political parties assumed authority and voted unanimously to curtail the monarch's political powers, effectively rendering him a ceremonial figure (Nepalnews, 2006).

Later, on 21 November 2006, the government of Nepal (led by the alliance of seven parties) and the Maoists signed a peace agreement, which cited the conditions for merging and forming an interim government. Both the Maoists and the Nepalese Army agreed an arms pact and locked up their weapons, with the United Nations acting as monitor (Zia-Zarifi, 2007: 3).

Despite the end of ten years of armed conflict, many challenges remained, including a plethora of economic, political and social issues. The damage caused by the violence in Nepal was unprecedented in the country's history. Estimates suggest that some 13,000 Nepalese were killed in the conflict; 100,000 were displaced, and approximately 1,700 people 'disappeared' (Zia-Zarifi, 2007: 4).

CHILDREN IN THE CONFLICT

Recruitment of children by the Maoists

The Maoists victimized children by targeting them as recruits, a practice that began to take place at such an alarming rate that Nepal was one of seven countries nominated by UN Security Council Resolution 1612 to establish a monitoring and reporting mechanism for grave violations against children in armed conflict (Zia-Zarifi, 2007: 6). In areas under their control, the Maoists operated a 'one family, one child' programme whereby each family was forced to provide a child recruit or face severe punishment (STC, 2007: 2). Once recruited, children were kept in the ranks through punishment or the fear of it; any children who wanted to escape had to consider the real possibility that the Maoists would exact reprisal upon their families (Zia-Zarifi, 2007: 5). The Maoists used a variety of techniques for recruiting children: the kidnapping of individual children, the abduction of large groups of children often from schools, and the use of propaganda campaigns to attract children as 'volunteers'. The Maoists frequently used compulsory educational sessions to recruit children as soldiers, sometimes simply by prohibiting the children from returning home.

It is estimated that at least 4,500 children were recruited by the Maoists, serving as porters, sentries, messengers and medical assistants (Zia-Zafari, 2007: 2). Most children served in local militias, but others held positions in the Maoists' core military wing, the People's Liberation Army (PLA). The majority of children in Maoist ranks received military training and were given weapons, ranging from fully fledged weapons, to a single grenade or improvised 'socket bombs'. Nepali NGOs estimated that over the past decade approximately 400 children were killed by the warring parties and more than 600 were injured. Nepali children also suffered the second highest global rate of injuries caused by landmines and unexploded ordinance left behind by the warring sides (CWIN, 2007).

The experience of child soldiers in Nepal differs from other armed conflicts. For example, unlike many of the conflicts in West Africa, children who were deployed by the Maoists were not subjected to mass rape or mutilation and forced to kill their families. However, the seriousness of the crimes against Nepali children should not be underestimated or brushed aside in comparison. All children used in armed conflict are placed in positions of danger, fear and isolation; they are separated from their families and miss schooling. 'For many children in the Maoists, their time with the armed group has been difficult, arduous, unpleasant and dangerous' (UNICEF, 2008: 27).

Why did children enlist?

Despite Maoist recruitment tactics, a study commissioned by Save the Children (STC) of a group of 914 former child soldiers revealed that 60 per cent of these children did not feel they had been forced to enlist (STC, 2008: 9). Nepal's conflict is unique not only for its lack of aggressive violence towards children, but also because many children voluntarily joined the forces. Most children recruited by the Maoists came from far-western and mid-western districts such as Rolpa, Rukum, and Jarjakot, where anti-state sentiment and underdevelopment were especially pernicious (Housden, 2009: 2).

According to the STC study, many children joined due to peer pressure and the appeal of cultural programmes. Other reasons included 'to earn money, poverty, interest in ideology, family member's involvement, abduction and revenge' (STC, 2009: 9). The study cites poverty, discrimination and a poor family/community environment as 'push' factors. With children's basic needs unmet, antipathy towards the state was exacerbated by the structural discrimination endemic in many rural communities particularly towards girls, marginalized ethnic minorities, and lower caste, or Dalit children. A report commissioned by the Transcultural Psychosocial Organization of Nepal showed that 24 per cent of children said they joined because of poverty, with 15 per cent joining from the belief that change within society (such as eliminating discrimination) was possible through the Maoists. Children also said that they joined because of family problems, and because of the lack of opportunities in their communities. Girls emphasized that they joined to escape abusive marriages or to avoid being forced into arranged marriages (Kohrt, 2007: 14).

'Pull' factors in recruitment

'Pull' factors included peer pressure, family involvement with the party and, as the conflict progressed, vengeance. The murder of a father or the rape of a mother or sister by the Royal Nepalese Army strengthened motivation to join the Maoists (Housden, 2009: 3). Personal advancement and personal interest was stated as a pull factor for 24 per cent of children who were later returned to their communities; they explained that they joined in the belief that they would be given opportunities to become leaders, politicians or army commanders. Other pull factors listed included interest in the party philosophy (10 per cent), and revenge on security forces (5 per cent) (Kohrt, 2007: 15).

The Maoists were successful in recruiting children because they implemented a strategy that tapped into their grievances. To give children a political voice and an outlet for their creativity, they organized cultural programmes of song and dance that were popular with children and contained clear messages expressing Maoist political ideology. The STC study showed that 72 per cent of people interviewed believed that cultural and political indoctrination activities carried out by the Maoists were the main attraction for children (STC, 2008: 6). Community members often described this recruitment as a *lahailahai* (children following one after the other). Recruits were also promised a guaranteed wage that often exceeded the average income. However, Housden argues it was the status and sense of empowerment gained by joining the Maoists that was particularly attractive. Maoist ideology was deeply rooted in equality and egalitarianism, which struck a chord with girls, lower castes and ethnic minorities (Housden, 2009: 3).

The inter-agency child protection database reported that 69 per cent of former child soldiers involved in the reintegration process considered that their enlistment with the Maoists was voluntary, while 31 per cent claimed that they were forced to join (IACP Database, 2009:3). This statistical outcome should be qualified: respondents might have been indoctrinated to believe they were not forced even if they were, and different people might define 'force' differently. A scenario where immense pressure is exerted might not be seen as force, yet such a situation might not present the child in question with any other options but to enlist.

Key motivation for joining

The wide ranges of motivations behind why children enlisted are presented in Figure 12.1. The Maoists used child soldiers to recruit new children, and schools were the main recruitment sites. The power that the child soldiers appeared to possess and would demonstrate in schools and communities, and the entertainment they enjoyed through the cultural programmes were key attractions for children who joined the Maoists. Of these range of motivations, it is worth highlighting that for both boys and girls the prime stimulus came from friends persuading them to join (CAAFAG, 2006: 7). Thus, the peer aspect was the main factor that contributed to the high recruitment of children to the Maoist movement.

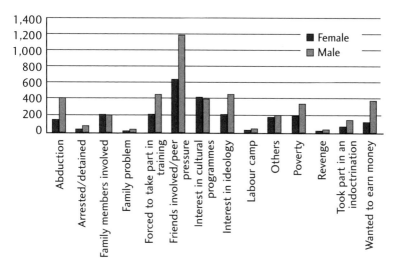

Figure 12.1 Reasons for joining

Source: Interagency Database (2009: 4).

The children left behind

Children left behind in their communities also suffered. In many places, schools closed down because of the destruction of premises, the lack of teachers, military operations and threats by the Maoists. In some areas during the conflict, children received less than 100 days' schooling a year because of strikes called by the Maoists and compulsory participation in activities run by them. Other children were kept at home for fear of abduction or were displaced to 'safer' areas – a tendency that caused severe overcrowding in urban schools (CAAFAG, 2006: 8).

REINTEGRATION OF CHILDREN AFTER THE CONFLICT

The response by NGOs

Until 2002, when the Maoists began recruiting children on a significant scale, the issue of child soldiers had not been considered a major problem and therefore was not a key issue for the child protection agencies in Nepal. Most agencies accommodated the issue within their ongoing development programmes, whose objectives were to mitigate the impact of armed conflict on children and to establish services for children, particularly in education and health. However, after 2002, the use of children in armed activities increased and became a cause for alarm. As a consequence of this, child protection agencies began direct interventions aimed at the reintegration of children who had been used by the security forces and the Maoists.

After 2002, several international and national agencies began addressing the protection issues of child soldiers through individual initiatives according to their own organizational mandates. Several had at least one programme for child soldiers, which fell into one of the following three categories:

- advocacy for the release and reintegration of children
- monitoring and reporting of violations of children's rights particularly by the conflicting parties
- awareness raising, community capacity building, and providing reintegration support to CAAFAG.

Joint efforts for advocacy

In 2003, STC and its local partner organizations initiated an advocacy campaign which later emerged as a national coalition called the National Coalition for Children as Zones of Peace (CZOP).[1] This coalition of 36 children's rights organizations, including UNICEF, initiated a range of advocacy measures jointly conducted at the national level.

Several organizations that were involved in CZOP also provided support to children and communities affected by conflict in areas such as education, income generation and livelihood support, psychosocial care and capacity building in child protection. At the same time, STC and its local partners were also monitoring grave violations of children's rights, such as the recruitment and abduction of children by conflicting parties, attacks on schools and the use of schools for armed activities.

STC, in partnership with SAHARA (a local NGO with child protection experience), established two transit centres – temporary shelters for children who had escaped from the Maoists – for 48 children, equipping staff with basic skills to provide the services required for reunification and reintegration. During a discussion with the author, Shiva Paudel, an STC programme officer stated:

> 48 children who sheltered in those transit centres for about three to six months reintegrated into their families successfully. Services also involved facilitating communication between children and their families prior to family reunion, carrying out assessments

of the family and neighbourhood environment, and creating a 'safety net' of several individuals in the neighbourhood. Families were also given support to build sustainable livelihoods based on their skills.

However, Paudel also noted:

[D]espite good preparation of family and children before reuniting, providing support to families for sustainable livelihood and linking children with school in their community, STC and its local partner could not conduct regular follow up of reunited children for at least two years in order to ensure their successful reintegration, which was lacking in the programme.

(Interview with the author, 2010)

In reality, preparing the family, the neighbourhood and the children themselves is as important as providing reintegration packages such as educational, livelihood and psychosocial support to children for their successful reintegration.

Addressing the issue on a wider scale

There is no doubt that individual efforts by organizations addressed the needs of conflict-affected children and contributed to bringing hope to their lives. Nonetheless, as the conflict escalated these efforts became insufficient to accommodate the increasing number of children affected, in part because efforts were confined within existing programmatic areas, but also because available resources (both human and financial) were inadequate to cover all geographical areas involved. The realization that joint working through the CZOP coalition had a more effective impact that any individual organizational efforts, prompted coalition agencies to explore working together under one 'umbrella' to ensure the successful reintegration of child soldiers in Nepal.

THE JOINT INITIATIVE: NEPAL'S REINTEGRATION PROGRAMME

The reintegration of former child soldiers is considered the responsibility of government. However, since 2006, in the absence of a Nepalese government body accepting responsibility, UNICEF and partners, including the UN Mission in Nepal, two UN agencies, six INGOs, three national NGOs and the CZOP coalition have implemented a programme for former child soldiers, aimed at their release and reintegration into civilian life.

The programme aims to support children who were used by armed groups and forces in Nepal in the decade-long armed conflict, in roles that included combatants, informers, cooks, porters and members of the cultural artists wing of the Maoists. The programme targets both CAAFAG, and other vulnerable and 'at risk' children, aiming to identify, trace and reunify them with their communities, to reintegrate them within their families and communities, and to strengthen social cohesion and community harmony among children and their communities through local peacebuilding initiatives. A further objective was to strengthen the child protection system at the national, district and community levels. All of these activities should promote the participation of children and youth in the process of building sustainable peace.

The organizations involved in the programme used to meet regularly as the CAAFAG Working Group, whose mandate was to provide:

> [A]forum to discuss, to analyse protection issues, to elaborate and to coordinate comprehensive and harmonized responses for the release, return and reintegration of CAAFAG, as well as to design common advocacy strategies with relevant stakeholders.
>
> (Housden, 2009: 5)

Practical support and advocacy

The Working Group operated in 34 districts in Nepal, working at a practical level to facilitate the release and reintegration of children and to prevent the recruitment of children (UNICEF, 2008: 3). It also provided immediate care, family tracing, reunification services and psychosocial training, as well as advocating at national and international levels for CAAFAG, and supporting families and communities to provide protection to returning former child soldiers, as well as building the child protection capacity of NGO partners and local communities.

The children involved in the programme included those who were in the cantonments (Maoist military camps), children who were 'self-released', including those who escaped from the Maoists during the conflict, children who might have been asked to leave the cantonment sites informally by the Maoists, and other vulnerable children, such as Dalit and children discriminated against on the basis of their ethnicity. Estimates suggest that this totals well over

11,000 children (UNICEF, 2008: 18). However, since no party to the conflict has admitted recruiting children or has released numbers of how many left their ranks, the true number involved is unknown. UNICEF estimated the numbers based on children visually identified at cantonments, whereas the true number will be substantially higher, as calculations would not have accounted for those children already back in their communities, those in village-based militias and those absent from cantonments on the days the children were counted. According to Inter Agency Child Protection Database,[2] by December 2009, the Working Group was providing cross-community support to 8,297 children and young people across 58 districts.

Was the reintegration programme a success?

UNICEF's report (2008) argued that the main strength of the reintegration programme is the fact that it exists at all:

> [T]hat it creates space to address child protection concerns in a context where child protection has not been at the top of any agenda and introduces the concepts and practice of child protection and child participation into the mainstream.
>
> (UNICEF, 2008: 32)

The fact that it existed is laudable, but this is certainly not enough alone to ensure the programme is a success. Positive feedback from children involved in the programme is a much stronger indication, and as evidenced in the two reports cited earlier, children feel the community-based nature of reintegration is the greatest strength of the programme.

COMMUNITY-BASED SUPPORT FOR REINTEGRATION

The reintegration programme was targeted not only at child soldiers in the cantonments, but also more broadly at children affected by the conflict and other vulnerable children in the community. It included development interventions, such as building community capacity in child protection and encouraging the participation of children in such initiatives, and the programme was designed to be community-based. Given that a large number of Nepali children joined the Maoists voluntarily, the community-based approach helped to avoid the perception of the community that child soldiers were being 'rewarded' by the programme; other vulnerable and conflict-affected children were also entitled to reintegration packages such as educational, livelihood and psychosocial support. Treating all vulnerable children, including CAAFAG, within the broader concept of 'children at risk' helped to avoid labelling specific children as 'CAAFAG'. It was demonstrated that stigmatization, discrimination and fragmentation were reduced when services such as education and health also benefited other children in the community. However, one former child soldier admitted in a discussion in 2010 with the author that she had faced discrimination both at school and in the community.

Building community capacity in child protection, as well as ensuring the wider engagement of children and community in the programme and bridging the gap between service providers and needy children in the community has helped to reduce the fear of re-recruitment. Many of the children interviewed during the mid-term evaluation of the programme expressed concern that without the continuation of the peace deal and increased community support, they would fear being re-abducted by the Maoists (CAAFAG, 2006: 6). Increasing awareness in the community of how recruiting children into armed activity violates their rights helps to reduce the chances of the Maoists abducting children, and consequently increases the safety and security of children.

The programme was indeed effective in increasing awareness of children's rights, and also of the roles played by elderly people and the community in protecting the rights of children affected by armed conflict (STC, 2008: 40). Children's clubs and drama productions offered through the programme not only raised awareness, but also allowed children an outlet for their creative talents – something that was sorely missing during the conflict and a contributing factor to why Maoist cultural programmes held such an appeal for Nepali children. Club activities included quiz contests, peace rallies, school sanitation programmes, village fairs, sports activities, peace initiatives, child protection awareness programmes and anti-discrimination campaigns (STC, 2007: 49). The children's clubs had a positive impact on their communities, many of whose members reached out to former child soldiers and encouraged them to return to school.

EMPOWERING CHILDREN AND PROVIDING PSYCHOSOCIAL CARE AND SUPPORT

A significant component of the programme was the recognition that young people can contribute productively to peacebuilding, and an accompanying focus on this:

[Y]outh returning from armed conflict of any political complexion often arrive home with skills, greater leadership potential and a sense of the imperative for peace. The UNICEF programme, therefore, offers an opportunity to focus on these youth as potential peace-builders.

(UNICEF, 2008: 19)

Psychosocial care was found to be a strong component of the programme in evaluations carried out by STC and UNICEF. During various psychosocial interventions, children disclosed problems such as nightmares, fears of re-attack, re-recruitment and re-kidnapping, guilt and regret through association with the party, the fear of losing face if they rejoined school and had to study with younger children, as well as restlessness, aggression, difficulty in concentration, loss of appetite and irritation. Such sharing helped children to vent their feelings and encouraged many of them to attend individual counselling sessions. The children acknowledged that they felt relaxed after articulating these deep emotions. After psychosocial support, positive changes were observed, such as the ability to integrate into the community, a sense of release from negative thoughts, increasing self-confidence, and a feeling of being accepted by the community (Kohrt, 2007: 4).

The provision of educational support to CAAFAG and other vulnerable children has been acknowledged as one of the most important components of the programme. Children receiving education support are universally positive, acknowledging that this has helped them to enrol in school or remain at school. The support helped children to gain confidence; many children were able to start a new life. Positive reintegration can also be seen in the engagement of many children in a variety of school-based activities. Educational support has reduced the likelihood of early marriage, as reported by some children (UNICEF, 2008; STC, 2008). One former child soldier noted: 'I sometimes felt like committing suicide. After getting reintegration support, I am now studying as well as creating environment for acceptance of girl CAAFAG. I now really feel better and content' (UNICEF, 2008: 19).

Schools receiving this support have also shared their positive experiences of children returning to education and appreciate that the support offered also helps other vulnerable children (UNICEF, 2008).

WHAT MORE COULD BE DONE?

There was a provision in the Comprehensive Peace Agreement that children would be released promptly from Maoist military camps, hence the reintegration programme was designed with the expectation that children would be discharged formally in huge numbers from the camps at once. It was expected that around 11,000 children would have to return to their communities and would need longer-term reintegration, creating the urgent need to prepare communities with poor infrastructure and economic capacity to receive thousands of children, possibly over a short time-scale (UNICEF, 2008: 18). Consequently, agencies involved invested huge resources in order to prepare for the majority of children who would be leaving the cantonment. In the event, child soldiers had to stay for more than three years in the cantonments and were released individually or in small groups, spread over more than two years. In the meantime, child protection agencies had no access to the child soldiers who were living in the cantonments and little was known by the agencies about conditions within the cantonments, nor about the needs of the children there. This resulted in a waste of resources on two fronts; first, in preparing for a formal and large-scale release of children and second, because the programme failed to take account of the children left behind in their communities, who also needed reintegration support. Unfortunately, the programme had failed to consider the scenario and consequences of a more gradual and protracted release of children from the cantonment.

In focusing solely on formal release from the cantonments, the programme missed the opportunity to provide community-based reintegration support to children who self-released, or who had escaped from the cantonments. Nonetheless, during the second phase of the programme, this situation was rectified and efforts were adapted to ensure sufficient support was offered to children already back in the community.

Compensation for former child soldiers

Contrary to international standards and good practice, the Maoists negotiated a fixed amount to be paid to their former soldiers, both adults and children, for the time they spent in cantonments. Both categories of former soldiers received NR27,000 (around US$40) for the period of time they spent in the cantonments. This is a vast sum of money in a country where a month's school fees are around NR35 and the average annual salary is approximately NR12,000 (UNICEF, 2008: 29). This made it difficult to reduce the distinction between returning children and other conflict-affected children in the community, and went against the principles of the community-based approach. Furthermore, it was difficult to monitor how children in particular spent the money they were given, and it was almost impossible for UNICEF and the other actors involved in Nepal's reintegration programme to ensure that children who received the stipends would give serious consideration to returning to school.

Vocational training and income generation

The intention of the programme with regard to investing in the children's future was positive: to provide older children with an alternative to education if they were reluctant to attend school, if they were experiencing pressure at home to begin earning, or if they were not comfortable at school for various reasons. The goal was to provide intensive, skills-based training for the children that would enable them to find work or to start their own business in the community. In particular for girls, the idea was that such skills would enable them to be independent if they had to leave their family or community; economic independence would additionally make it less likely for the girls to be married at an early age.

The Working Group lacked experience and expertise to implement the vocational education and income-generation component of the programme, and the programme exhibited several weaknesses in this area. Some children were incorrectly selected for particular vocational education and income-generation support; other children were offered training in specific areas without sufficient analysis of the likelihood of future relevant job opportunities. The programme raised expectations among children about what jobs they would find, or what entrepreneurial opportunities would be available, whilst support was inadequate to ensure that the children were indeed able to find the jobs they sought.

An additional problem was that what children wanted to do took precedence over realistic, sustainably targeted training:

> For instance, many boys stated that they wanted to become drivers and so they received a month's training. Many are now disappointed as they were either too young to obtain a driver's licence or are unable to obtain work that involves driving because they live far away from roads or cars. For girls, most accepted the offer of tailoring training, although again they are too young to set up their own business (in some cases too young to work).
>
> (UNICEF, 2008: 41)

One of the most profound problems with Nepal's child soldier reintegration programme was that a large number of children remained in cantonments for three years after the signing of the CPA, because of the lack of political will by the Maoists to release the children.

> [R]easons for this appear to be a combination of treating the children as an insurance against renewed conflict, using them as a negotiating tool for wider security system reform issues (the integration of Maoists cadres into the national security forces) and a belief that, once the elections have taken place, these children can be used to cement community allegiances to the Maoists through the Young Communist League or otherwise.
>
> (UNICEF, 2008: 28)

There was no evidence that the children were being subjected to violence or neglect while in the camps that were controlled by the Maoists. However UNICEF and other NGOs could not be sure of this, as they were denied access to the children. It was difficult to ensure these children had received information about the reintegration programme, or to understand what the children might need or want when they were released. This violated the Paris Principle of unhindered access to CAAFAG (UNICEF, 2008: 28). Finally, the lack of urgency about the children's situation in the cantonments was alarming; the older the children become, the more reluctant they might become to restart their schooling, and certainly the harder it becomes for them to return to their communities without stigmatization (UNICEF, 2008: 28).

Lack of involvement by the Nepali government

A major factor adversely affecting the programme was that the government of Nepal did not accept primary responsibility for the reintegration of child soldiers, and did not accept the financial burden of the programme. Consequently, there was concern that the longer-term dimensions of reintegration might be unsupported, particularly for children who left cantonments at a later date. If this were so, the programme would be more about 're-entry or reinsertion' than reintegration, and so would miss crucial ways of ensuring that children were not simply returned to their impoverished communities (UNICEF, 2008: 31).

> [O]ne of the biggest challenges for the CAAFAG programme is the short-term funding. During the various discussions in Nepal, concerns regarding limited and short-term funding were voiced by NGOs, CPC groups and the children themselves. All of the above

emphasized the need for long-term programming in order to effectively reintegrate CAAFAG into their community. A one-year programme does not allow enough time to train, identify and implement programmes to support these children.

(MacVeigh, Magure and Wedge, 2007: 38)

CONCLUSION

Although there is no concrete evidence about the exact number of children, various reports of child/human rights organizations estimate that around 11,000 children were involved in the armed conflict in Nepal in different capacities (UNICEF, 2008: 18).

Examining the efforts of the reintegration programme in Nepal, it is clear that successful reintegration requires an understanding of, and capacity to address, the underlying issues that fuel the conflict, such as caste/gender discrimination, poverty, and equitable access to services. Creating education, training and employment opportunities in the post-conflict setting is crucial, especially since many children joined the Maoists voluntarily from grievances such as poverty and discrimination. The sense of self-worth of many children will increase if they are able to enter education or a livelihoods programme, moreover children whose families benefited from an income-generation programme felt as though they were no longer a disgrace to their family. From this it is clear that providing children with a sense of self-worth and productivity is a key to successful reintegration. Interaction within the community also plays a role in ensuring the children feel safe from re-abduction and from discrimination. Finally, children's clubs have become a key aspect of NGO programmes due to their ability to engage children within their community, and their capacity to raise awareness and foster positive communication.

Improving the vocational training (livelihood) component, ensuring the involvement of government with its major role in the entire reintegration process, and increasing the involvement of children in the redesign of the ongoing reintegration programme are some of the other important, immediate challenges that still need to be addressed. Since the programme's Working Group members have accepted that they do not have enough expertise in creating livelihood opportunities for children and their families, it would be logical to team up with other organizations with expertise in this field such as the International Labour Organization (ILO), the World Bank, vocational training institutions and research-based organizations. Similarly, close collaboration with the Ministry for Women, Children and Social Welfare (MWCSW) and the Central Child Welfare Board (CCWB) must be initiated to ensure governmental involvement in the reintegration of CAAFAG.

Finally, it is of course important to provide reintegration packages such as educational, livelihood and psychosocial support to children. However, more efforts must be made to prepare the family, the neighbourhood and the children themselves for reintegration, something that is only possible if the provision of longer-term support is available. Hence, it will be critically important to redesign the reintegration programme to include community-based interventions and longer-term funding (three to five years) with the provision of follow-up support for a further two years, especially for children only recently released. This would contribute significantly to ensure the programme could effectively and sustainably support the reintegration of child soldiers in Nepal.

NOTES

1   Children as Zones of Peace is a national campaign as a joint efforts of 36 NGOs, INGOs and UN bodies working for promoting and protecting the rights of the children affected by armed conflict. During conflict time, the coalition effectively advocated against the use of children in armed activities.

2   The inter-agency child protection information system is managed by CAAFAG reintegration implementing organizations in Nepal, which include Save the Children, World Education and UNICEF. The system is a case management tool for the CAAFAG reintegration programme and UNICEF centrally hosts it. By the end of December 2009 information for 8,297 former child soldiers had been entered into the database.

REFERENCES

Aalen, L. (2002). 'Ethnic federalism in a dominant party state: the Ethiopian experience 1991–2000.' *Development Studies and Human Rights Report*, no. 2.

Abraham, A. (2001). 'Dancing with the chameleon: Sierra Leone and the elusive quest for peace.' *Journal of Contemporary African Studies*, 19(2), pp. 205–28.

Abu Amr, Z. (1994). *Islamic Fundamentalism in the West Bank and Gaza.* Bloomington, Ind., Indiana University Press.

Abu-Nimer, M. (2002). 'The miracles of transformation through interfaith dialogue: are you a believer?' In: Smock, D. (ed.), *Interfaith Dialogue and Peacebuilding.* Washington D.C., USIP Press.

Abu-Nimer, M. (2001) 'Conflict resolution and religion: toward a training model of interreligious peacebuilding.' *Journal of Peace Research,* 38(6), pp. 685–704.

Abu-Sitter, S. (2001). 'The right of return: sacred, legal and possible.' In: Aruri, N. (ed.), *Palestinian Refugees: The Right of Return.* London, Pluto Press.

Adlparvar, N. (2009). 'Democracy for Afghanistan?' *Arab News.* Available at <http://archive.arabnews.com/?page=7&section=0&article=128406&d=13&m=11&y=2009> Accessed May 14, 2010.

Afghanistan Ministry of Health (AMOH). (2005). 'A basic package of health service for Afghanistan.' Available at <www.msh.org/afghanistan/pdf/Afghanistan_BPHS_2005_1384.pdf> Accessed June 27, 2009.

AMOH and HANDS. (2002). 'Afghanistan national health resource assessment.' <online>. Available from <www.msh.org/afghanistan/ANHRA_2002_LITE.pdf> Accessed August 12, 2009.

Al-Zaytouna. (2007). *Palestinian Strategic Report.* Beirut, Lebanon, Al-Zaytouna Centre for Studies and Consultancies.

Aldred, R., LeBlanc, T. and Jacobs, A. (2010). 'Thoughts on forgiveness and Aboriginal residential schools', *Indian Life Newspaper.*

Alie, J.A.D. (2008). 'Reconciliation and traditional justice: tradition-based practices of the Kpaa Mende in Sierra Leone.' In: Huyse, L. and Salter, M. (eds), *Traditional Justice and Reconciliation after Violent Conflict: Learning from African Experiences.* Stockholm, International IDEA.

Allen, T. (2008). 'Ritual (ab)use? Problems with traditional justice in Northern

Uganda.' In: Waddell, N. and Clark, P. (eds), *Courting Conflict? Justice, Peace and the ICC in Africa*. London, Royal African Society.

Amis, M. (2008). 'Terrorism's new structure.' *Wall Street Journal*. Available at <http://online.wsj.com/article/SB121883817312745575.html>. Accessed July 2, 2012.

Anderson, B. M. (1999). *Do No Harm: How Aid Can Support Peace – or War*. London, Lynne Rienner.

Appleby, R. S. (2000). *The Ambivalence of the Sacred*. Lanham, Md. and Oxford, Rowman & Littlefield.

Armstrong, K. (2001). *The Battle for God: Fundamentalism in Judaism, Christianity and Islam*. New York, Harper Collins.

Arya, A. N. (2007). 'Peace through health.' In: Webel, C. and Galtung, J. (eds), *Handbook of Peace and Conflict Studies*. New York, Routledge.

Arya, A. N. (2008) 'Medical ethics.' In: Santa Barbara, J. and Arya, A. N. (eds), *Peace through Health: How Health Professionals can Work for a Less Violent World*. New York, Kumarian.

Ashplant, T., Dawson G. and Roper, M. (eds) (2000). *The Politics of War Memory and Commemoration*. London and New York, Routledge.

Assefa, H. (2005). 'Reconciliation: challenges, responses and the role of civil society.' In: Van Tongeren, P., Brenk, M., Hellema, M. and Verhoeven, J. (eds), *People Building Peace II*. London, Lynne Rienner.

Atmar, H. and Goodhand, J. (2002). 'Aid, conflict and peace building in Afghanistan: what lessons can be learned?' Available at <http://repository.forcedmigration.org/show_metadata.jsp?pid=fmo:2749> Accessed July 26, 2009.

Azar, E. E. (1990). *The Management of Protracted Social Conflict: Theory and Cases*, Aldershot, Hampshire, Dartmouth.

Azumah, J. (2002). 'The integrity of interfaith dialogue.' *Islam and Christian–Muslim Relations*, 13(3), pp. 269–80.

Baker, B. (1998). *Secession in Africa: A Doomed Escape Strategy*. Coventry, Coventry University.

Balkan Insight. (2011). 'Kosovo police seize northern border points.' Available at <www.balkaninsight.com/en/article/kosovo-police-seize-northern-border-points> Accessed July 2, 2012.

Ball, N. (1996). 'The challenge of rebuilding war-torn societies.' In: Crocker, C. A. et al. (eds), *Managing Global Chaos*. Washington, D.C., US Institute of Peace.

Bayfield, T. (2003) 'Sept. 11th – the case against us'. *Interreligious Insight* 1 (1), 20–33.

BBC. (2004). *Start the Week*. BBC Radio 4, broadcast on February 16, 2004.

BBC. (2007). BBC News Report, July 5, 2007.

Beha, A. and Visoka, G. (2010). 'Human security as ethnic security in Kosovo', *Human Security Perspectives*, 7(1).

Ben-Ami, S. (2006). *Scars of War, Wounds of Peace: The Israeli–Arab Tragedy*. Oxford, Oxford University Press.

Bennett, C., Wakefield, S. and Wilder, A. (2003). *Afghan Elections: The Great Gamble.* Afghanistan Research and Evaluation Unit (AREU).

Bercovitch, B. and Jackson, R. (2009). *Conflict Resolution in the Twenty-First Century: Principles, Methods, and Approaches.* Ann Arbor, Mich., University of Michigan Press.

Bergen, P. (2002). *Holy War, Inc.* Washington, D.C., Phoenix.

Bergner, D. (2004). *Soldiers of Light.* London and New York, Allen Lane.

Berhe, A. (2008). *A Political History of Tigray People's Liberation Front (1975–1991): Revolt, Ideology and Mobilization in Ethiopia,* Amsterdam, VRIJE University.

Bin Talal, E. H. (1996). Unpublished address to the Institute of Jewish Policy Research in London, June 25.

Blair, C. and Michel, N. (2007). 'The Aids Memorials Quilt and the contemporary culture of public commemoration.' *Rhetoric and Public Affairs,* 10(4), pp. 595–626.

Bloomfield, D. (2003). 'Reconciliation: An introduction.' In: Bloomfield, D. et al. (eds), *Reconciliation after Violent Conflict: A Handbook.* Stockholm, International IDEA (Institute for Democracy and Electoral Assistance) .

Boas, M. (2001). 'Liberia and Sierra Leone: dead ringers? The logic of neo-patrimonial rule.' *Third World Quarterly,* 22(5).

Bolton, G. and Visoka, G. (2010) 'Recognizing Kosovo's independence: remedial secession or earned sovereignty?' South East European Studies at Oxford (SEESOX) Occasional Paper no. 11/10. Oxford, SEESOX.

Borello, F. (2004). *A First Few Steps: The Long Road to a Just Peace in the Democratic Republic of the Congo.* New York, International Centre for Transitional Justice.

Boutros-Ghali, B. (1992). 'An Agenda for Peace.' A/47/277–S/24111. United Nations. Available at <www.un.org/docs/SG/agpeace> Accessed May 16, 2012.

Boutros-Ghali, B. (1995). 'Supplement to an Agenda for Peace.' A/50/60–S/1995/1. United Nations. Available at <www.un.org/Docs/SG/agsupp> Accessed May 16, 2012.

British and Irish Agencies Afghanistan Group (BAAG) and European Network of NGOs in Afghanistan (ENNA). (2008). *Aid and Civil–Military Relations in Afghanistan.* Policy briefing. London, BAAG/ENNA.

Buhmann, C. (2007). 'The possibilities for the health sector to actively contribute to peace processes.' *Danish Medical Bulletin,* 54(1).

Burton, J. (1990). *Conflict: Resolution and Prevention.* Basingstoke, Macmillan.

Calvert, J. (2007). *Islamism: A Documentary and Reference Guide.* Santa Barbara, Calif., Greenwood.

Carter, J. (2006). *Palestine: Peace Not Apartheid.* London, Simon & Schuster.

Caulker, J. (2009). Interview by S. Kaindenah.

Chaco, E. (2009). 'Debate over Truth Commission.' Available at <http://ipsnews.net/news.asp?idnews=46953> Accessed August 2010.

Chayes, A. and Minow, M. (eds) (2003). *Imagine Co-existence: Restoring Humanity after Violent Ethnic Conflict*. San Francisco, Calif., Jossey-Bass.

Chesse, S. G. (2012). 'Afghanistan casualties: Military forces and civilians.' Washington DC, Congressional Research Service.

Chesterman, S. (2004). *You, The People: The United Nations, Transitional Administration, and State-Building*. New York, Oxford University Press.

Children Associated with Armed Forces and Armed Groups (CAAFAG). (2006). *The Situation of Children Associated with Armed Forces and Armed Groups (CAAFAG)*. Nepal, CAAFAG Working Group.

Chomsky, N. (2000). *A New Generation Draws the Line: Kosovo, East Timor and the Standards of the West*. London, Verso.

Chrisjohn, R., Young, S. L. and Maraun, M. (2006). *The Circle Game: Shadows and Substance in the Indian Residential School Experience in Canada*. Penticton, BC, Canada, Theytus.

Christodulou, A. (2004). *Amputations in the Sierra Leone Conflict*. Accra, Sierra Leone Truth and Reconciliation Commission.

Churchill, W. (2008). 'Healing begins when the wounding stops: Indian residential schools and the prospects for "truth and reconciliation" in Canada.' *Briarpatch Magazine*.

Coburn, N. (2009). *Losing Legitimacy? Some Afghan Views on the Government, the International Community, and the 2009 Elections*. Kabul, Afghanistan Research and Evaluation Unit (AREU).

Commission on Human Security/United Nations Office for Project Services (UNOPS). (2003). Name of publication? New York. Available at <www.humansecurity-chs.org/finalreport/English/FinalReport.pdf> Accessed July 22, 2009.

Conibere, R.,Asher, J., Cibelli, K., Dudukovich, J., Kaplan, R. and Ball, P. (2004). *Statistical Appendix to the Report of the Truth and Reconciliation Commission of Sierra Leone*. Accra, Sierra Leone Truth and Reconciliation Commission. Report by the Benetech Human Rights Data Analysis Group and the American Bar Association Central European and Eurasian Law Initiative to the Truth and Reconciliation Commission. Available at <https://www.hrdag.org/resources/publications/SL-TRC-statistics-chapter-final.pdf> Accessed May 28, 2012.

Constitution of Federal Republic of Ethiopia. (1995).

Conteh, P. (2008). 'The place of African traditional religion in interreligious encounters in Sierra Leone since the advent of Islam and Christianity.' PhD thesis submitted to the University of South Africa, unpublished.

Cook, J. (2011). 'Here comes the non-violence resistance.' *Economist*. Available at <www.economist.com/blogs/democracyinamerica/2011/05/israel_and_palestine_0> Accessed August 16, 2011.

Corntassel, J., Chaw-win-is and T'lakwadzi. (2009).'Indigenous storytelling, truth-telling, and community approaches to reconciliation.' *ESC: English Studies in Canada*, 35(1), pp. 137–59.

Crisis Group (2010). 'Rule of law in independent Kosovo', Europe Report no. 204. Prishtina: International Crisis Group.

Crisis Group. (2012). 'Kosovo and Serbia: a little goodwill could go a long way.' Report no. 215, Pristina/Belgrade/Brussels, Crisis Group Europe.

Crocker, D. A. (2002). 'Punishment, reconciliation, and democratic deliberation.' *Buffalo Criminal Law Review*, 5, p. 509.

Child Workers in Nepal Concerned Centre (CWIN). (2007). 'Fact sheet: children in armed conflict.' Available at <www.cwin.org.np/press_room/fact_sheets/fact_cic.htm> Accessed May 25, 2010.

Davis, L. and Hayner, P. (2009). *Difficult Peace, Limited Justice: Ten Years of Peacemaking in the DRC*. Washington D.C., International Centre for Transitional Justice.

Deda, I, (2010). *Nations in Transition 2010 – Kosovo Report*. Washington, D.C., Freedom House.

De Rooij, P. (2004). 'The BBC and ethnic cleansing of Palestinians.' ZNet. Accessed at <www.zcommunications.org/the-bbc-and-ethnic-cleansing-of-palestinians-by-paul-de-rooij.pdf >. (No longer accessible.)

Department for International Development (UK) (DFID). (2004). 'Case study 1: A time-series analysis of health service delivery in Afghanistan.' London, DIFD Health Systems Report Centre. Available at <www.dfidhealthrc.org/publications/health_service_delivery/Afghanistan.pdf> Accessed July 3, 2009.

Dorrell, M. (2009). 'From reconciliation to reconciling: reading what "we now recognize". The Government of Canada's 2008 residential schools apology.' *ESC: English Studies in Canada*, 3(1), pp. 27–45.

Dowd, M. (2004). *Children of Abraham*. Broadcast on UK Channel 4, April 25, 2004.

Duffield, M. (2001). *Global Governance and the New Wars: The Merging of Development and Security*. London, Zed.

Economist (2001) 'The new enemy', *Economist*, September 13. Available at <www.economist.com/node/780351> Accessed May 28, 2012.

Eide, K. (2012). 'Power struggle over Afghanistan.' *Al Jazeera*. Available at <www.aljazeera.com/indepth/opinion/2012/01/2012116114410804972.html>. Accessed February 10, 2012.

Eldon, J., Waddington, C. and Hadi, Y. (2008). 'Health system reconstruction: can it contribute to state–building?' Available at <www.healthandfragilestates.org/index.php?option=com_docman&Itemid=38&gid=32&task=doc_download> Accessed July 28, 2009.

European Centre for Minority Issues (ECMI). (2009). 'Minority issues in Kosovo.' Available at <www.ecmi-map.com/map/index.php?option=com_content&view=category&layout=blog&id=30&Itemid=58&lang=en.> Accessed December 7, 2010.

European Commission (2008). 'Council Joint Action on the European Union

Rule of Law Mission in Kosovo, EULEX Kosovo.' Brussels: Official Journal of the European Union (2008/124/CFSP).

European Union (2011). *Key Findings of the 2011 Progress Report on Kosovo*. Brussels, European Commission.

Evaldsson, A. K. and Wessels, A. (2003).'To commemorate or not to commemorate: three important commemorative events in twentieth century South Africa.' *Journal for Contemporary History*, 28(1).

Firebrace, J. (1983). 'Tigray', Minority Rights Group Report no. 5, London, CIP.

Fisher, R. J. (1999) 'Social-psychological processes in interactive conflict analysis and reconciliation.' In: Jeong, H. (ed.), *Conflict Resolution: Dynamics, Process and Structure*. Aldershot, Ashgate.

Francis, D. (2002). *People, Peace and Power: Conflict Transformation in Action*. London, Pluto.

Freedom House. (2010). *Nations in Transition 2010: Kosovo Report*. Washington, D.C., Freedom House.

Freedom House. (2011). *Nations in Transition 2011: Kosovo Report*. Washington, D.C,. Freedom House.

Galtung, J. (1971). 'A structural theory of imperialism.' *Journal of Peace Research*, 8(2), pp. 282–304.

Galtung, J. (1975). 'Three approaches to peace: peacekeeping, peacemaking and peacebuilding.' In: Galtung, J., *Peace, War and Defence: Essays*. Oslo, Peace Research Institute.

Gazeta Express. (2010). 'UNMIK-u s'e ka kryer punën në veri.' *Gazeta Express*, October 13.

Gebreselassie, A. (2003). 'Ethnic federalism: its promise and pitfalls for Africa.' *Yale Journal of International Law*, 28(51).

Gilmour, D. (1980). *Dispossessed: The Ordeal of the Palestinians*. London, Sphere.

Giustozzi, A. and Ibrahimi, N. (2012). 'Thirty years of conflict: drivers of anti-government mobilisation in Afghanistan, 1978–2011.' Issues paper. Kabul, Afghanistan Research and Evaluation Unit (AREU).

Gongaware, B. T. (2003).'Collective memories and collective identities: maintaining unity in native American educational social movement.' *Journal of Contemporary Ethnography*, 32(5).

Gonzalez, E. (2008). 'Reconciliation, An International Perspective', Breaking the silence: International conference on the Indian residential schools commission of Canada, Montreal, PQ, Université de Montréal.

Goodhand, J. (2001). 'Violent conflict, poverty and chronic poverty.' Chronic Poverty Research Centre Working Paper no.6. Available at <www.chronicpoverty.org/uploads/publication_files/WP06_Goodhand. pdf> Accessed June 18, 2009.

Gopin, M. (2000). *Between Eden and Armageddon: the Future of World Religions, Violence and Peacemaking*. New York, Oxford University Press.

Gopin, M. (2002). 'The use of the word and its limits: a critical evaluation of religious dialogue as peacemaking.' In: Smock, D. (ed.), *Interfaith Dialogue and Peacebuilding*. Washington, D.C., USIP Press.

Governance and Social Development Resource Centre. (2006). 'Conflict-affected and fragile states (part I).' Available at <www.gsdrc.org/go/topic-guides/justice/conflict-affected-and-fragile-states-part-1> Accessed July 25, 2009.

Government of Canada. (2008). 'Report to parliament: Canada's engagement in Afghanistan.' Canada, Library and Archive Canada Cataloguing in Publication. Available at <http://www.afghanistan.gc.ca/canada-afghanistan/assets/pdfs/docs/reprap09_08_e.pdf> Accessed August 20, 2009.

Green, J. A. (2003). 'Decolonisation and recolonization in Canada.' In: Clement, W. and Voskko, L. F. (eds), *Changing Canada: Political Economy as Transformation*. Toronto, McGill-Queen University Press.

Guardian. (2010a).'Afghanistan elections postponed.' *Guardian,* January 24. Available at: <www.guardian.co.uk/world/2010/jan/24/afghanistan-elections> Accessed May 14, 2010.

Guardian. (2010b). 'Afghanistan war logs: the unvarnished picture.' Editorial, *Guardian.* Available at: <www.guardian.co.uk/commentisfree/2010/jul/25/afghanistan-war-logs-guardian-editorial> Accessed February 15, 2012.

Habtu, A. (2004). 'Ethnic pluralism as an organizing principle of the Ethiopian federation.' *Dialectical Anthropology,* 28(2), pp. 91–123.

Hamas. (1988). The Hamas Covenant/Charter. Yale Law School (translation), Avalon Project. Available at: <http://avalon.law.yale.edu/20th_century/hamas.asp> Accessed May 23, 2012.

Harff, B. and Gurr, T. R. (2004). *Ethnic Conflict in World Politics,* 2nd edn. Boulder, Colo., Westview Press.

Havermans, J. (2000). 'Africa's most worrying battle field.' Available at: <www.conflict-prevention.net/page.php?id=40&formid=73&action=show&surveyid=6> Accessed August 2010.

HealthNet TPO. (2008). 'Afghanistan country programme.' Available at <www.healthnettpo.nl/HealthnetTPO(EN)/DATA/Projects/Programme%20Information/Afghanistan%20Country%20Programme.PDF> Accessed June 25, 2009.

Henderson, J. and Wakeham, P. (2009). 'Colonial reckoning, national reconciliation? Aboriginal peoples and the culture of redress in Canada.' *ESC: English Studies in Canada,* 35(1), pp. 1–26.

Hoffman, M. (2009). 'What is left of the "liberal peace"?' *London School of Economics Connect,* 21.

Housden, O. (2009). 'In a weak state: status and reintegration of CAAFAG in Nepal.' Institute of Peace and Conflict Studies (IPCS) Research Papers, New Delhi, IPCS.

Hroub, K. (2006). *Hamas: A Beginner's Guide*. London, Pluto Press.

Humper, J. (2004).*Witness to the Truth: Report of the Sierra Leone Truth and Reconciliation Commission, Vol. 2*. Accra, Graphic Packaging.

Human Rights Watch (HRW). (2012). 'World Report 2012: Afghanistan.' Country summary. Available at: <www.hrw.org/world-report-2012/world-report-2012-afghanistan> Accessed February 10, 2012.

Huntingdon, S. P. (2004). *The Clash of Civilizations and the Remaking of World Order.* New York, Free Press.

Ibrahim, R. (2008). 'An analysis of Al-Qa'ida's worldview: reciprocal treatment or religious obligation?', *Middle East Forum.* Available at: <www.meforum.org/2043/an-analysis-of-al-qaidas-worldview> Accessed January 15, 2011.

Ignatieff, M. (2003). *Empire Lite: Nation-building in Bosnia, Kosovo and Afghanistan.* London, Vintage.

Independent Election Commission of Afghanistan. (2009). 'Presidential and provincial council elections Afghanistan 2009 election.' Available at: <www.iec.org.af/results/index.html> Accessed August 28, 2009.

Inter Agency Child Protection Database (IACP Database). (2009). Inter Agency Child Protection Database Report. Kathmandu, CAAFAG Working Group.

International Committee of the Red Cross (ICRC). (2008). 'ICRC Annual Report 2008: Afghanistan.' Available at: <www.icrc.org/web/eng/siteeng0.nsf/html/section_annual_report_2008> Accessed June 27, 2009.

International Crisis Group (ICG). (2004). 'Dealing with Hamas.' ICG Middle East Report no. 21, Amman, ICG.

ICG. (2004). 'Palestinian refugees and the policy of peacemaking.' ICG Middle East Policy Paper no. 22, Amman, ICG.

ICG. (2005). 'Understanding Islamism.' ICG Middle East/North Africa Report no. 37. Available at: <www.crisisgroup.org/library/documents/middle_east___north_africa/egypt_north_africa/37_understanding_islamism.pdf> Accessed February 27, 2009.

ICG. (2007). 'Afghanistan's endangered compact', Asia Policy Briefing no. 59, Brussels, ICG.

ICG. (2009). 'Ethiopia: ethnic federalism and its discontents.' Africa Report no. 153, Nairobi, ICG. Available at: <www.crisisgroup.org/en/regions/africa/horn-of-africa/ethiopia-eritrea/153-ethiopia-ethnic-federalism-and-its-discontents.aspx> Accessed July 2, 2012.

ICG. (2009). 'Security in Afghanistan.' Available at: <www.crisisgroup.org/home/index.cfm?id=3071#Background> Accessed August 10, 2009.

ICG. (2009). 'Afghanistan: elections and the crisis of governance.' Asia Briefing no. 96. Brussels, ICG.

ICG. (2010). *Rule of Law in Independent Kosovo.* Prishtina, ICG.

International Rescue Committee. (2006). 'Mortality in the Democratic Republic of Congo: a nationwide survey', *The Lancet,* 367(9,504), pp. 44–51.

Ipsos and ICRC. (2009). 'Our world: views from Afghanistan.' Available at: <www.icrc.org/web/eng/siteeng0.nsf/htmlall/views-from-field-report-240609> Accessed August 15, 2009.

IRIN. (2009). 'Afghanistan: little health care for women in Paktika Province.'

IRIN. Available at: <www.irinnews.org/report.aspx?ReportId=82638> Accessed May 9, 2012.

Jarstad, A. K. (2008). 'Dilemmas of war-to-democracy transitions: theories and concepts.' In: Jarstad, A. K. and Sisks, T. D. (eds), *From War to Democracy: Dilemmas of Peacebuilding*. Cambridge, Cambridge University Press.

Johnston, D. (1994) 'The churches and apartheid in South Africa.' In: Johnston, D. and Sampson, C. (eds), *Religion, the Missing Dimension of Statecraft*. New York and Oxford, Oxford University Press.

Johnson, C. and Leslie, J. (2004). *Afghanistan: The Mirage of Peace*. London, Zed.

Jones, S. G. and Libicki, M. C. (2008). *How Terrorist Groups End: Lessons for Countering al Qa'ida*. Santa Monica, RAND.

Kahora, J. and Kumakana, H. (2009). 'Talk of reviving Truth Commission to deal with legacy of civil war.' Available at: <http://www.iwpr.net/report-news/congolese-push-reconciliation> Accessed August 2010.

Kambala, O. and Savage, T. (2008). 'Decayed, decimated, usurped and inadequate: the challenge of finding justice through formal mechanisms in the DR Congo.' In: Aertsen, I. et al. (eds), *Restoring Justice after Large-Scale Violent Conflicts*. Cullompton and Portland, Ore., Willan, pp. 336–58.

Kamwimbi, T. (2006). 'The DRC elections, reconciliation and justice.' Available at: <www.ictj.org/en/news/coverage/article/986.htmlICTJ in the News> Accessed August 2010.

Kantor, P. and Pain, A. (2011). 'Rethinking rural poverty reduction in Afghanistan.' In: *Afghanistan Looking Ahead. Challenges for Governance and Community Welfare – Research Briefs for the 2011 Bonn Conference*. Kabul, Afghanistan Research and Evaluation Unit (AREU): 7–10.

Karki, A. and Seddon, D. (eds). (2003). *The People's War in Historical Context*. Delhi, Adroit.

Kasimow, H. (2003) 'Swami Vivekananda and Rabbi Abraham Joshua Heschel: standing on the shoulders of giants.' *Interreligious Insight,* 1(3), pp. 8–15.

Kasuku, J. (2010). 'Analysing the progress of the reconciliation process in the Democratic Republic of Congo, 2002 to 2010', interview by V. Mould. Coventry, August 25, 2010.

Keen, D. (2005). *Conflict and Collusion in Sierra Leone*. Oxford and New York, Palgrave Macmillan.

Kepel, G. (2003). *Jihad: The Trail of Political Islam*. London, I B Tauris.

Kessler, E. (2003). '"I am the way, the truth and the life" (John 14:6) and Jewish-Christian Dialogue.' *Interreligious Insight,* 1(3), pp. 25–31.

Khashan, H. (1994). *Palestinian Resettlement in Lebanon: Behind the Debate*. Montreal, Montreal Studies on the Contemporary Arab World.

Khelwatgar, N. (2008). 'Open market and poverty increase in Afghanistan.' Available at: <www.intermedia.org.pk/pdf/pak_afghan/Najibullah.pdf> Accessed May 14, 2010.

Kilcullen, D. (2008). *Countering Global Insurgency*. Available at: <small-

warsjournal.com/documents/kilcullen.pdf>. Accessed January 15, 2011.

Kingston, P. and Spears, I. (eds). (2004). *States Within States: Incipient Political Entities in the Post-Cold War Era*. Basingstoke and New York, Palgrave Macmillan.

Klugman, J et al. (2010). *Human Development Report 2009. The Real Wealth of Nations: Human Pathways to Human Development*. Basingstoke and New York, Palgrave Macmillan.

Knitter, P. F. (1985).'Doing before knowing – the challenge of interreligious dialogue.' In: *No Other Name? A Critical Survey of Christian Attitudes Toward the World Religions*. London, SCM Press.

Koha Ditore. (2010a). 'UNMIK-u takohet me strukturat paralele.' Available at: <www.koha.net/index.php?cid=1,22,38685> Accessed November 29, 2010.

Koha Ditore. (2010b). 'Daka: Procesi është devijuar.' Available at: <www.kohaditore.com/index.php?cid=1,70,43936> Accessed December 19, 2010.

Kohrt, B. (2007). *Recommendations to Promote Psychosocial Well-Being of Children Associated with Armed Forces and Armed Groups (CAAFAG) in Nepal*. Kathmandu, Transcultural Psychosocial Organization (TPO).

Kosovo Assembly. (2008). 'Kosovo Declaration of Independence', 17 February. Prishtina, Kosovo Assembly. Available at: <www.assembly-kosova.org/?cid=2,128,1635> Accessed November 14, 2010.

Kosovo Institute for Policy Research and Development (KIPRD). (2009). *Kosovo at a Crossroad: Decentralization and the Creation of New Municipalities*, Policy brief no. 14. Prishtina, KIPRD.

Kreisberg, L. (2001). 'Changing forms of coexistence.' In: Abu-Nimer, M. (ed.), *Reconciliation, Justice, and Co-Existence*, Lanham, Md., Lexington.

Kung, H. (1993) *Declaration Toward a Global Ethic*. Chicago, Parliament of the World's Religions. Available at <www.cpwr.org/resource/ethic.pdf> Accessed July 2, 2012.

Kung, H. (2002). 'Preface.' In: Tehranian, M. and Chappell, D. W. (eds), *Dialogue of Civilizations: A New Peace Agenda for a New Millennium*. London and New York, I B Tauris.

Kung, H. (2003). 'A global ethic: development and goals.' *Interreligious Insight*, 1(1), pp. 8–19.

Lamey, J. and Winterbotham, E. (2011). 'Painful steps – justice, forgiveness and compromise in Afghanistan's peace process.' In: *Afghanistan Looking Ahead. Challenges for Governance and Community Welfare – Research Briefs for the 2011 Bonn Conference*. Kabul, Afghanistan Research and Evaluation Unit (AREU).

Landmine and Cluster Munition Monitor. (2010). 'Causality and victim assistance: Afghanistan.' Available at: <www.themonitor.org/custom/index.php/region_profiles/print_theme/477> Accessed March 28, 2011.

Laqueur, W. (1998). 'Terror's new face: the radicalization and escalation of modern terrorism.' *Harvard International Review,* 20(4), pp. 48–51.

Lederach, J. P. (1997). *Building Peace: Sustainable Reconciliation in Divided Societies.* Washington D.C., US Institute of Peace Press.

Lederach, J. P. (2001). 'Civil society and reconciliation.' In: Crocker, C. A., Hampson, F. O. and Aall, P. (eds), *Turbulent Peace.* Washington D.C., US Institute of Peace Press.

Lederach, J. P. (2005). *The Moral Imagination: The Art and Soul of Building Peace.* Oxford, Oxford University Press.

Lederach, J. P. (2010). *Building Peace: Sustainable Reconciliation in Divided Societies* Washington, D.C., US Institute of Peace Press, p. 29.

Lewis, I. M. (1989). 'The Ogaden and the fragility of Somali segment nationalism.' *International African Institute Papers,* Vol. 88.

Levy, G. (2010). *The Punishment of Gaza.* Verso, London.

Licklider, R. (2001). 'Obstacles to peace settlements.' In: Crocker, C. A., Hampson, F. O. and Aall, P. (eds), *Turbulent Peace: The Challenges of Managing International Conflict.* Washington, D.C., US Institute of Peace, pp. 697–718.

Liden, K. (2009). 'Building peace between local and global politics: the cosmopolitical ethics of liberal peacebuilding.' *International Peacekeeping,* 16(5).

Liechty, J. (2002) 'Mitigation in Northern Ireland: a strategy for living in peace when truth claims clash.' In: Smock, D. (ed.), *Interfaith Dialogue and Peacebuilding.* Washington, D.C., USIP Press, pp. 89–101.

Lord, D. (2000). 'Paying the price: the Sierra Leone peace process.' Available at: <www.c-r.org/our-work/accord/sierra-leone/contents.php> Accessed March 15, 2010.

Lough, O. (2011). 'Practicing democracy in Afghanistan – key findings on perceptions, parliament and elections.' *Afghanistan Looking Ahead: Challenges for Governance and Community Welfare – Research Briefs for the 2011 Bonn Conference.* Kabul.

Maass, G. and Mepham, D. (2004) 'Promoting effective states: a progressive policy response to failed and failing states.'<online> London: Institute for Public Policy Research and Friedrich Ebert Stiftung. Available at: <www.ippr.org.uk/ecomm/files/promotingeffectivestates.pdf > Accessed August 21, 2009.

Mac Ginty, R. (2006). *No War, No Peace: The Rejuvenation of Stalled Peace Processes and Peace Accords.* Basingstoke, Palgrave Macmillan.

Mac Ginty, R. and Williams, A. (2009). *Conflict and Development.* Abingdon, Routledge.

MacQueen, G. (2008). 'Setting the role of health in context: multi-track peace work.' In: Arya, A. N. and Santa Barbara, J. (eds), *Peace through Health: How Health Professionals Can Work for a Less Violent World.* New York, Kumarian.

MacQueen, G. and Santa Barbara, J. (2000). 'Conflict and health: peace building through health initiatives.' *British Medical Journal*, 321(7,256), pp. 293–6.

Mackenzie, I. (2009). 'For everything there is a season.' In: Younging, G., Dewar, J. and DeGagné, M. (eds), *Response, Responsibility, and Renewal: Canada's Truth and Reconciliation Journey*. Ottawa, Aboriginal Healing Foundation, pp. 87–93.

MacVeigh, J., Maguire, S. and Wedge, J. (2007) *Stolen Futures: The Reintegration of Children in Armed Conflict*, submission to the 10-year review of 1996 Machel study on the impact of armed conflict on children. London, Save the Children UK.

Magonet, J. (2003) *Talking to the Other: Jewish Interfaith Dialogue with Christians and Muslims*. London and New York, I.B. Tauris.

Malan, J. (1997). *Conflict Resolution Wisdom from Africa*. Durban, ACCORD.

Malešsevic, S. (2004) *The Sociology of Ethnicity*, London, Sage.

Mani, R. (2002). *Beyond Retribution: Seeking Justice in the Shadows of War*. Cambridge, UK, Polity Press.

Markakis, J. (1996). 'The Somali in Ethiopia.' *Review of African Political Economy*, 23(70).

Martin, K. (2009). 'Truth, reconciliation, and amnesia: porcupines and china dolls and the Canadian conscience.' *ESC: English Studies in Canada*, 35(1), pp. 47–65.

Massad, J. (2001). 'Return of permanent exile?.' In: Aruir, N. (ed.), *Palestinian Refugees: The Right of Return*. London, Pluto.

Masterton, G. (2006) 'Defining civil society in the context of an African peer review mechanism.' Available at: <www.eisa.org.za/aprm/pdf/Resources_Bibliography_Masterson3.pdf > Accessed August 2010.

Malan, J. (1997). *Conflict Resolution Wisdom from Africa*. Durban, ACCORD.

Mawdudi, A. A. (1980). *Jihad in Islam*. Lahore: Islamic Publications.

McIntosh, J. (2009). 'Elders and "frauds": commodified expertise and politicized authenticity among Mijikenda.' *Africa*, 79(1).

Medija Centar. (2010). 'Security and perspectives in the north of Kosovo.' Available at: <www.medijacentar.info/en/mc-debates/reports/298-qse-curity-and-perspectives-in-the-north-of-kosovoq-16072010> Accessed December 27, 2010.

Milton-Edwards, B. and Farrell, S. (2010). *Hamas: The Islamic Resistance Movement*. Cambridge, Polity Press.

Mishal, S. and Sela, A. (2000). *The Palestinian Hamas: Vision, Violence and Coexistence*. New York, Columbia University Press.

Møller, B. (2009). 'The Somali conflict: the role of external actors', *DIIS Report*.

Mould, V. (2010). Survey carried out by author in June.

Muni, S. D. (2003). *Maoist Insurgency in Nepal: The Challenge and the Response*, New Delhi, Rupa.

Murray, C. J. L., King, G., Lopez, A. D., Tomijima, N. and Krung, E.

(2002). 'Armed conflict as a public health problem.' *British Medical Journal*, 324(7, 333), pp. 346–9.

NATO. (2009). 'NATO Afghanistan Report 2009.' *Afghan Conflict Monitor*.

Napoleoni, L. (2003a). 'Modern jihad: the Islamist crusade.' *SAIS Review*, 23(2), pp. 53–69.

Napoleoni, L. (2003b). *Modern Jihad: Tracing the Dollars Behind the Terror Networks*. London, Pluto.

Napoleoni, L. (2003c) 'Rapid rise of the economy of terror', *Guardian Online*. Available at: <www.guardian.co.uk/world/2003/nov/03/terrorism.alqaida> Accessed January 10, 2011.

Nepalnews. (2006) .'Chronology of decade-long conflict.' Available at: <www.nepalnews.com/archive/2006/nov/nov22/news08.php> Accessed July 10, 2010.

Ngolahun Leader. (2009). Interview by S. Kaindenah.

Nolte-Schamm, C. (2006) 'The African traditional ritual of cleansing the chest of grudges as a ritual for reconciliation.' *Religion and Theology*, 13(1).

Osberg, S. (2009). 'Did the PLO die in Lebanon?' Available at: <http://english.aljazeera.net/programmes/plohistoryofrevolution/2009/07/20097 2855032594820.html> Accessed July 29, 2009.

Paris, R. (2006). *At War's End: Building Peace After Civil Conflict*, 3rd edn. New York, Cambridge University Press.

Parsons, A. (1997). 'The United Nations and the Palestine refugees with special reference to Lebanon.' *Journal of Refugee Studies*, 10(3), pp. 228–42.

Payne, L. A. (2004). 'In search of remorse: confessions by perpetrators of past violence.' *Brown Journal of World Affairs*, 11(1).

Peterson, S. and Shellman, S. M. (2006). 'Aids and violent conflict: the indirect effects of disease on national security.' College of William and Mary. Available at: <http://web.wm.edu/irtheoryandpractice/security/papers/AIDS.pdf?svr=www>. Accessed July 2, 2012.

Physicians for Human Rights (PHR). (1998). 'The Taliban's war on women: a health and human right crisis in Afghanistan.' <Online> Washington D.C., Physician for Human Rights. Available at: <http://physiciansforhumanrights.org/library/documents/reports/talibans-war-on-women.pdf> Accessed August 20, 2009.

Pressman, J. (2003). 'The second intifada: background and causes of the Palestinian Israeli conflict.' *Journal of Conflict Studies*, 22(2), 114–41.

Probst, P. (2007). 'Picturing the past: heritage, photography and the politics of appearance in a Yoruba City.' In: Jong, F. D. and Rowlands, M. (eds), *Reclaiming Heritage: Alternative Imaginaries of Memory in West Africa*. Walnut Creek, Calif., Left Coast Press.

Poole, L. (2011). *Afghanistan: Tracking Major Resource Flows*. London: Global Humanitarian Assistance.

Qutb, S. (2006). *Milestones*. New Delhi, Islamic Book Services.

Ramsbotham, O., Woodhouse, T. and Miall, H. (2011). *Contemporary Conflict Resolution: The Prevention, Management, and Transformation of Deadly Conflicts,* 3rd edn. Cambridge, Polity Press.

Ranger, T. (2004). 'Dignifying death: the politics of burial in Bulawayo.' *Journal of Religion in Africa,* 34(1–2).

Regan, P. (2006). 'Unsettling the settler within: Canada's peacemaker myth, reconciliation, and recolonization.' PhD dissertation, University of Victoria.

Riaz, A. and Basu, S. (2007). *Paradise Lost? State failure in Nepal.* Plymouth, Lexington.

Richmond, O. P. (ed.) (2010). *Palgrave Advances in Peacebuilding.* Basingstoke and New York, Palgrave Macmillan.

Richmond, O. (2008). *The Transformation of Peace.* Basingstoke, Palgrave Macmillan.

Rigby, A. (2010). *Palestinian Resistance and Non-violence,* Jerusalem, PASSIA.

Rigby, A. (2011). 'How do post-conflict societies deal with a traumatic past and promote national unity and reconciliation?' In: Webel, C. and Johansen, J. (eds), *Peace and Conflict Studies: A Reader.* London and New York, Routledge.

Roeder, P. G. and Rothchild, D. (eds) (2005). *Sustainable Peace: Power and Democracy after Civil Wars.* Ithaca, N.Y., Cornell University Press.

Rotberg, R. I. (2006). 'Creating robust institutions: preparing secure governance foundations.' Research Partnership on Postwar State-building. Available at: <http://statebuilding.org/resources/Rotberg_RPPS_October 2006.pdf> Accessed June 20, 2008.

Roy, S. (2007). *Failing Peace: Gaza and the Palestinian-Israeli Conflict.* London, Pluto.

Rubin, A. (2011). 'World Bank issues alert on Afghanistan economy.' *New York Times.* Available at: <www.nytimes.com/2011/11/23/world/ asia/world-bank-issues-alert-on-afghanistan-economy.html> Accessed February 10, 2012.

Rubin, B. R. (2004). 'Creating a constitution for Afghanistan.' *Journal of Democracy,* 15(3).

Rubenstein, L. S. (2010). 'Humanitarian space shrinking for health program delivery in Afghanistan and Pakistan.' Available at: <www.usip.org/ publications/humanitarian-space-shrinking-health-program-delivery-in-afghanistan-and-pakistan> Accessed January 4, 2011.

Rushton, S. (2005). 'Health and peace building: resuscitating the failed states in Sierra Leone.' *International Relations,* 19(4), pp. 441–56.

Sacks, J. (2002). *The Dignity of Difference: How to Avoid the Clash of Civilizations.* London and New York, Continuum.

Said, E. (2001). 'The right of return at last.' In: Aruri, N. (ed.), *Palestinian Refugees: The Right of Return.* London, Pluto.

Saltmarshe, D. and Medhi, A. (2011). 'Local governance for local needs.' In: *Afghanistan Looking Ahead. Challenges for Governance and*

Community Welfare – Research Briefs for the 2011 Bonn Conference. Kabul, Afghanistan Research and Evaluation Unit (AREU).

Santa Barbara, J. (2008) 'Peace Education as a Primary Prevention.' In: Santa Barbara, J. and Arya, A. N. (eds), *Peace through Health: How Health Professionals can Work for a Less Violent World.* New York, Kumarian.

Santa Barbara, J. and Arya, A. N. (eds) (2008). *Peace through Health: How Health Professionals Can Work for a Less Violent World.* New York, Kumarian.

Savage, T. (2006). *In Quest of a Sustainable Justice: Transitional Justice and Human Security in the Democratic Republic of the Congo.* Pretoria, Institute for Security Studies.

Savage, T. and Vanspauwen, K. (2008). 'The conflict in the Democratic Republic of Congo.' In: Aertsen, I. et al. (eds), *Restoring Justice after Large-Scale Violent Conflicts: Kosovo, DR Congo and the Israeli-Palestinian Case.* Cullompton, UK and Portland, Ore., Willan.

Save the Children (STC). (2007). *Release, Return and Reintegration (RRR) of Former CAAFAG (Children Associated with Armed Forces and Armed Groups) in Nepal: A Field Guide.* Kathmandu, STC.

STC. (2008). *Reintegration of Former CAAFAG (Children Associated with Armed Forces and Armed Groups) in Nepal, an evaluation report submitted to AusAID.* Kathmandu, STC.

Sayigh, R. (2007). *The Palestinians: From Peasants to Revolutionaries,* 2nd edn. London, Zed.

Schanzer, J. (2008). *Hamas vs. Fatah: The Struggle for Palestine.* Basingstoke, Palgrave Macmillan.

Schirch, L. (2004). *The Little Book of Strategic Peacebuilding: A Vision and Framework for Peace with Justice.* Intercourse, Pa., Good Book.

Schmidt, H. (1997). 'Healing the wounds of war: memories of violence and the making of history in Zimbabwe's most recent past.' *Journal of Southern African Studies,* 23(2).

Schmidt-Leukel, P. (2004). *War and Peace in the World's Religions: The Gerald Weisfeld Lectures 2003.* London, SCM Press.

Schneier, A. (2002). 'Religion and interfaith conflict: appeal of conscience foundation.' In: Smock, D. (ed.), *Interfaith Dialogue and Peacebuilding.* Washington DC, USIP Press.

Schulz, H. L. and Hammer, J. (2003). *The Palestinian Diaspora: Formation of Identities and Politics of Homeland.* London, Routledge.

Sedra M. and Middlebrook, P. J. (2005).'Beyond Bonn: revisioning the international compact for Afghanistan.' Policy briefing. Silver City, N.M. and Washington, D.C., Foreign Policy in Focus.

Shakdiel, L. (1991). 'Dialogue as an opportunity for spiritual growth: linking tradition with creativity.' In: Gordon, H. and Gordon, R. (eds), *Israel/Palestine: The Quest for Dialogue.* Maryknoll, N.Y., Orbis.

Shepard, B., O'Neil, L. and Guenetter, F. (2006).'Counselling with First Nations women: considerations of oppression as renewal.' *International Journal for the Advancement of Counselling,* 28(3), pp. 227–40.

Short, D. (2005). 'Reconciliation and the problem of internal colonialism.' *Journal of Intercultural Studies*, 26(3), pp. 267–82.

Sifaoui, M. (2008). 'Interview with Mohamed Sifaoui.' Available at: <www.meforum.org/1870/mohamed-sifaoui-i-consider-islamism-to-be-fascism>. Accessed January 15, 2011.

Sisk, T. (2008). 'Power sharing after civil wars: matching problems to solutions.' In: Darby, J. and Mac Ginty, R. (eds), *Contemporary Peacemaking: Conflict, Peace Processes and Post-War Reconstruction*, 2nd edn. Basingstoke, Palgrave Macmillan.

Slater, J. (2001). 'What went wrong? The collapse of the Israeli–Palestinian peace process.' *Political Science Quarterly*, 116(2), pp. 171–99.

Slye, R. (2000). 'Amnesty, truth and reconciliation.' In: Rotberg, R. and Thompson D. (eds), *Princeton Truth v. Justice: The Morality of Truth Commissions*. Princeton, N.J. and Oxford, Princeton University Press.

Smith, B. C. (2007). *Good Governance and Development*. Basingstoke, Palgrave Macmillan.

Solana, J. (2006). 'The health dimension to security.' In: Mellbourn, A. (ed.), *Conflict Prevention and Health, Health and Conflict Prevention*, Anna Lindh Programme on Conflict Prevention, 2006 edn. Sweden, Gidlunds.

Stephens, J. (2007). 'Memory, commemoration and the meaning of a suburban war memorial.' *Journal of Material Culture*, 21(3).

Sternberg, S. (1997). 'Interfaith dialogue and world peace.' Unpublished address given at the Crans Montana Forum, 26 June .

Strong, L., Wali, A. and Sondorp, E. (2005). 'Health policy in Afghanistan: two years of rapid change a review of the process 2001–2003.' Available at: <www.dfid.gov.uk/r4d/SearchResearchDatabasePrint.asp?OutputID=172824> Accessed July 25, 2009.

Sudan Tribune. (2010). 'Ethiopian gov't remarks on peace deal plan misleading-rebel group.' *Sudan Tribune*. Available at <www.sudantribune.com/Ethiopia-gov-t-remarks-on-peace,35282>. Accessed July 2, 2012.

Suhrke, A. (2006).'When more is less: aiding statebuilding in Afghanistan.' Working Paper 26, Madrid, Fundacion para les Relaciones Internacionales y el Dialogo Exterior .

Suhrke, A. (2007a). 'Democratization of a dependent state: the case of Afghanistan.' Working Paper 10, Bergen, Chr. Michelsen Institute.

Suhrke, A. (2007b). 'Reconstruction as modernisation: the "post-conflict" project in Afghanistan.' *Third World Quarterly*, 28(7), pp. 1291–308.

Swanström, N. L. P. and Cornell, S. E. (2005). 'A strategic conflict analysis of Afghanistan.' Available at: <www.silkroadstudies.org/new/docs/publications/2005/050820AFGHAN.pdf> Accessed August 10, 2009.

Tamimi, A. (2007) *Hamas Unwritten Chapters*. London, Hurst.

Teshome, W. B. (2009).'Ethiopian opposition political parties and rebel fronts: past and present.' *International Journal of Social Science*, 4(1).

Thabat. (2006). 'Free market economy, reinforcement of class system.' Thabat. Available at <www.accessmylibrary.com/article-1G1-142236461/afghan-paper-says-free.html> Accessed May 14, 2010.

Thompson, G., Gutlove, P. and Russell, J. H. (2003). 'Social reconstruction in Afghanistan through the lens of health and human security.' Available at: <www.irss-usa.org/pages/documents/afg-16jun03-3.pdf> Accessed August 12, 2009.

Trocaire. (2008). 'DR Congo: peace process fragile, civilians at risk.' Available at <www.trocaire.org/news/2008/07/29/dr-congo-peace-process-fragile-civilians-risk> Accessed August 2010.

Tronvoll, K. (2000). *Ethiopia: A New Start?* London, Minority Rights Group International Report.

Trouillot, M. R. (1995). *Silencing the Past: Power and the Production of History.* place?, Beacon Press, University of Michigan.

Tutu, D. (1999). *No Future without Forgiveness*, London, Rider & Co.

United Nations. (2000). Report of the Panel on United Nations Peace Operations (the Brahimi report)**A/55/305 S/2000/809**. Available at: <www.un.org/peace/reports/peace_operations/> Accessed May 22, 2012.

United Nations. (2006). 'Rule of law tools for post-conflict states: monitoring legal systems.' Geneva, Office of the UN High Commissioner for Human Rights. Available at: <http://www.ohchr.org/Documents/Publications/RuleoflawMonitoringen.pdf> Accessed July 25, 2009.

United Nations. (2007). 'Governance strategies for post conflict reconstruction, sustainable peace and development.' Available at: <http://unpan1.un.org/intradoc/groups/public/documents/un/unpan028332.pdf> Accessed August 10, 2009.

United Nations Children's Emergency Fund (UNICEF). (2008). *Programme for the Reintegration of Children Associated with Armed Forces and Armed Groups in Nepal.* New York, United Nations.

United Nations Conference on Trade and Development (UNCTAD). (2010). '"New development paths" urged in wake of global crisis.' Information note UNCTAD/PRESS/IN/2010/014. Geneva, UNCTAD.

United Nations Development Programme (UNDP). (2002). 'Preliminary needs assessment for recovery and reconstruction.' January. Available at: <www.adb.org/Documents/Reports/Afghanistan/pnarr.pdf> Accessed July 27, 2009.

UNDP. (2006). 'Kosovo internal security sector review.' Kosovo, UNDP.

UNDP. (2010). 'Early warning reports #28.' Available at: <www.ks.undp.org/repository/docs/EWR_eng_web-opt.pdf> Accessed December 18, 2010.

United Nations High Commissioner for Refugees (UNHCR). (2012). '2012 UNHCR country operation profile: Afghanistan.' Available at: <www.unhcr.org/cgi-bin/texis/vtx/page?page=49e486eb6> Accessed February 8, 2012.

United Nations Relief and Works Agency for Palestine Refugees in the Near East (UNRWA) (2008). Official website. Available at <www.unrwa.org> Accessed June 5, 2009.

United Nations Secretary-General. (2007). 'Report of the Special Envoy of the Secretary-General on Kosovo's future status.' S/2007/168. New York, United Nations.

UN Secretary-General. (2008). 'Report of the Secretary-General on the United Nations Interim Administration mission in Kosovo.' Report, S/2008/354. New York, United Nations.

UN Secretary-General. (2010). 'Report of the Secretary-General on the United Nations Interim Administration Mission in Kosovo.' Report S/2010/169. New York, United Nations.

United Nations Security Council. (1999). Resolution 1244. S/RES/1244. New York, United Nations.

UN Security Council. (2002). 'UN Security Council Meeting.' Available at <www.securitycouncilreport.org/atf/cf/%7B65BFCF9B-6D27-4E9C-8-CD3-CF6E4FF96FF9%7D/Kos%20SPV4559.pdf> Accessed December 29, 2010.

UN Security Council. (2010). 'UN Security Council Meeting.' S/PV.6353. New York, United Nations.

Université de Montréal. (2008). 'Breaking the silence: International conference on the Indian residential schools commission of Canada.' Available at <www.creum.umontreal.ca/spip.php?article900> Accessed November 3, 2010.

United States Department of State. (2001). 'The Taliban's war against women.' Available at: <www.state.gov/g/drl/rls/6185.htm> Accessed August 18, 2009.

Utstein Peacebuilding Study. (2004). Oslo, Peace Research Institute Oslo (PRIO).

Van Tongeren, P. (1999). 'Reflections on peacebuilding.' *People Building Peace,* pp. 124–9. Utrecht, European Centre for Conflict Prevention.

Vetevendosje (2006) *Serbia's Plan for Kosova.* Prishtina, Levizja Vetevendosje. Available at: <www.vetevendosje.org/repository/docs/decentralizimi.pdf> Accessed May 5, 2012.

Vinck, P., Pham, P., Baldo, S. and Shigekane, R. (2008). *Living with Fear: A Population-based Survey on Attitudes about Peace, Justice and Social Reconstruction in the Democratic Republic of Congo.* Berkeley, Calif., University of California Human Rights Centre.

Visoka, G. (2011). 'International governance and local resistance in Kosovo: the thin line between ethical, emancipatory and exclusionary politics.' *Irish Studies in International Affairs,* 22, pp. 99–125.

Waldman, M. (2008). 'Falling short: aid effectiveness in Afghanistan', *ACBAR Advocacy Series*, Kabul, Agency Co-ordinating Body for Afghan Relief (ACBAR).

Waldman, R., Strong, L. and Wali, A. (2006). *Afghanistan's Health System Since 2001: Condition Improved, Prognosis Cautiously Optimistic.* Kabul, Afghanistan Research and Evaluation Unit.

Wallensteen, P. (2007). *Understanding Conflict Resolution: War, Peace and the Global System,* 2nd edn. Thousand Oaks, Calif., Sage.

Warner, M. (2006). 'Hope and fear in Palestine: Online News Hour.' Available at: <www.pbs.org/newshour/bb/middle_east/jan-june06/palestine_1-24.html> Accessed January 24, 2006.

Weighill, M. L. (1997). ' Palestinians in Lebanon: the politics of assistance.' *Journal of Refugee Studies,* 10(3), pp. 294–313.

Wiggins, J. (2003) 'In praise of religious diversity and friendship'. *Interreligious Insight* 1 (3), 32–8.

Wijeyaratne, S. (2008). 'Afghanistan: a study on the prospects for peace.' Discussion paper, Ottawa, Canadian Council for International Co-operation.

Wilder, A. (2007). 'Cops or robbers? The struggle to reform the Afghan national police.' Issues Paper Series. Kabul, AREU.

Woodhead, L (ed.) (2001). *Religions in the Modern World: Traditions and Transformations.* London, Routledge.

World Bank. (2007). 'Review of technical assistance and capacity building in Afghanistan.' Discussion paper for the Afghanistan Development Forum. Available at: <www.cdc-crdb.gov.kh/cdc/twg/Afghanistan%20TA%20 study%202006.pdf> Accessed July 29, 2009.

World Bank. (2011). 'Afghanistan country overview 2011.' .Available at <www.worldbank.org.af/WBSITE/EXTERNAL/COUNTRIES/ SOUTHASIAEXT/AFGHANISTANEXTN/0,,contentMDK:20154015~ menuPK:305992~pagePK:141137~piPK:141127~theSitePK:305985,00. html> Accessed February 10, 2012.

World Health Organization (WHO) (2002) '25 questions and answers on health and human rights.' Health and human rights publication serious issue no. 1. Geneva, WHO. Available at: <www.who.int/hhr/ NEW37871OMSOK.pdf> Accessed July 14, 2009.

WHO. (2010). 'Afghanistan, the role of contractual arrangements in improving health sector performance.' Available at <http://gis.emro. who.int/HealthSystemObservatory/PDF/Contracting/Afghanistan.pdf>. Accessed March 31, 2011.

WHO. (2011). 'Health action in crises.' Available at <www.who.int/hac/ techguidance/hbp/en/> Accessed March 27, 2011.

Yav, J. (2007). 'DRC: healing the wounds of war through repara-tions.' Available at: <www.internationalpeaceandconflict.org/profiles/ blogs/780588:BlogPost:9744> Accessed August 2010.

Young, J. (1996). 'Ethnicity and power in Ethiopia.' *Review of African Political Economy,* 23(70), pp. 531–42.

Young, R. (2002) 'American Jews, Christians and Muslims working together for peace in the Middle East.' In: Smock, D. (ed.), *Interfaith Dialogue and Peacebuilding.* Washington D.C., USIP Press, pp. 63–71.

Zaum, D. (2007). *The Sovereignty Paradox: The Norms and Politics of International Statebuilding,* Oxford: Oxford University Press.

Zewde, B. (1991). *A History of Modern Ethiopia: 1855–1974.* London, James Curry.

Zia-Zarifi, S. (2007). 'Children in the ranks: the Maoists' use of child soldiers in Nepal.' *Human Rights Watch,* 19(2).

Zollner, B. H. E. (2009). *The Muslim Brotherhood: Hasan Al-Hadaybi and Ideology.* Basingstoke, Routledge.

INDEX

Soviet Union (former), 56, 121,
    145–6
state building, third–party control
    of, 17–18
Steiner, Michael, 33
structural violence, 3
Sudan, 144
Suhrke, A., 23, 26, 28, 31n6
Sun City talks/Accord, 63, 68
sustainable development theory,
    2, 3
Syria, 152, 155, 161

T
T'lakwadzi, 100
takfir, 142
Taliban, 18–19, 121, 128, 139
Taylor, Charles, 73
terrorism, 9, 51, 56, 114, 168
    main areas of, 144–5
    new economy of, 137–50
    overriding aim of destroying,
        23, 29
Tewdros II, emperor of Ethiopia, 46
Thaci, Hashim, 38
themes of the book, 1
Tigrean People's Liberation Front
    (TPLF), 48, 49, 52–3
torture, 24
Transcultural Psychosocial
    Organization of Nepal, 187
Trouillot, M. R., 97
trust
    building of, 57–8
    horizontal and vertical, 5
truth
    claims, comparing, 115–16
    claims, mitigation of, 111
    importance of, 5
truth and reconciliation
    commissions, 5–6, 7
    in Canada, 87–8
    and community–based
        arrangements, 79
    in DRC, 63–6, 70
    problems and criticisms of, 6

in Sierra Leone, 74–5
Tutu, Archbishop Desmond, 79,
    105

U
unemployment, 41
United Kingdom, 165n2
United Nations, 2, 183
    in Afghanistan, 15, 17–18, 20,
        22–4, 29, 30
    attitude to Israel/Palestine,
        154, 180
    Children's Emergency Fund
        (UNICEF), 190–1, 193,
        195–8, 200n2
    Declaration of Human Rights,
        51
    Declaration of the Rights of
        Indigenous Peoples, 93
    Development Programme
        (UNDP), 24
    General Assembly resolutions,
        154, 159–61, 164
    Institute of Peace, 26
    in Kosovo, 7, 32–8
    Mission in Kosovo (UNMIK),
        33, 36–7, 39
    in Nepal, 185
    peacebuilding unit, 2
    Relief and Works Agency for
        Palestinian Refugees in the
        Near East (UNRWA), 152,
        154, 165n1, 165n3
    role of, 15, 17, 22
    Security Council resolutions,
        33, 186
    standard operating procedure,
        6–7, 15–16, 27–8, 31n7
United States
    and the Cold War, 145–6
    expenditure on aid, 25
    and Israel/Palestine, 154, 174,
        176, 180
    and Kosovo, 34
    role/policy in Afghanistan, 7,
        18, 21, 22–7, 121